OTHER BOOKS BY JERRY AND CATHERINE GRAHAM

Jerry Graham's Bay Area Backroads, Revised and Updated
Jerry Graham's More Bay Area Backroads

JERRY GRAHAM'S

Bay Area Backroads

FOOD AND LODGING GUIDE

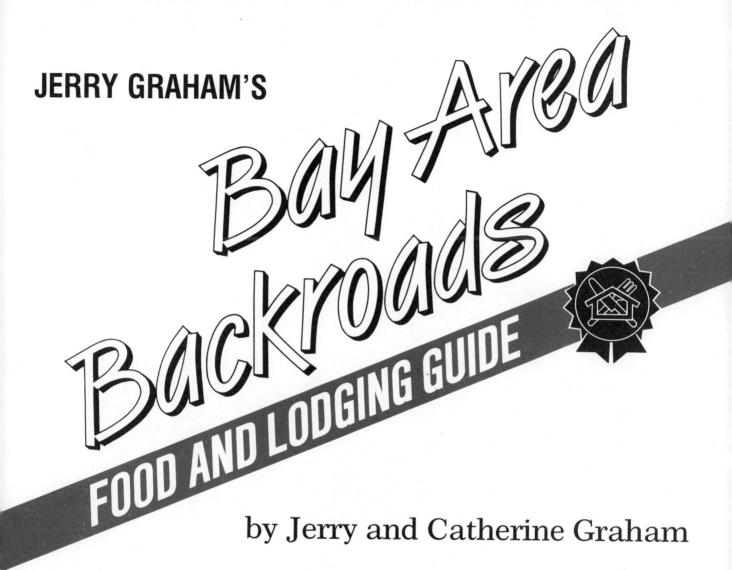

by Jerry and Catherine Graham

PERENNIAL LIBRARY

HARPER & ROW, PUBLISHERS, NEW YORK
Grand Rapids, Philadelphia, St. Louis, San Francisco
London, Singapore, Sydney, Tokyo, Toronto

FIRST EDITION

Designed by Barbara DuPree Knowles

Maps by Ron Lang

LIBRARY OF CONGRESS CATALOGING-IN-PUBLICATION DATA

Graham, Jerry.
    Jerry Graham's Bay Area backroads food and lodging guide/Jerry and Catherine Graham.
      p.   cm.
    ISBN 0-06-096451-0
     1. Restaurants, lunch rooms, etc.—California—San Francisco Bay Area—Guide-books.
    2. Hotels, taverns, etc.—California—San Francisco Bay Area—Guide-books.
    3. San Francisco Bay Area (Calif.)—Description and travel—Guide-books.
    I. Graham, Catherine, 1955– . II. Title.
TX907.3.C22S364 1990
647.94794'61—dc20   89-45659

90 91 92 93 94 DT/RRD 10 9 8 7 6 5 4 3 2 1

Contents

BACKROADS FOOD *North Bay*

 OVERVIEW *1*

BACKROADS FOOD South Bay

OVERVIEW *151*

BACKROADS LODGING *North Bay*

BACKROADS LODGING *South Bay*

BACKROADS LODGING *East Bay*

BACKROADS LODGING *Beyond the Bay*

Acknowledgments

We wish to offer many "thank-yous" to friends and colleagues for their support and encouragement.

Thanks to the staff and management of KRON-TV, and especially to the crew of "Bay Area Backroads"; Jessica Abbe, Paul Ghiringhelli, Vicky Collins, Peter Hammersly, Jeff Pierce, Stan Drury, Dave Vandergriff, Jim Morgan, plus the many other station people who from time to time work on the weekly show. Thanks especially to Bob Klein, who conceived the TV show and suggested that it might be nice to include recommendations for places to eat and stay.

Thanks to the loyal viewers of "Bay Area Backroads" and their many suggestions. They have been valuable tipsters.

Thanks to Larry Ashmead and John Michel at Harper & Row in New York for their encouragement and counsel. They have made the author-editor relationship a great pleasure. Thanks to Joseph Montebello for his appealing cover design. Thanks also to copy editor Shelly Perron for her meticulous eye, and for "getting the jokes." And thanks to Peter Ginsberg, our agent, who has graciously volunteered to do restaurant research for future editions.

Back in California, thanks to Sayre Van Young for her skill at creating indexes, and to Jean Haseltine for plunging through the unbelievable task of checking all addresses, hours, and prices.

Finally, thanks to all the brave people who decided to defy the odds and face the impossible work of opening a restaurant or inn. Because of them, Northern

California is blessed with some of the finest, most interesting places to eat on earth and with some of the most hospitable and rejuvenating getaways one could hope to find anywhere in the world.

Jerry Graham
Catherine Graham

MAY 1989

Introduction

Congratulations! The mere fact that you are reading this book means you are likely to head out on the Backroads of the Bay Area. Not only will you encounter wonderful scenery, unforgettable characters, and memorable attractions, but you'll eat and sleep well, too.

Some background about this book and its authors: Since 1984, Jerry Graham (that's me) has been the host of the top-rated series on KRON-TV in San Francisco "Bay Area Backroads." In each half-hour program, I visit four or five interesting locations and then follow those stories with recommendations of places to eat and stay in the area. Because of the success of that program, I and my wife, Catherine (and that's me), collaborated on our first book, *Jerry Graham's Bay Area Backroads*, published in the summer of 1988. In that book, there was a small section of food and lodging recommendations.

This book takes off from there. In addition to restaurants and inns that have been recommended on the TV show, we have expanded our research to include more than 300 places to eat and more than 115 places to spend the night, material that would only fit in a separate book.

As with our other books, the food and lodging guide will be divided first into broad geographical areas—North Bay, South Bay, East Bay, and Beyond the Bay—and then, in alphabetical order, by communities within those areas. There is no attempt at a uniform length for the entries. Some are brief and some are more wordy, but that is not a barometer of quality or our enthusiasm. Some stories can be told well in a few lines. Others may involve historic buildings, interesting anecdotes, or just be the result of wordy writers with nothing better to do.

Important: Between publication and the time you read this, any number of changes could happen. A restaurant could close, a chef could quit, Anthony Perkins might have taken over that sweet little motel. Do whatever you can to try to verify that the place is still as we described it. We have included phone numbers and addresses.

Yolo

Sonoma

Napa

Solano

Marin

Contra Costa

San Francisco

Alameda

San Mateo

Santa Clara

The Bay Area

Santa Cruz

JERRY GRAHAM'S BAY AREA BACKROADS FOOD AND LODGING GUIDE

Backroads FOOD

This is a book of recommendations. The 300 or so restaurants, cafes, diners, bakeries, and fruit stands in this book are places we like and think you would enjoy, too. This is not a book of reviews. In fact, we don't even like the idea of restaurant reviews. Why should the livelihoods and dreams of so many people hinge on whether or not a critic had what he or she considered to be a good meal? Why bother even to print a negative review? Sure, in the four or more years we've been sampling restaurants on the Backroads, we've eaten some awful meals, but you won't find out about them in this book.

Our criteria are rather simple: We like good, well-prepared food, the fresher the better and the healthier the better. We love places that frown on preservatives and cheap ingredients. We search out cooks who put a little bit of themselves into every dish, whether it's a bowl of soup, a slab of ribs, or a delicately poached fish. If a place serves great desserts, so much the better. And if they have an espresso machine or serve great coffee, they are to be blessed. Decor counts, too, and atmosphere, and the friendliness of the place. Most of all, though, it's the food. One of our great pleasures in life is eating a good meal, and that's the ultimate measure for this book.

It is difficult to report specific hours and menu prices since they change so often. Instead of hours we will indicate which meals are served, unless the hours of operation are unusual or the place is a bakery or coffee shop that does not serve regularly scheduled meals. Instead of fixed dollar amounts we will use the

1

categories Inexpensive, Moderate, and Expensive. We realize these are relative terms, determined by one's own wallet and by how you order. A restaurant offering entrees in the $12 range could be Moderate for one diner, but for another, who adds an appetizer, a salad, a dessert, and a bottle of wine to the tab, the same place could become an Expensive proposition.

As a rule of thumb, Inexpensive will mean that there are currently (1989) many lunch entrees $7 and under, sandwiches are no more than $4 or $5, and desserts cost $2.50 or less. For dinner, Inexpensive means there are entrees priced at $7 and $8 and that two people can feel satisfied and still get out of the place with a tab of from $15 to $20.

Moderate means that there are many lunch items from $8 to $11. Sandwiches are offered for around $6 and desserts are priced at about $3 to $4. For dinner, Moderate means that entrees average $10 to $14 and that two people can dine for $30 to $40, exclusive of wine.

Expensive is anything above the Moderate category.

We've skipped the price category altogether for places that serve only coffee and baked goods; however, as a matter of convenience, we've listed these in the index under inexpensive.

Keep in mind that because there are so many restaurants in the Bay Area, competition is intense and changes are frequent. Chefs move on to new jobs, quality can vary, and yesterday's hit can be history by the time you get there. Please, please call ahead to check current hours and prices.

North Bay

BMWs or no BMWs, for years Marin was a culinary wasteland. One either left the county for a great meal or settled for expensive if mediocre food. But in the mid-1980s the culinary trends that began in Berkeley and San Francisco finally moved across the Golden Gate and San Rafael bridges. Now there are several fine places to eat in Marin, taking advantage of the produce grown in nearby Sonoma and Napa counties. Today you can get everything from a great hamburger to fine Chinese, Thai, Italian, California-French, and even Caribbean food.

CHAPTER **1** Marin County

✔ Bolinas Bay Bakery.   Bolinas is considered a mystical power-spot by those who pay attention to such things. On the streets, you will see lots of tie-dyed fabric and beads and may experience some not-so-good vibrations from locals who wish visitors would stay off their cloud.

   But, if you find yourself in Bolinas and you're hungry and in need of hospitality, head to the Bolinas Bay Bakery. The people are genuinely friendly and help-

BOLINAS
①

3

ful, and they really know how to bake. The New York cheesecake reminded us of the heyday of Lindy's, the pecan pie is filled with nuts instead of syrupy glop, and the more health-conscious items are good, too. Most items are made with organic flours, and all ingredients are cheerfully reported. They are known for the "seeds and stems" loaf—sandwich-style bread filled with sunflower seeds and the like. You can also get a slice of whole-wheat crust pizza and a bottle of fruit juice to take outside and eat on the steps; they have an espresso machine, too. Monday evening is Pizza Night, and the bakery stays open until 9 P.M.

They also sell tie-dyed T-shirts, so if you want to fit in among the locals, you can do some wardrobe shopping, too.

BOLINAS BAY BAKERY, *15 Wharf Road; (415) 868-0211. Open 7 A.M. to 6 P.M. weekdays (to 9 P.M. Mondays); 8 A.M. to 6 P.M. Saturday and Sunday. No alcohol. MC (MasterCard), Visa, Am Ex (American Express). Inexpensive.*

CORTE MADERA ②

✔ **Il Fornaio.** Il Fornaio began as a bakery chain in Italy before opening its first American venture, in San Francisco. In the Bay Area, the chain started off well, but was in a business downturn.

Enter local entrepreneur Larry Mindel, who had run a successful chain of restaurants. He bought the American bakeries and established a chain of Il Fornaio (which means "the baker") restaurants in California. The one in Corte Madera was built first, probably because Mindel lives nearby. The place, with etched-glass partitions and generous use of Carrara marble and terra cotta, was built to resemble an elegant Italian trattoria.

The kitchen, which specializes in Northern Italian cuisine, gets going early in the morning and keeps going into the night. Breakfast might be two eggs baked on a six-inch pizza lined with asparagus and pancetta. For lunch: sandwiches on freshly baked focaccio bread, a variety of salads, calzone. Dinner might feature one of the ducks or chickens seen roasting over the open-fire rotisserie behind the counter. Baked goods—breads, breadsticks, biscotti, and pastries—are displayed like art objects on shelves behind the cash register; you can drop in just to pick up baked goods to enjoy later.

Il Fornaio has its own garden in Sausalito for growing the herbs and vegetables served in the restaurant, so you know you're getting quality ingredients. Prices are reasonable, and the service is excellent; no matter how busy the place is, the waitpersons are friendly, helpful, and they never ever tell you their names.

IL FORNAIO, *223 Town Center; (415) 927-4400. Breakfast, lunch, and dinner daily, plus Sunday brunch. Full bar. MC, Visa. Moderate.*

✔ **Savannah Grill.** The Savannah Grill was one of the first places to qualify Marin for a place on the Bay Area culinary map. It's still a fun place, with a sophis-

Marin

Point Reyes Station

Novato

Sir Francis Drake Blvd.

San Rafael

Mill Valley

Tiburon

Sausalito

ticated atmosphere created by lots of dark wood, white tablecloths, marbled overhead lamps, dim lighting, and an exposed grill area. In fact, if the place is crowded and if you don't mind sitting at the counter you can get a ringside seat and watch the grill cooks at work.

Given the name, it's not surprising to find a southern influence on the menu: barbecued baby back ribs, Gulf prawns with spicy red curry cream, pork tenderloin with grilled apples and onions.

But the menu is extensive and you'll find influences from around the globe: chicken salad with Thai vinaigrette (Catherine almost always orders this); quesadillas with black beans and chorizo; ravioli with Provini veal, swiss chard, roasted garlic, and basil pesto. Highly recommended is a side order of the rosemary polenta—cornmeal mush cut into a triangle and fried in olive oil, seasoned with fresh herbs.

No matter what the ethnic origin, all the menu offerings are very California, meaning most of the ingredients are grown locally and specials are based on what's freshest that day. You will always have a choice of fresh fish plus other typical California Cuisine items such as baked Sonoma chevre.

In this health-and-calorie-conscious area of the world, it is not unusual for customers to order just an appetizer or a small plate of pasta and salad instead of an entree and dessert. Reservations are advised.

SAVANNAH GRILL, *55 Tamal Vista; (415) 924-6774. Lunch Monday through Saturday, dinner nightly, brunch on holidays, Sundays. Full bar. MC, Visa, Am Ex. Moderate.*

FOREST KNOLLS
③

✔ **Two Bird Cafe.** If anyone ever asks you to describe the cultural differences between rural West Marin and the rest of this affluent county, you could say it's the difference between the 1990s and the 1960s, or, to look at it another way, the difference between BMWs and a VW Bug. Or you could point to the Two Bird Cafe in Forest Knolls, a remote little town in West Marin. This is sort of the VW Bug of cafes, reflecting some of the best aspects of the "mellow" good old days of the sixties, featuring good, wholesome food, a very laid-back scene, and a woody and communal atmosphere. It's the kind of place where people linger awhile and read the paper or discuss the timeless merits of the early works of the Grateful Dead.

Breakfast is your best bet, and it's served all day. With egg dishes you get excellent home fries and dense, whole-grain muffins and breads. Coffee is strong and plentiful. You can also choose from a variety of sandwiches, salads, and daily specials that often include thick soups and stews.

TWO BIRD CAFE, *6921 Sir Francis Drake Boulevard; (415) 488-9952. Breakfast and lunch Tuesday through Friday, dinner Thursday through Sunday, brunch*

Saturday and Sunday; closed Mondays. Beer and wine only. MC, Visa. Inexpensive.

✔ **Joe LoCoco's.** From the exterior of the modern business park where the restaurant is located, you'd never expect the elegant interior of LoCoco's. But once you enter the reception area, you are transported into a gracious world of white tablecloths, Italian tiles, and the ambiance of a special occasion—a birthday, an anniversary, a first date. A fabulous display of salads, antipasti, and desserts is strategically located between the front door and the maître d's station, so right away you are hooked.

GREENBRAE

The LoCocos started with a popular pizza joint in the suburb of Terra Linda, to the north. Their ristorante is geared for Northern Italian cuisine with a very large selection of dishes. There are more than a dozen pastas alone, and several chicken, veal, and beef dishes, plus fresh fish. LoCoco's has a bustle to it that is reminiscent of New York or Chicago hangouts. This is not a subtle place. The atmosphere is festive, the waiters love to joke a bit and direct your order, and the portions are sizeable and satisfying. When your aunt and uncle from Syracuse visit, take them here.

JOE LOCOCO'S, *300 Drake's Landing Road; (415) 925-0808. Lunch Monday through Friday, dinner nightly. Full bar. MC, Visa. Moderate to Expensive.*

✔ **Ristorante Dalecio.** Now here's yet another symbol of how things have changed in the suburbs. For years, there was an old family Italian restaurant called Galli's, just south of Novato in the little village of Ignacio. You know the kind of place: huge portions of food covered with gobs of tomato sauce. Well, you wouldn't recognize old Galli's now. It's been transformed into a ristorante, which in Italian means this ain't no diner.

IGNACIO
⑤

Instead of the usual spaghetti and veal cutlet offerings, the menu now features pasta fresca della casa; homemade cappellini, fettuccine, linguine, rigatoni, and tortellini. The rest of the menu reads along these lines. Instead of roast chicken, there's pollo alla griglia: grilled boneless chicken breast with virgin olive oil and lemon. In other words, this is an Italian-Italian restaurant, rather than an American-Italian restaurant. And it's very good.

At lunch, when the prices are a few dollars less, you can also get a half order of pasta with a salad as opposed to a full order. Everything is indeed fresh, and the best available ingredients are used.

A few years ago, this would have been a silly statement, but today it's a compliment to say in all seriousness that this might well be the best restaurant between San Rafael and Petaluma.

RISTORANTE DALECIO, *340 Ignacio Boulevard; (415) 883-0960. Lunch Monday through Saturday, dinner nightly. Full bar. MC, Visa, Am Ex, Diners. Moderate.*

INVERNESS

(6)

✓ **Barnaby's.** This is the restaurant connected to the Golden Hinde Motel, right on Tomales Bay in Inverness. You can eat inside in an airy dining room with floor-to-ceiling windows overlooking the water, or you can be served outside on the deck.

The menu features fresh fish and seafood, salads, and barbecued items like chicken and ribs. There's also a selection of appetizers such as stuffed potato skins filled with enough stuff to make an entire lunch.

BARNABY'S, *in the Golden Hinde Motel, 12938 Sir Francis Drake Boulevard; (415) 669-1114. Lunch and dinner daily, though closed on Wednesday during the winter, plus Sunday brunch. Beer and wine only. MC, Visa. Moderate.*

✓ **Vladimir's.** This Czech restaurant is right in the center of town, such as it is, right on the main road. The owner and the food are authentic Czech. You'll get dumplings with everything, including such specials as roast duck and schnitzel. You'll also be in for a treat if you are a beer fancier. There's an extensive selection of European beers, featuring the brew named for the Czech city of Pilsen. The food and drink are good, and Vladimir is a congenial host. The decor is what one would imagine to find in the countryside of Czechoslovakia: dark wood, lots of beer steins, and a general atmosphere of *gemütlichkeit*. You'll also find many pictures of Vlad himself on horseback. Your host is a champion equestrian as well as war hero, and he has many a story to tell.

This is one of two Czech restaurants in the small town of Inverness. It's also the better of the two, for our tastes. The food is heavy on starches and thick sauces, a far cry from spa cuisine. You won't lose weight here, but you will not leave hungry.

And yes, you will get a friendly chuckle when you shout to the waiter, "Check, please." He may respond, "Double Czech."

VLADIMIR'S, *12785 Sir Francis Drake Boulevard (at Inverness Way); (415) 669-1021. Lunch Wednesday through Sunday, dinner Tuesday through Sunday; closed Mondays. Full bar. No credit cards. Moderate.*

KENTFIELD

(7)

✓ **Half Day Cafe.** When this cafe opened in 1985, the idea was to have a place for locals to hang out, have meetings, and eat inexpensively but well. It was open for breakfast and lunch only, thus the name Half Day Cafe. The idea worked so well that dinner five nights a week was added, but the name has remained the same.

This is the sort of place we're always thrilled to find: good food for cheap in a friendly atmosphere. The menu is basic cafe food made with high-quality ingredients; so even a mundane item like a turkey sandwich ends up being a great turkey sandwich. Breakfast includes a variety of egg dishes (huevos rancheros, florentine scramble), French toast, freshly baked muffins and scones, and parfaits of granola, yogurt, and seasonal berries. Lunch features housemade soups, salads, egg dishes, and a variety of hamburgers served with crispy french fries. At dinner the menu expands to include pasta and fish entrees.

The restaurant is located right across the street from the College of Marin and it attracts a mixed crowd: students and professors, wealthy Marin ladies between shopping sprees, and rolfers between appointments. It is housed in a large, barnlike structure built in the thirties. When purchased by the current owner the building was being used as an automotive body shop. In its reincarnation as a restaurant, the place has high ceilings with skylights—very cheerful even on rainy days. This is an ideal place to go with a small child; there's lots of room and a normally high noise level so Junior can't really disturb anyone.

HALF DAY CAFE, *848 College Avenue; (415) 459-0291. Breakfast and lunch daily, dinner Tuesday through Saturday. Beer and wine only. MC, Visa. Inexpensive.*

✔ **La Lanterna.**   This small, neighborhood restaurant is very popular, and for good reason. La Lanterna serves authentic Northern Italian cuisine at reasonable prices. In addition to the regular menu, the chef offers a special selection of dishes that are either low in cholesterol, fat, or sodium, or a combination thereof. Chef Jim Brewn calls this type of cuisine *il coure sano*, or "the healthy heart." You can indeed have tasty Italian food without loading it with salty cheese and fattening sauces. On the weekends, the entire restaurant is a nonsmoking establishment.

LA LANTERNA, *799 College Avenue, in a small shopping center; (415) 258-0144. Dinner Tuesday through Sunday; closed Monday. Beer and wine only. MC, Visa, Am Ex. Moderate.*

✔ **Lark Creek Inn.**   Bradley Ogden became one of the "star" chefs of the Bay Area when he moved from the Midwest to set up the restaurant at the plush Campton Place Hotel in San Francisco. His innovative creations of American cuisine were hailed by the critics, and folks would spend large sums of money to eat in the elegant dining room. In the fall of 1989, Ogden left the city to open his own place on the Backroads, and his food is better than ever. What's more, the prices are downright reasonable, especially at lunch.

The new location is an old inn, set back from the main street of the quiet town of Larkspur. At first glance, the place looks like the kind of country inn or restaurant that you used to see all over the East Coast and Midwest, usually a converted old mansion. But upon closer inspection there is an air of hipness, perhaps due to the modern ceramic art decorating the walls and the smartly dressed

LARKSPUR
⑧

waiters and waitresses gliding past the tables with heaping plates of glorious-looking food. Part of the show is to see what everybody else is eating.

Whatever you choose, it will be terrific and there will be lots of it; portions are generous. The menus change daily, but at lunch you will probably find such items as a baked meatloaf sandwich with romaine on grilled brioche, Southern fried chicken salad with blue cheese and red wine vinaigrette, or Yankee pot roast with onion dumplings. At dinner, you will find items along the lines of pan-fried trophy trout with BBQ chive glaze, braised escarole, and sweet potato and beet chips; grilled beef liver steak with country bacon and oak-fired onions; and oven-roasted salmon with corn spoonbread and chervil tomato broth. Fresh seafood, pasta, and other selections are also available on a menu that will cater to every taste, all of it seemingly prepared by a culinary magician.

Desserts are outrageously good, and like everything else at the restaurant, are served in huge portions. Two of us shared the dark devil's food cake with home-made buttermilk ice cream. Amazing!

This is a special place. Reservations for lunch and dinner are recommended. A tip to those who can't get around to making reservations: The bar does serve a limited menu of light dinner items and reservations are not necessary. The beverage menu offers some selections of nonalcoholic beer, wine, and blender drinks; a virgin Lark Creek fizz is quite delicious!

LARK CREEK INN, *234 Magnolia Avenue; (415) 924-7766. Lunch Sunday through Friday, dinner nightly. Full bar. Smoking permitted in bar area only. MC, Visa, Am Ex. Moderate.*

✔ **Marvin Gardens.** If you have ever played Monopoly, you will probably be tempted to try a place that calls itself Marvin Gardens. You won't be sorry. Tucked away off the street in a little shopping center, Marvin's is a comfortable neighborhood cafe offering an unusual selection of dishes.

Daily specials always feature an Indian curry, a Mexican dish or two, and an Italian frittata in addition to the regular fare of burgers, omelets, soups, and salads. All the food is well prepared. Try the desserts, especially the chocolate mousse cake.

MARVIN GARDENS, *1000 Magnolia Street; (415) 461-2241. Lunch Monday through Saturday, dinner Thursday through Saturday; closed Sunday. Beer and wine only. MC, Visa. Inexpensive to Moderate.*

MARSHALL
⑨

✔ **Tony's.** One of the favorite outings for people in the Bay Area is to head to Point Reyes for a day at the beach and then drive up the coast to the town of Marshall for barbecued oysters. Tony's is a charming place offering this specialty for you oyster lovers.

Overlooking Tomales Bay, Tony's also offers fresh seafood and Italian specialties to go along with the main attraction. The atmosphere is very informal, with red-checkered tablecloths, big outdoor grills, and mounds of empty oyster shells lying around.

TONY'S, *11863 Highway 1, just south of the town of Marshall; (415) 663-1107. Lunch and dinner Friday, Saturday, and Sunday; open Monday in summer. Beer and wine only. No credit cards. Moderate.*

✔ **Avenue Grill.** From the decor you might think the Avenue Grill is a bit fancy and stiff, but no; despite the snazzy decor it's an informal place with prices in the moderate-plus range.

The food is California Cuisine, meaning they specialize in whatever is freshest that day. You can always get a juicy, upscale burger here, and they also experiment with unusual food combinations and change their specials with great regularity. Selected menu items include Thai-fried calamari, crab and cheddar quesadilla with salsa, fresh fish, brisket, chicken pot pie, and touches of the diner revival such as meatloaf. If you like garlic, you'll want to try the house mashed potatoes, guaranteed to keep vampires away for centuries.

AVENUE GRILL, *44 East Blithedale Avenue; (415) 388-6003. Dinner nightly. Beer and wine only. MC, Visa. Moderate to Expensive.*

✔ **Cafe Renoir.** It takes a bit of persistence to find Cafe Renoir, but it's worth the effort. This itsy-bitsy jewel box of a cafe is situated in the rear of an office complex at the end of Shoreline Highway north of Sausalito. There are not a lot of tables, and much of one wall is taken up by a mural based on one of Auguste Renoir's masterpieces. (If you'll look closely, you find the owners' faces in the crowd.)

Open 7 A.M. to 7 P.M. for breakfast, lunch, and light, early dinners, Cafe Renoir specializes in such fare as fresh muffins and egg dishes at breakfast, housemade soups, gargantuan salads, pasta, and light entrees at lunch. By all means, try the chicken salad, our favorite: It is lightly curried and served on a variety of very fresh lettuces and seasonal vegetables. Coffees and pastries are also top-notch, and you can sit on the patio on a warm day. Owners Jerry Mulroney and Phil Thomas—remember them from the mural?—are among the friendliest guys in town, and they've opened a similar place up the road in San Rafael (see Cafe Monet, page 17). Reservations are advised.

CAFE RENOIR, *100 Shoreline Highway, near Route 101; (415) 332-8668. Breakfast, lunch, and early dinner (7 A.M. to 7 P.M.) Monday through Friday. Beer and wine only. All nonsmoking. MC, Visa. Inexpensive to Moderate.*

MILL VALLEY
⑩

✔ **Depot Bookstore and Cafe.** For years, the semiseedy Book Depot in the center of town was the place where the literati and filmmakers of southern Marin hung out. Then in 1987, the place was purchased, spruced up, and turned into the new, improved Depot Bookstore and Cafe. You can still get a good cappuccino and pastry while rubbing elbows with writers and filmmakers, and you can also have a nice lunch and a light dinner. As the name implies, this coffeehouse was fashioned from the town's old train depot and is an excellent bookstore. The cafe area also serves as a gallery for local artists; the exhibit changes every month or so. It's a very pleasant place to browse or read while enjoying a cup of coffee.

DEPOT BOOKSTORE AND CAFE, *87 Throckmorton Avenue; (415) 383-2665. Breakfast, lunch, and light dinners daily, 7 A.M. to 10 P.M. Beer and wine only. All nonsmoking. No credit cards. Inexpensive to Moderate.*

✔ **Dipsea Cafe.** This is the place to go when you're looking for a fast and friendly short-order breakfast or lunch. We're talking eggs, pancakes, hamburgers, and BLTs, Mill Valley style. That means the lettuce on your sandwich is more likely to be Romaine than iceberg; the vinegar served with fish 'n' chips will be balsamic. And, of course, there's an espresso machine on the premises.

Located just off the main square in a brick minimall called El Paseo, the Dipsea Cafe is named after the famous annual runners' race that takes place on Mt. Tam. It's worth dropping by just to see the gallery of photographs chronicling the history of the grueling endurance test. Lots of locals patronize the cafe, and it's so small that you're likely to be drawn into a conversation with the person at the table or in the counter seat next to you.

DIPSEA CAFE, *1 El Paseo; (415) 381-0298. Breakfast and lunch daily, plus Sunday brunch. Beer and wine only. All nonsmoking. No credit cards. Inexpensive.*

✔ **Jennie Low's Chinese Cuisine.** When she arrived in America from Hong Kong, Jennie Low couldn't even cook rice. Her uncle was a master chef and on his days off he would prepare food for the family. He told his impetuous young niece to pay attention. Fortunately for us all, she did.

Since learning to cook everything Chinese, Jennie Low has authored three cookbooks and now teaches cooking and leads culinary tours to China. Best of all, she started her own restaurant, which became an immediate and on-going hit from the second the doors opened.

Before going into rapturous praise of the food, we must mention the unpretentious, aesthetically pleasing, and humorous environment Ms. Low has created for presenting her food. Three things might catch your eye. One is what we jokingly refer to as "the kitchen under glass"; you can watch the cooks, woks, and cleavers in action through a plate glass window, safely protected from splattering and the heat. Then you might notice the abundance of purple and lavender. These are Jennie's good-luck colors; the walls, waiters' and busboys' shirts, menus, even Jennie's lipstick have a purple hue. Last but not least, on the menu you might observe that every dish is priced ending with the number eight (for example, clams in black bean sauce is priced at $8.18). In many Asian cultures, eight is like the Western number seven, an omen of good luck and fortune. Nobody ever accused Jennie Low of not being superstitious.

And now, the food. Let's start with appetizers. We know people who would drive for hours to get an order of crab puffs, which are deep-fried won tons filled with a mixture of walnuts, crabmeat, jicama, water chestnuts, and cream cheese. Jennie offers both pork and vegetarian pot stickers, both kinds wrapped in skins made fresh that day.

And then there are the Jennie's specials: her lemon chicken, deep-fried nuggets of chicken breast served with a thick, tangy sauce; Jennie's beef, stir-fried with snow peas and bamboo shoots in brown bean sauce; Jennie's broccoli, served crisp and flavored with sesame oil and garlic.

The menu is extensive, featuring dishes from the Cantonese, Mandarin, Hunan, and Szechuan regions of China. Familiar offerings include hot and sour soup, mu shu pork, hot spicy eggplant, and Hunan prawns, all excellently prepared without the aid of MSG.

The kitchen is very accommodating to individual tastes; you can request degrees of spiciness and heat. Best of all, the prices are reasonable, with most entrees priced at about seven or eight dollars, and all items can be prepared to go.

JENNIE LOW'S CHINESE CUISINE, *38 Miller Avenue; (415) 388-8868. Lunch Monday through Saturday, dinner nightly. Beer and wine only. All nonsmoking. MC, Visa, Am Ex. Inexpensive to Moderate.*

NOVATO
(11)

✓ **The Hilltop Cafe.** A lovely spot for lunch in Novato sits high on a hill overlooking the city and the valley below. The Hilltop Cafe is a rather large restaurant, with a bar in the center and all the tables situated so you can gaze out of the huge picture windows that dominate the building. With such a setting, it would be logical to expect that the food would be something of an afterthought. Happily, that is not the case.

There's a standard menu offering several pasta dishes, plus a few chicken, fish, and veal dishes. Sandwiches are also available. Each day an additional menu of specials is printed that offers an even bigger selection. Our party of four had grilled, peppered salmon in cilantro lime sauce; pork filet, pan roasted with garlic and mushrooms; cold poached salmon and prawns in a mustard dill dressing; and veal piccatta, and all were very good. For the adventurous, you can start with the house soup, which is cream of garlic and is served in a carved-out miniloaf of sourdough bread.

Dinners are a bit more traditional, featuring steaks, lobster tail and prime rib, along with several pasta, chicken, and veal dishes.

THE HILLTOP CAFE, *850 Lamont Road; (415) 892-2222. Lunch, Monday through Friday, dinner nightly, Sunday brunch. Full bar. MC, Visa, Am Ex. Moderate.*

✔ **Santa Fe Mary's.** You wouldn't expect to find a New Mexico–style restaurant in the center of the suburban town of Novato, but that's exactly what Santa Fe Mary's is. We use the term New Mexico–style because the food is not as spicy as the authentic food of the Southwest, but it is good, and the place is attractive. You can order everything from typical Mexican specialties to mesquite-grilled items. Some customers settle for Coronas and nachos or other appetizers. Santa Fe Mary's can be jammed in the evenings, as it's probably the liveliest spot in town. Lunchtimes are usually less crowded.

SANTA FE MARY'S, *1200 Grant Avenue; (415) 898-2234. Lunch Tuesday through Saturday, dinner nightly, Sunday brunch. Beer and wine only. No non-smoking section. MC, Visa, Am Ex. Moderate.*

OLEMA
⑫

✔ **Chez Madeleine.** This is a very pleasant little country French restaurant, serving unpretentious dinners. One of the nicest things about it is that you'll feel like you're eating in someone's home, and that someone happens to know her way around the kitchen. This isn't a California adaptation of French cuisine. Madeleine grew up in France and cooks as she was taught. She will probably greet you at the door, then run back to check things in the kitchen. The menu offers items you find on most French menus in the United States, all of them well prepared. It's a very informal place, bustling with locals and tourists.

CHEZ MADELEINE, *10905 Highway 1; (415) 663-9177. Dinner Wednesday through Sunday, and Sunday brunch. Beer and wine only. MC, Visa. Moderate.*

✔ **Olema Inn Wine Bar and Restaurant.** The Olema Inn originally opened on the Fourth of July, 1876. In those days, Olema was a rough-and-tumble logging town, and the inn served triple duty as a stagecoach stop, tavern, and overnight resting spot. In more recent years, several folks tried their hands at running a restaurant on the premises, but the place would close down every few years. Its most recent incarnation began in mid-1989. If quality and comfort are any measure, the Olema Inn Wine Bar and Restaurant should do well.

The menu offers traditional French and Italian dishes—coquille St. Jacques, and veal and spinach cannelloni, for example—plus modern California concoctions like endive and radicchio salad with crab and walnut vinaigrette. This salad is a good example of the attention to detail here. First of all, it is an aesthetically impressive offering, the various ingredients arranged artfully on the plate. It is also huge, a meal in itself; and true to the idea of California Cuisine the ingredients are very fresh. Even the more modest salade maison of seasonal greens is of the same high quality. Served with an excellent vinaigrette, it is priced at $3 (the going rate is more like $5 or more for a dinner salad of this quality).

The poulet roti grandmère, the simplest of chicken dishes, is another test of the kitchen, and it is wonderful, served brimming with juice and flavored with garlic. The daily seafood specials are very good—as they should be, given the Inn's proximity to the ocean. Dessert eaters take note of the house specialty: chocolate cake resembling a fudge brownie served warm.

Saturday and Sunday brunch offerings are not for the dieters in your group. The menu features such items as salmon Benedict, shrimp and crab en croute, and pear and camembert quiche.

The atmosphere is casually elegant, and in good weather you may dine outdoors.

By the way, the Olema Inn offers bed and breakfast accommodations upstairs (see Lodging section, page 158).

OLEMA INN WINE BAR AND RESTAURANT, *10000 Sir Francis Drake Boulevard; (415) 663-9559. Lunch Tuesday through Friday, dinner Tuesday through Sunday, brunch Saturday and Sunday; closed Mondays. Full bar. MC, Visa, Am Ex. Moderate.*

✔ **Drake's Beach Cafe.** When you're out at Point Reyes National Seashore, you are a long way from a restaurant. Fortunately, the cafe adjoining one of the Seashore's visitors' centers is surprisingly good. The Drake's Beach Cafe ought to be the model for luncheonettes and snack bars at every beach in the United States.

It's a small place with a few tables inside and lots of tables outside overlooking the ocean. Just like every other snack bar in the world, they have burgers and hot dogs, except these are thick, hand-pressed real beef burgers served on great whole-wheat buns from a local bakery and juicy, well-seasoned franks. Both the New England clam chowder and the split pea soup were definitely homemade. Also featured are vegetarian specials and really good coffee from Graffeo's, in San Francisco, and great desserts. Every Saturday and Sunday you can get barbecued local oysters and corn.

Prices are inexpensive, and the only disadvantage is that the cafe can be crowded when the weather is good at Drake's Beach.

DRAKE'S BEACH CAFE, *at the end of Sir Francis Drake Boulevard at the ocean's*

POINT REYES NATIONAL SEASHORE

edge, adjoining the visitors' center; (415) 669-1297. Open 11:30 A.M. to 6 P.M. weekdays; 10 A.M. to 6 P.M. weekends; closed on stormy days. No alcohol served. All nonsmoking. No credit cards. Inexpensive.

POINT REYES STATION
(13)

✔ **Station House Cafe.** If we had only one mealtime to spend in the Inverness–Point Reyes area we would eat at the Station House Cafe. This is an informal place in the center of Point Reyes Station. It looks like a glorified coffee shop, and the waitresses bop around in kind, but something else entirely is going on in the kitchen. The surprise is the variety of selections offered for lunch or dinner.

If you are searching for a romantic spot in the country, move on. This is a no-frills family restaurant. The food here is terrific. You can get egg dishes, great hamburgers on homemade buns, pasta, grilled fresh fish, wonderful salads, and it's all prepared perfectly and the service is very friendly. Be sure to save room for one of their desserts and a cappuccino.

STATION HOUSE CAFE, *11180 State Highway 1 (Main Street); (415) 663-1515. Breakfast, lunch, and dinner Wednesday through Monday; closed Tuesday. Full bar. All nonsmoking, except at the bar. MC, Visa. Inexpensive to Moderate.*

SAN ANSELMO
(14)

✔ **Bubba's Diner.** This is a wonderful place to have breakfast or lunch and to be coddled. The same folks who run the Marin establishments Coco Nuts (see Sausalito, page 20) and Santa Fe Mary's (see Novato, page 14) run this place; apparently it's part of their scheme to offer the customer more fun per calorie than any other places in Marin.

Though one might think that the "Bubba" in the name is the nickname for a former defensive tackle, here they are referring to the Yiddish word for grandmother. When you come in here, you are almost ordered to eat and eat a lot so that if you're not careful you could end up looking like a former defensive tackle.

Breakfasts feature a variety of egg dishes with half a plate full of hash browns. You can have muffins or bagels or huge fluffy biscuits. At lunch, you might want some homemade soup, a giant salad, or one of their unusual sandwich combinations (they get especially creative during the holidays and election time).

We dare ya, just try to get out without having dessert . . .

BUBBA'S DINER, *566 San Anselmo Avenue; (415) 459-6862. Breakfast and lunch daily, dinner Friday through Sunday. No alcohol served. MC, Visa. Inexpensive.*

✔ **Comforts.** San Anselmo may lead the nation in the number per capita of incredibly cute restaurants and cafes featuring espresso machines. One of the nicest is called Comforts, and it is located right on the main drag of the downtown area. When you walk in, the first thing you see is the deli counter filled with a beautifully displayed array of salads, casseroles, and pastas you can take out, or you can be seated for lunch and choose from an ever-changing seasonal menu of soups and daily specials.

In this pleasant, pastel-colored dining room a curiously international array of items is offered, items from all over the map that may include black bean chili, Thai lemon-lime chicken soup, or pasta primavera. The chef is on a low-sodium diet so the food sometimes comes out of the kitchen lightly salted, which may be troublesome for those accustomed to salting their food. However, if you request low-sodium preparation you will have an empathetic cook.

The same chef obviously has no problem with sugar so you will find a fine assortment of sweets. Chocoholics should ask for the karioka—dark chocolate cake with alternating layers of white and dark chocolate mousse filling.

COMFORTS, *337 San Anselmo Avenue; (415) 454-6790. Breakfast and lunch served; deli open 9 A.M. to 6 P.M. daily. Beer and wine only. All nonsmoking. MC, Visa over $15. Moderate.*

✔ **Cafe Monet.**   The owners of Cafe Renoir (see Mill Valley, page 11) have followed up on their success with Cafe Monet, and thus have covered the French Impressionist food market in Marin. Both restaurants have large copies of famous paintings by their namesake artists, and both are comfortable, attractive, and affordable cafes. This is a place where you can be served quickly if you need to catch the opening of a movie across the road, or if you just want to have a sandwich or salad and hang out.

SAN RAFAEL
⑮

Like Cafe Renoir, Cafe Monet is located in a large office complex; this one is called Regency Center. You have to make an effort to find the neon sign over the counter area, which can be seen from the parking lot in front of the building. As you enter you see most of the food being prepared behind the large counter and a copy of Monet's famous water lilies adorning a wall.

The menu is posted on a chalkboard each week, and it shows the sense of humor of the proprietors. One day it read: roasted chicken breast with black beans and rice; a turkey-melt sandwich; a barbecued pork sandwich; Sicilian pasta; and shoulder massage ($1).The massages are actually ordered and given while you sit at the table and await your order, and have become one of the hits of the Cafe. Another example of the proprietors' touch of whimsy is the use of cartoon-decorated glasses for beverages. We had Perrier in a Pepe le Pew tumbler.

Prices are scaled so that everything is priced under $10. There are also extremely rich and fattening desserts and good coffee drinks.

CAFE MONET, *in the Regency Center, 100 Smith Ranch Road; (415) 479-8668. Open 9:30 A.M. to 4 P.M. Monday, 9:30 A.M. to 9 P.M. Tuesday through Friday, 5 P.M. to 9 P.M. Saturday, closed Sunday. Beer and wine only. All nonsmoking. MC, Visa. Inexpensive to Moderate.*

✔ **Cafe Tango.** This was one of the first places in the Bay Area, certainly in Marin, to feature tapas, "little tastes" of wonderful food that are served in bars and cafes throughout Spain. Now the tiny bar has been expanded into a small restaurant, and the new owners have expanded the menu as well. Still, you can't go wrong making a meal out of their tapas, which include espinadas catalana (sautéed spinach with raisins, pine nuts, apricots), calamares à la plancha (grilled squid with garlic and parsley), tortilla espanola (Spanish potato and onion omelet), and albondigas (Spanish meatballs in almond sauce).

While waiting for the food to arrive a small basket of bread is served with salsa romesco (a sweet red pepper and almond sauce) instead of butter. Afterward, you can indulge in espresso and a small selection of classic desserts, including flan, crema catalana, and chocolate mousse.

CAFE TANGO, *1232 Fourth Street; (415) 459-2721. Lunch and dinner Tuesday through Saturday. Beer and wine only. MC, Visa. Inexpensive to Moderate.*

✔ **Milly's.** Even if you don't care a fig about fiber and sodium and complex carbohydrates, you can have a lovely meal at Milly's, a dinner spot on the far reaches of San Rafael's main drag, Fourth Street. Milly's slogan is "gracious vegetarian dining." This means variations on traditional menu items like tofu piccata, tempeh Oscar, and a warm cobb salad (sans meat, of course). Even the most committed carnivore can order a satisfying meal of hearty soups, enchiladas, and pasta, all well-seasoned with herbs instead of lots of salt. The alcoholic beverages offered are along the lines of saki, plum wine, and beers, plus nonalcoholic wines made from wine grapes; these wines are not sweet like grape juice.

MILLY'S, *1613 Fourth Street; (415) 459-1601. Dinner nightly. Beer and wine only. MC, Visa, Am Ex. Inexpensive to Moderate.*

✔ **Panama Hotel.** If you love vintage Hawaiian shirts, art deco bric-a-brac, and slowly revolving overhead fans à la *Casablanca*, then you'll love the ambiance of the Panama Hotel. This is an operating bed-and-breakfast inn hidden away in a residential neighborhood.

The dinner menu changes nightly, taking advantage of seasonal offerings from the nearby farms in Sonoma and Napa. A typical evening's menu might include linguini with duck sausage, grilled ribeye steak with pine nut sauce, Thai squid salad, and grilled organic chicken with tomatillo sauce.

The lunch menu remains constant and it includes a soup, salad, and pasta of the day. You can also get Thai coconut curried chicken salad, Panama burritos with homemade black bean frijoles and fresh salsa, a Cajun meatloaf sandwich with crisp pan-fried potatoes and Caesar salad, big enough for two, heavy on the

Parmesan. Both lunch and dinner are moderately priced, especially given the high quality of the ingredients.

If at all possible, eat in the courtyard. Once you step through the wrought-iron gate suddenly you're on a garden terrace with strings of little white lights in the trees creating a fairyland effect. There are ample heaters, so you can dine comfortably outside most of the time.

Don't be surprised if a swing band arrives and starts playing Cole Porter tunes.

PANAMA HOTEL, *4 Bayview Street; (415) 457-3993. Lunch Tuesday through Friday, dinner Tuesday through Sunday, brunch Sunday; closed Monday. Beer and wine only. MC, Visa, Am Ex, Diners. Moderate.*

✔ **Phyllis' Giant Burgers.**   This looks like a place you'd find in the Midwest instead of Marvelous Marin. But here it is, with nothing on the menu but hamburgers and companions like grilled onions, fries, cole slaw, and milkshakes. The giant burgers are just that, and you can have them with bacon and/or your choice of four kinds of cheeses. Phyllis' wins the Best Hamburger category every year in a local paper, and we have friends from the city who will drive all the way to Marin to have one. These are not gourmet, fresh-ground sirloin tip; these are old-fashioned, greasy affairs served on a soft white bun. The only concession to gourmet tastes is the optional sourdough roll, with sautéed onions and Dijon mustard. Junior-size burgers are also available. Phyllis also has a place in Mill Valley.

PHYLLIS' GIANT BURGERS, *2202 Fourth Street; (415) 456-0866. Open 11 A.M. to 9 P.M. daily. No alcohol served. No credit cards. Inexpensive.*

✔ **Royal Thai.**   Marin is developing a new reputation as a place to find interesting ethnic restaurants, and some of the best Thai cuisine in the Bay Area can be found in a little shopping center called the French Quarter.

If you have never had Thai food, this is a good place for an initiation. Try the satays, or anything flavored with lemon grass or mint. Be sure to tell them how tolerant you are of hot and spicy foods.

ROYAL THAI, *in the French Quarter, 610 Third Street; (415) 485-1074. Lunch Monday through Friday, dinner nightly. Beer and wine only. MC, Visa, Am Ex, Diners. Inexpensive to Moderate.*

✔ **Caffe Trieste.**   This is the Marin branch of the famous North Beach institution in San Francisco. The Trieste makes some of the best coffee drinks to be found anywhere. They will also make you a sandwich, and have Italian pastries on hand. The atmosphere is conducive to sitting and reading or having a political

SAUSALITO
⑯

discussion with anyone who will listen. This is not a fancy place for a special meal; it's where you can get a continental breakfast, a light lunch or dinner, or quick pick-me-up any time of day. It's also a good place to soak up some local atmosphere.

CAFFE TRIESTE, *1000 Bridgeway; (415) 332-7770. Open 7 A.M. to 11 P.M. daily. Beer and wine only. No nonsmoking section. No credit cards. Inexpensive.*

✔ **Coco Nuts.** What a fun place to go! Coco Nuts serves breakfast and lunch items best described as "Caribbean food with a sense of humor." These include rasta pasta (saffron fettuccine with sun-dried tomatoes, roasted garlic, eggplant, and black beans tossed with extra virgin olive oil and aged Gouda); dread lox (smoked yellow fin tuna with hearts of palm, papaya, and onion on salad greens); and the tourist burger (flame broiled, with french fries, and, to quote the menu "other burger-type stuff"). Maybe the funniest thing is that it all tastes so good.

A section of the menu is named "Big tastes, little plates," which struck us as being a variety of Caribbean tapas. Highly recommended are the pinonos—a slice of grilled plantain encircling a stuffing of roasted pork, almonds, golden raisins, and dried mango, topped with a dollop of sour cream.

Breakfast items include whole-grain pancakes with macadamia nuts, Creole beignets, corn muffins, and waffles topped with cinnamon, raisins, nuts, and berries. Thus, both health-conscious eaters and those persons who simply want to play with their food can find something satisfying. Clearly this place is run by folks who know how to create theme restaurants. (See Bubba's Diner, San Anselmo, page 16, and Santa Fe Mary's, Novato, page 14).

COCO NUTS, *3001 Bridgeway; (415) 331-7515. Breakfast and lunch daily. Beer and wine only. All nonsmoking. MC, Visa. Moderate.*

✔ **Fred's Place.** Want to have breakfast where the locals who don't care about cholesterol go? It's said that five hundred people compete daily for the restaurant's thirty seats, and we believe it. Not only is the food good and plentiful, but this is also an informal community center where you can pick up all the gossip, avoid the tourist rush, and read the newspaper with your coffee for as long as you'd like. Large portions of eggs and pancakes are the breakfast specialty, hamburgers are the sort of fare at lunch. Nothing fancy, just good eats and plenty of it. Payment is on the honor system. Just tell the cashier what you had.

FRED'S PLACE, *1917 Bridgeway; (415) 332-4575. Open from 6:30 A.M. to 2:30 P.M. Monday through Friday, 7 A.M. to 3 P.M. Saturday and Sunday. Beer and wine only. No nonsmoking section. No credit cards. Inexpensive.*

✔ **Gatsby's.** Another local neighborhood hangout, removed from the tourist scene around Bridgeway and the waterfront, is on Caledonia Street, where residents can not only go to the drugstore or grocery but also have an informal dinner at Gatsby's. This is a friendly and busy place that specializes in Chicago-style pizza—in other words, stuffed and huge. You can also get pasta, a meatball sandwich, salads, and other such fare. This is a good place to take the kids, particularly if they tend to make noise. With the sound of the TV and/or the music system, no one will notice the tykes.

GATSBY'S, *39 Caledonia Street; (415) 332-4500. Lunch and dinner daily. Full bar. No nonsmoking section. MC, Visa. Inexpensive to Moderate.*

✔ **Parkside Cafe and Snack Bar.** Stinson Beach is a little surfside town with a grocery, art gallery, real estate office, surf shop, and, on warm days, hordes of sunbathers. We've been there dozens of times over the years, but only recently did a local tell us about the Parkside Cafe. From the outside it looks like a typical hot dog and burger snack bar and we didn't even realize there was a sizeable cafe inside.

STINSON BEACH
⑰

Surprise! This is a great place. They offer old-fashioned home-style cooking with items like muffins, breads, cookies, and pastries baked on the premises, plus burgers, great omelets, bulging sandwiches, and strong coffee. The owner is the grill chef, and he or his wife will probably be there to greet you when you arrive. They also prepare daily specials, including a soup and fresh fish. It's an informal kind of place, where you can arrive windswept and wet from the beach and feel right at home. The tables are covered simply with oilcloths, and you help yourself to water and coffee. Another nice touch: There's a baby grand piano just sitting there waiting for someone to play it.

The Parkside Cafe also functions as a community center. Posted by the front door is the current schedule of the Exercise with a Friend program; neighbors meet each morning at the cafe and go for a hike, bike ride, or whatever the day's activity is. The outside terrace (where lettuces, herbs, and other items for the cafe are grown) is sometimes used for community theater and other such events.

The snack bar is open in summer and makes burgers, fries, and really good milkshakes (try the banana) to go. The giant oatmeal cookies are just like the ones we wish mom had made.

PARKSIDE CAFE AND SNACK BAR, *43 Arsenal Avenue, just off the main drag; (415) 868-1272. Cafe hours: 7:30 A.M. to 2 P.M. weekdays, 8 A.M. to 2 P.M. weekends all year. Snack Bar open seasonally, usually March through October, 11 A.M. to 8 P.M. weekdays, 11 A.M. to 9 P.M. weekends. Beer and wine only. No credit cards. Inexpensive.*

✔ **The Sand Dollar.** This little bar and cafe has been there forever, a Stinson Beach tradition that has withstood the changing trends in food and fashion. Located right on Route 1 in the center of town, the Sand Dollar has a limited selection at lunch, basically burgers and salads. The dinner menu is more extensive and usually includes fresh fish, fried chicken, steak, and nightly specials. It's all surprisingly good, and if you have their mud pie for dessert you will remember the place fondly.

Weather permitting, you can have your meal outside on the large patio.

THE SAND DOLLAR, *3458 Shoreline Highway (Route 1); (415) 868-0434. Lunch and dinner daily. Full bar. No nonsmoking section. No credit cards. Inexpensive for lunch, Moderate for dinner.*

TIBURON

(18)

✔ **Sweden House.**   The Main Street waterfront of this picturesque village is home to several big restaurants, all with decks overlooking the bay. This is where folks come when the fog enshrouds San Francisco and everyone freezes in the summer. In Tiburon, it's likely to be sunny and delightfully warm, and places like Sam's and Guyamas are jammed with folks who will drink and lunch on the deck. Our favorite spot is smaller and less a "scene." Sweden House is a bakery-cafe with about ten tables inside and four or five out on a small deck.

When you enter, you have to walk past a glass case filled with enticing pastries. Don't worry. You can come back after lunch. The menu is limited, with sandwiches, salads, and maybe a special of the day. Everything is good, particularly the Swedish-style open-face sandwiches.

SWEDEN HOUSE, *35 Main Street; (415) 435-9767. Open 8 A.M. to 5 P.M. Monday through Friday, 8:30 A.M. to 7 P.M. Saturday and Sunday. Beer and wine only. No nonsmoking section. No credit cards. Inexpensive to Moderate.*

CHAPTER **2** Sonoma County

Since we have been combing the Backroads, beginning in 1984, the number of new and good restaurants that have opened is nothing short of astounding. There always were a few top-notch places; a couple in Santa Rosa, a few in Petaluma, one or two in Sonoma, but now wonderful restaurants and cafes are turning up in very small communities like Sebastopol, Healdsburg, and Glen Ellen. One of our pleasures is to discover an ambitious new enterprise, elevating the quality of eating in its town.

BODEGA BAY

(1)

✔ **The Tides.**   This restaurant is part of a busy tourist complex right on the water. You'll see a gift shop, a tackle-and-bait store, a fish market—all the trappings of hokeyness that couldn't possibly lead to a decent meal, right? Wrong. The

Healdsburg

Santa Rosa

Sebastopol

Petaluma

Sonoma

Sonoma

food at The Tides is very good, in fact, it may be the best in town.

The Tides is a large rambling restaurant with several rooms filled with locals and tourists. Many of the seats have views of the ocean, so if your timing is right, you may get a window table. There, amidst the hoopla of a busy institution, you'll be served fresh fish, cooked as you order it, along with decent side dishes. The best thing is that if you order your fish rare, or undercooked, that's how you'll get it. And if you want it dry—that is, without sauce—no problem.

THE TIDES, *853 Highway 1; (707) 875-3652. Breakfast, lunch, and dinner daily. Full bar. MC, Visa, Am Ex. Moderate.*

BOYES HOT SPRINGS ②

✔ **Big Three Cafe.** This is the coffee shop for the fancy Sonoma Mission Inn. Located near the highway in front of the hotel, this remodeled glitzy diner serves not-so-typical coffee shop lunch and dinner items such as saffron fettuccine with pesto and fresh tomato, housemade Dungeness crab ravioli, cold smoked chicken salad with Sonoma baby greens, and low-cal spa cuisine entrees designed for persons attending the Inn's spa program.

The breakfast menu more closely resembles a traditional coffee shop's, offering pancakes, French toast, Belgian waffles, and egg dishes. You can make your own toast in the little toaster provided in each booth; I'm not sure why that is so appealing, but it is.

Breakfast is the bargain if you order correctly. For $3.95 you can order eggs any style, with a buttermilk biscuit and wonderful pan-fried potatoes. The apple oat cakes, made with special batter that needs to be made a day ahead and served with crème fraîche and chopped walnuts, is a filling meal for $4.95. On the other hand, the juices and espresso drinks are expensive ($2.25 for a small glass of juice; $2.75 for a double shot of espresso).

The Big Three Cafe has the same chef as the fancy restaurant in the hotel lobby (see The Grille, which is the next entry). The place is huge, with counter, table, and booth service. Half of the space is given to a gourmet food market.

BIG THREE CAFE, *Sonoma Mission Inn, 18140 Sonoma Highway (Highway 12); (707) 938-9000. Breakfast, lunch, and dinner daily, plus Sunday brunch. Full bar. MC, Visa, Am Ex, Diners. Inexpensive to Moderate.*

✔ **The Grille.** If you're watching your weight but you're dining out with people who aren't watching theirs, this is a good place to satisfy the entire party. Located off the lobby of the luxurious Sonoma Mission Inn, The Grille is a very attractive restaurant offering some spa cuisine items and many un-spa cuisine items.

This is a white linen tablecloth kind of place; men may want to wear a jacket and tie to dinner. The food is based on the cuisines of Italy and California; offerings of angel hair pasta with fresh tomatoes and extra virgin olive oil sit comfortably on the menu next to grilled Petaluma duck breast and the hamburger with goat cheese. An asterisk appears on the menu next to items with lowered fat and salt content.

Lunch can be a good deal if you order right, avoiding such overpriced items as bottled water and espresso drinks. You have your choice of a variety of sandwiches (the roasted chicken with apricot chutney in pita bread is especially nice), grilled and poached fish, pasta, chicken tostadas, spit-roasted leg of veal, and the aforementioned California burger (with goat cheese, wild mushrooms, and sun-dried tomatoes).

Dinner is a more formal and costly event. Main courses include such items as Pacific sea bass, sautéed in a cast-iron skillet and served with white corn ragout; roasted free-range chicken breast with pinto beans, tomatillos and basil aioli; filet of Black Angus beef with rosemary and garlic oil grilled over mesquite and served with corn pancakes. Dinner can cost twice as much as lunch.

In addition to the rich, gooey high-cal desserts, The Grille offers some delicious-sounding low-cal desserts. Many of these treats are sweetened with artificial sweeteners, which leave a funny aftertaste in some people's mouths. If you have an unpleasant reaction to artificial sweeteners, you will want to question your waitperson about ingredients.

THE GRILLE, *Sonoma Mission Inn, 18140 Sonoma Highway (Highway 12); (707) 938-9000. Lunch and dinner daily, plus Sunday brunch. Full bar. MC, Visa, Am Ex, Diners. Moderate for lunch, Expensive for dinner.*

✔ **Blue Heron Restaurant and Black Bart Tavern.** The Russian River is one of those places you go for the scenery and recreation, not necessarily for the food. In fact, at least two of the nicer inns in the area have started serving breakfast *and* dinner to their overnight guests because good places to eat are few and far between around here. One of the places innkeepers do recommend is the Blue Heron.

At one time, this was known as a vegetarian restaurant, back in the days when wood panelling, stained-glass windows, and lots of God's Eyes were hip. It was kind of a community center in the seventies. In 1986 it was purchased by several partners, including the very successful San Francisco architect Piero Patri, who may well be the world's foremost expert on Black Bart. It seems the famous bandit had been in town well before the hippies, and Patri wanted to restore Bart's legend. The tavern section in front was renamed for Black Bart and now serves several namesake cocktails. The restaurant portion looks like the sort of place that would still serve tofu burgers (it doesn't). But the new owners are trying to make the cuisine reflect the lifestyle of the nineties. Though

DUNCAN'S MILLS
③

some vegetarian specialties are offered, most of the very pleasant fare is along the lines of baked brie, fish, chicken, and pasta.

BLUE HERON RESTAURANT AND BLACK BART TAVERN, *Moscow Road at Route 116; (707) 865-2225. Lunch Saturday and Sunday, dinner nightly. Full bar. MC, Visa. Moderate.*

GEYSERVILLE
(4)

✔ **Catelli's, The Rex.**   Now, really—isn't this a great name for a restaurant? Catelli's is the self-proclaimed king of downtown Geyserville eating places. In fact, it's the only one we know of. This is actually two places: the old-fashioned Italian-American restaurant, featuring stuff like spaghetti and meatballs and a daily special or two; and the large and noisy bar in front, where locals play Liar's Dice and tell loud stories to anyone who will listen. The scene is great, a real touch of local color that shouldn't be missed. The food ain't bad, either, mostly king-size portions of down-home Italian specialties. Nothing fancy, just plain good eating. The pasta dishes are particularly plentiful, the waitresses friendly and efficient, and you'll have the experience of visiting a local tradition.

CATELLI'S, THE REX, *21047 Geyserville Avenue, off Highway 128; (707) 857-9904. Lunch Monday through Friday, dinner nightly. Full bar. MC, Visa. Inexpensive to Moderate.*

✔ **Chateau Souverain Restaurant.**   The Chateau Souverain winery is a stately presence to the west of Route 101 near the town of Geyserville. It is designed to resemble a large French country estate, and the beautiful drive up to the headquarters sets up great expectations.

After you climb the outdoor stairs to the main building, you'll enter a lovely reception area. To the left is the winery tasting room, where you can pass the time if you have to wait for a table; to the right is the entrance to the dining room. Whichever direction you take, save some time to enjoy one of the most pleasant and fulfilling dining experiences available in the wine country.

If the weather is warm, you may wish to dine on the patio overlooking the vineyard. However, our preference is the dining room. It is spacious and beautiful, with a high-peaked ceiling, exposed beams, and skylights. One wall features a walk-in fireplace. Art hangs on other walls and all around is a staggering array of flowers. The tables are set with china and linen tablecloths and napkins, and the service is both elegant and friendly.

But you came to eat, right? No problem. Lunch and dinner menus offer a wonderful selection of unusual dishes that combine California Cuisine with French cooking. The California part is expressed in the unusual combinations of foods and in the immediate freshness of the produce and other ingredients. French tradition shows up in the extensive use of butter and cream. Needless to say, this is not an ideal place for those watching their waistlines and cholesterol, though if you choose carefully you can be served items with less emphasis on the butterfat.

The lunch menu features such items as poached chicken in puff pastry with tarragon cream sauce or ravioli stuffed with scallops and leeks with red pepper sauce. Daily specials usually include several grilled fish offerings. The dinner menu changes weekly and features dishes like pan-fried Muscovy duck breast with garlic purée or loin of lamb with artichoke hearts, hazelnut coriander butter and lamb essence. Appetizers and desserts are lavish productions.

Another notable feature of this restaurant is the free tastes of Souverain wines brought in from the tasting room, plus a complete and reasonably priced selection of Sonoma County wines on the wine list.

CHATEAU SOUVERAIN RESTAURANT, *400 Souverain Road, off Highway 101; (707) 433-8281. Lunch Tuesday through Saturday, dinner Thursday through Saturday, Sunday brunch. Wine only. MC, Visa, Am Ex. Moderate to Expensive for lunch; Expensive for dinner.*

✔ **Glen Ellen Inn.** What a lovely restaurant! This is the sort of petite, elegant restaurant where you can see the owners' dream coming true. There's just enough room for about eighteen diners, almost all of whom will have a view of the kitchen, which is the size of a galley on a modest yacht. Two or three people will be working furiously; one of them will be chef-owner Bob Rice. If you sit on the left side of the restaurant you can chat with him all evening while he cooks and you eat.

More than likely you will be seated by Bob's wife, Lynda, the restaurant's co-owner, who loves to tell the story of falling in love with her husband over his chicken salad.

The two put their heads and talents together to open this place, which serves some of the best food in the area. The menu changes each week to take advantage of the freshest ingredients available. As you might expect, a kitchen that small can produce only a limited selection of items, but what is offered is excellent. Usually there are two appetizers; one will probably be a soup. Three entrees are offered, one starring chicken, another fish, the third meat. After the entree comes an excellent salad of mixed lettuces, Asiago cheese, toasted pecans, and raspberry vinaigrette included in the price; most fine restaurants would charge $5 if this salad was ordered à la carte. Entrees run about $16 to $18.

Then there's dessert. The selection depends on what the chef or his assistants feel like making that day. Usually there's something chocolate, perhaps there will be a cheesecake or bread pudding, plus something fresh and wonderful based on whatever fruit is in season. Whatever you choose will be a satisfying and comforting way to end a lovely meal.

GLEN ELLEN INN, *13670 Arnold Drive; (707) 996-6409. Dinner only, Wednes-*

GLEN ELLEN
⑤

day through Sunday. *Beer and wine only. All nonsmoking. No credit cards. Moderate to Expensive.*

<table>
<tr><td>

GUERNEVILLE
⑥

</td><td>

✔ **Coffee Bazaar.**   The town of Guerneville is the main metropolis of the Russian River Resort area and, unfortunately, does not have a restaurant that has moved us to write about it. It does, however, have a haven for cappuccino addicts like your humble wide-awake guides, and that is the Coffee Bazaar, a place that also serves soup and tasty treats like carrot cake imported from Just Desserts in San Francisco. There are tables inside and out on the sidewalk, so you can watch the world go by. There's also a good newsstand-bookstore next door.

</td></tr>
</table>

COFFEE BAZAAR, *in the Cinnabar Street Shops minimall, 14045 Armstrong Woods Road; (707) 869-9706. Open 6:45 A.M. to 9 P.M. Monday through Thursday, 6:45 A.M. to 10 P.M. Friday, 8 A.M. to 10 P.M. Saturday, and 8 A.M. to 9 P.M. Sunday. No alcohol. No credit cards. Inexpensive.*

<table>
<tr><td>

HEALDSBURG
⑦

</td><td>

✔ **Downtown Bakery and Creamery.**   Across the street from the plaza in the heart of town is a good spot to enjoy an afternoon cappuccino and pastry or take home some baked goods for breakfast. It's a very attractive place owned by Lindsey Shere, longtime pastry chef at Chez Panisse and author of *Chez Panisse Desserts.*

</td></tr>
</table>

To the right as you enter is a glass display case with a heart-stopping arrangement of tarts with polenta crust, biscotti, and cakes like works of art. Behind the counter where you order is an attractive display of baskets containing breads, morning buns, and croissants; just beyond that is the kitchen, where pastry chefs are busy carrying sacks of flour, rolling out dough, and practicing culinary magic. For the best selection of baked goods, get there early in the day.

In addition to baked goods the Downtown Bakery and Creamery offers housemade sherberts and gelati made with seasonal fruits.

There are no tables or chairs, just a marble counter; as in the coffee bars of Italy, you stand up to partake in whatever morning or afternoon delight you choose.

DOWNTOWN BAKERY AND CREAMERY, *308-A Center Street; (707) 431-2719. Open 8 A.M. to 5:30 P.M. Wednesday through Monday; closed Tuesday. No credit cards. Inexpensive to Moderate.*

✔ **40 Karrots Diner.**   The Healdsburg town square is blessed with three good places to sit down and eat. The most frivolous place is the hip little diner called 40 Karrots Diner. The design alone is worth the trip, with its black and white floor tile and long lunch counter. The specialty of the house is huge stuffed salads, but you can get all sorts of diner food items. They make a mean milkshake, too.

40 KARROTS DINER, *109 Plaza Street; (707) 431-8181. Breakfast and lunch daily, dinner Friday and Saturday. Beer and wine only. No nonsmoking section. MC, Visa. Inexpensive.*

✔ **Jacob Horner.**   Jacob Horner is the largest of the three busy restaurants on the town square. It is probably most appealing to those who have come to Sonoma for the wine. In addition to their extensive wine list, Horner's offers seventeen different wines by the glass.

The food is in the California Cuisine mode, and it's all prepared very well. The selection of dishes is as extensive and varied as the wine list, featuring such items as fresh fish, pasta, salads, and meat courses. This is where you go if you have a large party or want the ambiance of a traditional upscale-looking city restaurant, with a large bar, comfortable tables and chairs, carpeting, and efficient, friendly service.

JACOB HORNER, *106 Mateson Street, on the plaza; (707) 433-3939. Lunch and dinner Tuesday through Saturday. Full bar. MC, Visa. Moderate.*

✔ **Plaza Grill.**   Right next door to 40 Karrots is a tiny cafe with an attractive art deco influence. It looks like a chic New York jazz club, without the music. As the name suggests, the emphasis here is on grilled items—chicken, fish, beef—cooked to perfection. The salads are also noteworthy. There is a relaxed, cozy charm about the place that is very inviting. Because there are so few seats and the food is so good, reservations are advised.

PLAZA GRILL, *109-A Plaza Street; (707) 431-8305. Lunch Tuesday through Friday, dinner Tuesday through Sunday. All nonsmoking. MC, Visa, Am Ex. Moderate.*

✔ **Kenwood Restaurant and Bar.**   You may recognize the chef, Max Schacher. Formerly of Marin's Le Coqliquet, he was featured on the PBS series "The Great Chefs of San Francisco." A few years ago, he opened this unimposing-looking restaurant right on Highway 12. A classical French cook, Schacher has not lost his knack for rich sauces. This is definitely not spa cuisine, though it is easy to order healthfully, given the selection of fresh ingredients from the farms of the surrounding countryside.

KENWOOD
⑧

Main course offerings run along the lines of fresh fish, a daily pasta, New York steak, and local rabbit, sausage, and duck. Appetizers include such items as escargot and fried polenta with wild mushrooms. Everything we had was very good and beautifully presented. The menu and prices are the same at lunch and dinner. Wine lovers will be interested in the Kenwood's large and fairly priced wine list, featuring an impressive array of local labels, many offered by the glass.

KENWOOD RESTAURANT AND BAR, *9900 Highway 12; (707) 833-6326. Lunch and dinner Tuesday through Sunday; closed Monday. Full bar. MC, Visa. Moderate to Expensive.*

OCCIDENTAL

⑨

✔ **Occidental Cafe.**   This is the newest place in town, a very good place to have breakfast, lunch, and dinner, or grab a bite on the run. Breakfast items include banana pancakes, eggs any style, eggs with salsa and guacamole, eggs with spinach and ricotta, and toast made from bread baked on the premises. Lunch and dinner offerings are along the lines of sautéed tiger prawns, veggie stir frys, chile rellenos, and salads made from organically grown lettuces.

If it's pizza you're after, they make their dough from scratch and top it with just about anything that suits your mood. You can create your own, starting with or without cheese and proceeding through a list of choices that includes Canadian bacon, pineapple, pine nuts, sun-dried tomatoes, zucchini, and pesto. You may have to wait a while; pizzas are made to order.

Out front by the cash register is a bakery case filled with muffins, brownies, and other sweet things you can get with a cappuccino to go.

OCCIDENTAL CAFE, *3688 Bohemian Highway; (707) 874-2894. Breakfast and dinner daily, lunch Monday through Friday, Sunday brunch. Beer and wine only. All nonsmoking. No credit cards. Inexpensive to Moderate.*

PETALUMA

⑩

✔ **Aram's.**   This is an unusual find in the middle of downtown Petaluma: a deli–coffee shop that serves Mediterranean food. The owners are a married couple—she's from Barcelona, he's half Armenian, and his mom makes almost everything back in the kitchen. For breakfast, you can choose from an international cornucopia of baked goods, including croissants, scones, and bagels. For lunch or an early light dinner, the choices seem infinite: lasagna, dolmas, baba ghanoush, falafels, hummus, tabouleh, homemade soup, and, last but not least, aram sandwiches—those little sandwiches with turkey, roast beef, or vegetables, each with cream cheese and rolled in pita bread.

You can stop in at any time of the day just for a coffee drink and a Middle Eastern dessert. In addition to cappuccino and espresso, Aram's also makes "Armenian coffee," sweet and spicy, and so thick with sediment your spoon can stand up straight.

ARAM'S, *122-A Kentucky Street; (707) 765-9775. Open 10 A.M. to 6 P.M. Monday through Saturday. Beer and wine only. All nonsmoking. No credit cards. Inexpensive.*

✔ **Christine's Cafe.**   Christine's is a perfect example of the old rule of thumb: If you want a successful business the top three considerations are location, location, and location. This sweet cafe is right in the center of town, next to the classic old Plaza Movie Theater and across the street from the popular shopping mall built inside an old mill.

Fortunately, Christine's has more going for it than just the location. The food is also very good. This is the kind of place we long for when we are in a hurry. You place your order at the counter, then after passing the time in front of some very tempting desserts inside a display case, your name is called and your order is ready. Food is mostly light fare like housemade soups, salads, quiches, sandwiches, and daily specials. And they have an espresso machine. There are plenty of tables available for your comfort while enjoying your quick lunch or for lingering over a newspaper.

CHRISTINE'S CAFE, *17 Petaluma Boulevard North (near B Street); (707) 778-7105. Lunch and dinner Monday through Saturday; closed Sunday. Beer and wine only. MC, Visa over $20. Inexpensive to Moderate.*

✔ **De Schmire.** With a name like that, we knew this place had to be really awful or truly wonderful. Fortunately for us all, it is the latter. De Schmire is short for "De whole schmire," and when you walk in, you see de whole schmire—kitchen, dining room, and art gallery in one—shall we say—"intimate" space.

This is the sort of place we love: The food is wonderful, the atmosphere fun, and prices moderate. This is also the sort of place lots of people love, which becomes obvious on a Saturday night when every table is full and every inch of standing room is taken up by people waiting for a chance to sit.

In addition to nightly specials, the regular menu includes items like red snapper with almonds and mushrooms, prawns flamed with Pernod, and roast duckling with honey lemon sauce. Though we rarely eat meat, our instincts convinced us to order the filet mignon. It was excellent, with a buttery texture and served with a flavorful green peppercorn sauce, mashed carrots-and-potatoes, and stem broccoli with a light, lemony hollandaise, all for $14, including the soup and salad that accompanies all entrees.

The atmosphere is casual, though some folks do get quite dressed up. Reservations, especially on weekends, are a good idea.

DE SCHMIRE, *304 Bodega Avenue; (707) 762-1901. Dinner nightly. Beer and wine only. No credit cards. Moderate.*

✔ **Fino.** Once upon a time, two guys from Italy met onboard a cruise ship. They went to San Francisco and worked at such high-class joints as Ernie's and Modesto Lanzone's. They teamed up with a third *paisano*, and together they opened their own place in late 1987.

What you will get here is food that is Italian-Italian, as opposed to California Italian—the sort of pasta, chicken, and veal dishes you would expect to be served in a neighborhood trattoria in Italy, or perhaps San Francisco's North Beach. One owner is from Sicily, another from Venice, and the third from Central Italy, so there is an interesting selection of dishes from most regions of the mother country. It's all moderately priced, and entrees can be served as part of a full dinner (with pasta plus soup or salad) or à la carte, for smaller appetites.

This is a very friendly place, with a large dining room simply but tastefully decorated with white tablecloths and a mixture of Italian rock 'n' roll and opera piped through the sound system. The owners are also the waiters and they keep a steady patter going with every customer.

FINO, *208 Petaluma Boulevard, at Washington Street; (707) 762-5966. Lunch Tuesday through Friday, dinner Tuesday through Sunday. Beer and wine only. MC, Visa, Am Ex. Moderate.*

✔ **Markey's Cafe.**   Just a few blocks from downtown is a place where you can have a tasty vegetarian meal or simply a good cup of coffee or tea. Markey's Cafe is a very informal, hangout type of place serving soups, salads, vegetarian sandwiches, and daily specials like curry, mushroom stroganoff, lasagne, and tofu pot pie. They also feature many kinds of natural juice drinks, as well as an espresso bar. Adding to the pleasure of being there is the classical music playing on the sound system at all times. Take-out service is available.

MARKEY'S CAFE, *316 Western Avenue, next door to the Chamber of Commerce; (707) 763-2429. Open 8:30 A.M. to 9:30 P.M. daily. Beer and wine only. All non-smoking. No credit cards. Inexpensive.*

✔ **Marvin's.**   South of the town center is a cozy local institution called Marvin's. It could best be described as a coffee shop—diner that happens to be built into an old small house. Here, while the music blares and the locals exchange gossip, you can get good and large omelets, sandwiches, salads, and daily specials served by incredibly energetic people. The owner doubles as an aerobics instructor as do most of her waitresses, so the entire staff seems to bounce around the place.

MARVIN'S, *317 Petaluma Boulevard South; (707) 778-8611. Breakfast and lunch daily, dinner Wednesday, Thursday, and Friday. Beer and wine only. MC, Visa, Am Ex. Inexpensive.*

✔ **Millie's Chili.**   There is a trend around the country to re-create diners of the 1950s, and suddenly people are rushing to stand in line for meatloaf sandwiches, mashed potatoes with gravy, and BLTs. Well in Petaluma, just south of the main drag, there is such a place that is not a re-creation; it is the real thing.

We first heard of Millie's Chili from the film crew working on Francis Coppola's film *Peggy Sue Got Married*. They converted it for the film into a 1950 doughnut shop, changing the name and the food. Pity; you can't improve on the genuine article, and you could probably make the most entertaining movie ever made just by watching Millie and her twin sister, Vickie, in action.

Millie and Vickie live in back of the diner. They're in their late sixties, maybe early seventies now. They're up by 5:30 A.M., getting the chili on the stove, making salads, peeling onions. By opening time (11 A.M.) you'd better be ready to operate at their pace. Millie stands behind the little cooking area, flipping burgers and stirring her chili; Vickie's right there, order pad in hand, ready to take your order. All the time, they go at each other, bickering, teasing, laughing, and having the time of their lives. If they're really busy they'll tell you not to bother them; they have to concentrate!

It seems that no matter what you order, it's going to have chili on it. I'm not going to tell you this is the best chili in the world, but I promise you won't ever forget a visit with these memorable people. By the way, make sure you eat everything on your plate or else Vickie will give you the dickens.

Better hurry. They may not stay open much longer. Their hours are now down to three days a week, Monday through Wednesday, lunch only.

MILLIE'S CHILI, *Petaluma Boulevard South, at H Street; no phone. Lunch only, Monday through Wednesday. Beer and wine only. No credit cards. Inexpensive.*

✔ Three Cooks Cafe. There's a new sign on Route 101 that calls Petaluma "a city of restaurants"—more than 140 of them in a town with a population of about 42,000. Maybe that's why it took us so long to get around to finding the Three Cooks Cafe, which is located out on the north end of town, sharing a parking lot with an auto repair shop. We look forward to going back, because this is a terrific place, especially when we're in the mood for huge portions of good food at bargain prices.

As the location would indicate, this is hardly a haven of chic dining. This is a down-home diner with a large counter and several Formica-top tables decked out with white paper placemats. Customers range from businessmen in suits and ties to highway construction workers in their bright orange safety jackets. The common bond is people with hearty appetites.

The menu is extensive, with at least a dozen kinds of burgers served with soup, salad of the day, or a heaping helping of home fries. (Say that fast, three times.) You have a choice of at least two dozen different types of sandwiches, from the familiar (grilled cheese, BLT) to the original (how about the Foo Foo, which is roast beef, chili, onions, and cheese served open-face on a French roll; or the Big E, which is barbecued pork shoulder with volcano sauce). By the way, this hot, hot volcano sauce is offered with ribs, chicken hot links, and ham and beef sandwiches; you may also choose two milder sauces instead.

Breakfast is served throughout the day, with huge omelets, Texas-style French toast, and enormous pancakes, plus daily specials.

If you can resist the temptations on the menu, you could eat very well with just an order of one pancake for one dollar; a cup of coffee will cost an additional forty-seven cents.

THREE COOKS CAFE, *841 North Petaluma Boulevard; (707) 762-9886. Open 6 A.M. to 3 P.M. daily; dinner served until 10 P.M. on Friday. Beer and wine only. MC, Visa. Inexpensive.*

SANTA ROSA
⑪

✔ **Fonseca's.**   Like many other towns with a history, Santa Rosa has re-created its original "old" section, which is called Old Railroad Square. There are several decent restaurants here, including a really good Mexican restaurant called Fonseca's. The menu offers all the traditional fare—tacos, enchiladas, burritos, etc., plus the kinds of beef, chicken, and fish dishes you are likely to find in vacation spots south of the border. Everything is made to order, very tasty, and served in such bountiful quantities that you probably won't be able to eat it all at once. The burritos are exceptional, stuffed to the limit with meat.

FONSECA'S, *117 Fourth Street; (707) 576-0131. Lunch and dinner daily. Beer and wine only. No nonsmoking section. MC, Visa, Am Ex, Diners. Inexpensive.*

✔ **John Ash and Company.**   John Ash is often credited with upgrading the quality of food in Santa Rosa. In his rather plain-looking restaurant in the Montgomery Village shopping center, he capitalized on the interest in fine wines in the region, selling local vintages in the front room of the establishment, then featured the marriage of fine wine and gourmet food in the restaurant. It worked, and still does, only now he has a showplace in the Vintner's Inn on the north side of town.

The new John Ash restaurant is all elegance and style, housed in a spacious building with curved reddish stucco walls and terra cotta tile floors. In fact, it could be a little intimidating, especially when you find the headwaiter in a tux at lunch. Perhaps he has lightened up his wardrobe since our last visit.

The food is still adventurous, with items like pheasant and squab served with imaginative combinations of vegetables and sauces. The menu almost always has interesting selections using fish, chicken, beef, and veal. The food is best described as California French. This is fine, leisurely dining.

JOHN ASH AND COMPANY, *4330 Barnes Road, at Vintner's Inn; (707) 527-7687. Lunch Tuesday through Friday, dinner Tuesday through Sunday, brunch Sunday; closed Monday. Full bar. All nonsmoking, except at bar. MC, Visa, Am Ex, Diners. Moderate to Expensive for lunch; Expensive for dinner.*

✔ **La Grande's.**   On the southern outskirts of town is a restaurant that serves food that I call old-fashioned Italian. In other words, instead of the lighter Northern

Italian places that are the rage now, La Grande's serves the Italian food I remember as a kid: spaghetti with meatballs, spaghetti with chicken livers, and ravioli, all loaded with a thick sauce. They also have veal and chicken dishes, beef braciole, and steaks, all served in portions you cannot possibly finish. What's more, it's good.

La Grande's is a hangout for the nontrendy, a family place where the kids can play a video game or listen to a live rock band on weekends while the parents eat in peace in another of the restaurant's many rooms or out on the patio. *Mangia!*

LA GRANDE'S, *3660 Stony Point Road; (707) 584-8803. Lunch Monday through Friday, dinner nightly, brunch Sunday. Full bar. MC, Visa, Am Ex. Inexpensive to Moderate.*

✔ **Lisa Hemenway's.** As is often the case with pioneering restaurants, one success story spawns several spin-offs. Such is the case with Lisa Hemenway, who is a former employee of John Ash and Company (see page 34). Lunch features items from the mesquite grill, including hamburgers, the fresh fish of the day, and daily specials. Savories, such as torta Milanese and brioche stuffed with tarragon chicken, are offered at lunch, as are large main course salads. At dinner the menu emphasizes the grill and daily pasta specials. There's also a take-out section called Tote Cuisine.

Those in need of a quick snack might also want to know about their oyster bar and deli, open all day long, but closed Mondays.

LISA HEMENWAY'S, *714 Village Court, in the Montgomery Village, Montgomery Street and Route 12; (707) 526-5111. Lunch Monday through Saturday, dinner Tuesday through Saturday, closed Sunday. Beer and wine only. MC, Visa, Diners. Moderate.*

✔ **Matisse.** Another of the first restaurants on the Backroads to start serving food that could compete with the San Francisco biggies is Matisse. This is another example of California freshness and lightness meeting French tradition, and the result is a success. Matisse is a fairly small place, staffed by a young and eager group of food lovers. The menu changes often, but there is always a fresh fish selection, interesting salads, and a group of imaginative entrees. And as the name suggests, the decor is arty. Once a month, the restaurant opens on Sunday night to prepare a special menu.

The same owners have an Italian place in another part of Santa Rosa (see Ristorante Siena, page 36).

MATISSE, *620 Fifth Street; (707) 527-9797. Lunch Monday through Friday, dinner Monday through Saturday. Beer and wine only. All nonsmoking, except for bar. MC, Visa, Am Ex, Diners. Moderate.*

✓ Omelette Express. In the historic section of Santa Rosa called Old Railroad Square is a refreshingly unhip place called the Omelette Express. Nothing tricky or trendy here, just a very large selection of omelets and other light dishes, prepared well and without pretense.

OMELETTE EXPRESS, *112 Fourth Street, in Old Railroad Square; (707) 525-1690. Breakfast and lunch daily. Beer and wine only. MC, Visa. Inexpensive to Moderate.*

✓ Polka Dot's. This is a fun, informal spot in Old Railroad Square owned by the same folks who run 40 Karrots in Healdsburg. This is yet another re-created fifties diner with vinyl booths, little jukeboxes on the Formica tables, and plenty of glass bricks. But, really: During the Eisenhower administration were there any diners that served turkey pecan sandwiches, pesto chicken, and baked brie?

But have no fear. This modern cuisine and the traditional fare (burgers, chicken-fried steak, meatloaf, BLTs) are delicious and moderately priced. The menu says "Lunch served any time" and that means you can get their "testimonial" onion rings first thing in the morning if you wish. Another specialty of the house is called "triplets": three smaller "slider" hamburgers, each topped with a different sauce. Dinner entrees like mom would want you to eat are served after 5 P.M.

Each table is covered with white butcher paper and comes equipped with crayons for expressing oneself accordingly; the hallway to the restrooms is wallpapered with the best drawings left by past customers.

POLKA DOT'S, *115 Fourth Street; (707) 575-9080. Breakfast and lunch daily; dinner Tuesday through Saturday. Beer and wine only. MC, Visa. Inexpensive to Moderate.*

✓ Ristorante Siena. The folks who brought us Matisse (see page 35) also operate an Italian cafe in a shopping center—industrial park on the outskirts of town. Don't get the idea that this is some tacky joint, sandwiched between stores. Ristorante Siena is a sprawling space decorated with blond furniture and white walls. It's a very pleasant and attractive restaurant. The menu features fresh pasta dishes, salads, and grilled items. The accent is on light cooking, free of heavy sauces. The food is very good. Reservations are recommended.

RISTORANTE SIENA, *1229 North Dutton Avenue; (707) 578-4511. Lunch Monday through Friday, dinner Wednesday through Sunday, brunch Sunday. Beer and wine only. MC, Visa. Moderate.*

SEBASTOPOL

✓ Chez Peyo. This is a French restaurant owned by a Basque named Pierre whose nickname is Peyo. This is also a very popular spot for lunch and dinner. Fresh fish and pasta are featured daily, and the American favorite, the hamburger, is served with a bearnaise sauce. One day for lunch I had a very nice fresh trout in lemon cream sauce, with properly steamed vegetables (still crisp, not soggy).

At dinner the prices jump up a bit but are still in the moderate range. Light and inexpensive suppers are also offered, featuring such things as pumpkin ravioli and broccoli with ricotta wrapped in puff pastry.

CHEZ PEYO, *2295 Gravenstein Highway South (Route 116); (707) 823-1262. Lunch and dinner Tuesday through Saturday, brunch and dinner Sunday; closed Monday. Beer and wine only. All nonsmoking, except for bar. MC, Visa. Inexpensive to moderate.*

✔ **East-West Cafe.**   The East-West Cafe is a fairly ordinary-looking place, with many tables and comfortable seats. This is also Sebastopol's first Syrian restaurant. In fact, it may be Sonoma County's first Syrian restaurant. As the cafe's name would suggest, the food has a Middle Eastern accent, though this could also be described as a New Age restaurant, with an emphasis on vegetarian items.

For breakfast and lunch, the service is cafeteria style, and a surprising variety of choices is offered, including housemade soups, organic salads, plus many dishes utilizing tofu. You can also get falafel, hummus, stuffed grape leaves, and other Middle Eastern items, plus such East-West hybrids as pasta with yogurt and garlic cream sauce. Also available are fresh juices, specialty coffees, and freshly baked pastries. Most items for lunch go for $5 and under. Dinner is a sit-down affair and features various kabobs.

EAST-WEST CAFE, *128 North Main Street; (707) 829-2822. Breakfast and lunch Monday through Saturday, dinner Tuesday through Saturday. No alcohol served. All nonsmoking. No credit cards. Inexpensive.*

✔ **The Gallery Cafe.**   As we've stated elsewhere in this guide, when we pull into a new town we always keep our eyes peeled for the best place in town for an afternoon coffee. In Sebastopol we found it at The Gallery Cafe, which also happens to serve very nice breakfasts and light lunches: housemade soups, good sandwiches, and the like. This is a very informal place, nothing fancy; service is quick and the food is good. The surprise is that there is a very nice patio and deck out back where you can eat and relax.

About that coffee: It's from Peet's in Berkeley, which means it is good and strong. There will be no fighting a nap on the way back to the city.

THE GALLERY CAFE, *305 North Main Street; (707) 823-4458. Open 7:30 A.M. to 5 P.M. weekdays, 9 A.M. to 3 P.M. weekends. Beer and wine only. All nonsmoking inside. No credit cards. Inexpensive.*

✔ **Katie Jean's.** This is a very congenial little spot, near the main intersection in town. I'm always amazed by the amount of food they serve from their tiny space behind the counter.

As you enter you gaze upon the desserts in the cooler. Then you will see the day's hot specials, which might be a tamale pie, a quiche, and a lasagne, maybe even a vegetarian casserole. You can order any number of sandwiches, including the house specialty, which is turkey, cheese, and cranberry sauce. Whatever you choose will be good.

After you order, take a seat at a table and your food will be brought to you.

KATIE JEAN'S, *6961 Sebastopol Avenue; (707) 823-1324. Breakfast and lunch Monday through Saturday. Beer and wine only. All nonsmoking. No credit cards. Inexpensive.*

✔ **Mom's Apple Pie.** One day in the height of the apple season, we were driving along the Gravenstein Highway and saw a little cabin with a big sign: MOM'S APPLE PIE. Even though we had always followed the maxim "Never eat at a place called Mom's or play cards with a guy called Pop," we couldn't resist stopping in. Boy, were we sorry. It was so good that we nearly ate ourselves into a bigger pants size.

Mom is a lovely lady who came to the United States from Asia a few years ago and somehow ended up creating a prize-winning example of the typically American dessert. Using local apples, she makes a wonderfully rich pie, complete with flaky, buttery crust. You can usually get a piece hot out of the oven, which you can enjoy at one of the few tables in front of the counter. Pies are sold to take home, too, and apple is just one of the varieties.

Since we last visited, Mom's has started serving lunch and dinner. We haven't yet had the chance to have a meal there, but if they are anything like the pie, you're in good hands.

MOM'S APPLE PIE, *4550 Gravenstein Highway; (707) 823-8330. Lunch and dinner daily. No alcohol served. No credit cards. Inexpensive.*

✔ **Pack Jack Bar-b-Que.** If the wind is blowing right, you can smell the smoke from the Pack Jack Bar-b-Que about a mile before you get there. That's great news for everyone who loves ribs and chicken. This is the genuine article. A few hours before the place opens owners Donnie and Marie Harris arrive to start a wood fire in a deep brick oven. Once started, the fire will go until closing, cooking up three kinds of ribs—pork, lamb, and beef—plus chicken and Donnie's own hot links. They also make their own beans, salads, and sweet potato pie.

Donnie and Marie (no Osmond jokes, please) started this place as a take-out joint with a few seats and have expanded to include a full dining room seating thirty-five.

If you're wondering why your ribs on the backyard grill never taste as good as the ones in the rib joints, we can share the secret passed on by Donnie: The meat should never be flamed. Donnie says that when you put ribs or chicken directly on a grill with a flame or hot coals underneath you cook the fat and lose a lot of taste. Instead, Donnie slow cooks everything in the hot smoky oven next to the wood fire. The closest you can come to this technique at home is to use the indirect heating method on a covered grill. Using Donnie's method, pork ribs take as long as four hours; chicken, about an hour and a half.

But at home you won't have Donnie's special sauces, and he's not passing out his secret recipe.

The Bay Area is blessed with many wonderful barbecue restaurants, especially around Oakland, Berkeley, and San Francisco. Finding one in Sebastopol is rare, and this place rates with the best of them.

PACK JACK BAR-B-QUE, *3963 Gravenstein Highway South (Route 116); (707) 823-9929. Open 2 P.M. to 9 P.M., Tuesday through Thursday, 11 A.M. to 11 P.M. Friday, Saturday, and Sunday. Beer and wine only. No credit cards. Inexpensive.*

✔ **Truffles.**   Someone once listed this restaurant as one of the reasons to live in Northern California. It's easy to understand why. The food is imaginative and wonderful, and people drive all the way from San Francisco just to eat here.

The restaurant originated with a group of partners involved in mushroom farming. Hence the name, plus the appetizer offering of sautéed mushrooms. The chef is Mark Malicki, who worked in the chic New York kitchens of Odeon and the River Cafe. His wife, Jenny, used to be a hostess at the Four Seasons in New York; chances are she'll be the one to graciously seat you.

Sebastopol is located right in the heart of produce paradise, and the staff at Truffles makes the most of this location. One local farmer grows exclusively for them (during the summer try his golden raspberries). Fruits and vegetables too fragile to ship outside the area make their way into the daily specials.

The food is a unique blending of Asian, Indian, Mediterranean, French, and American. As an appetizer, the chicken satay sticks with a pungent peanut dipping sauce are a must, as are the aforementioned sautéed mushrooms. Of course the menu adapts to what's in season, but what we ate the last time we were there illustrates the sort of fare that can be expected: grilled chicken with salsa on a bed of crispy steamed vegetables of the season, surrounded by a halo of paper-thin slices of cucumber, each dotted with pieces of red and yellow pepper and black sesame seeds; and elegantly poached salmon on a bed of baby greens. When the food arrives it is a feast for the eyes; each plate looks so beautiful that it is almost painful to disrupt the pattern with a fork and knife.

The menu also offers pasta and meat dishes plus a two-course spa meal, low in salt and fat and high in flavor. This is available at both lunch and dinner. Also, many of the entrees are marked with the red heart seal of approval of the American Heart Association.

Like the food, the decor is a perfect marriage of East and West. Paintings from the American Southwest hang on peach-colored walls; dramatic bamboo and floral displays, arranged with Japanese simplicity, stand in large Chinese food crocks used as vases.

The best news of all is that the prices are remarkably fair for the quality. Those wonderful satay sticks we recommended for appetizers are only one dollar each, and you can eat well and inexpensively if you order carefully.

TRUFFLES, *234 South Main Street; (707) 823-8448. Lunch Tuesday through Friday, dinner nightly. Beer and wine only. All nonsmoking, except for the bar. MC, Visa. Moderate to Expensive.*

SONOMA
(13)

✔ **L'Esperance.** Tucked away in a courtyard behind the French Bakery on the town square in Sonoma is a sweet little French restaurant called L'Esperance. Many of the people working here used to be at a place called Sharl's, which used to be *the* in place to eat in town.

You can have a light lunch or dinner or a full-course meal. Everything will be prepared well and will be made of the freshest ingredients available. Reservations are suggested.

L'ESPERANCE, *464 First Street, on the square; (707) 996-2757. Lunch Monday through Saturday, dinner nightly, brunch Sunday. Beer and wine only. MC, Visa. Moderate to Expensive.*

✔ **Moosetta's.** On the one hand, the town of Sonoma is quickly filling up with very chic restaurants; on the other hand, fast-food chains are invading the territory. Therefore it was downright refreshing to discover Moosetta's, the most untrendy and down-home place you could imagine. The specialty of the house is piroshki, which is Eastern Europe's answer to the burrito. Here you have the choice of beef, beef and cheese, mixed vegetable, or mushroom and cheese fillings inside a doughy pastry.

Each day a freshly made soup is offered; a light lunch of soup and piroshki will cost you about two dollars. Best of all, you can get cookies and little dessert pastries for fifty cents each; in an area where a dessert in a restaurant costs three to five dollars, there is something positively thrilling about ordering *ten* lemon puffs or walnut shortbreads for the same price.

Moosetta's sells both hot-and-ready-to-eat and frozen take-home items, so if you have an oven available, check out the cabbage rolls, beef stroganoff, and turkey pot pies. If you order ready-to-eat items, you have the option of sitting outside on a deck overlooking the parking lot of the McDonald's next door or you can eat in your car.

MOOSETTA'S, *18976 Sonoma Highway (Highway 12); (707) 996-1313. Open 10 A.M. to 7 P.M. Tuesday through Saturday. No alcohol. No credit cards. Inexpensive.*

✔ **Pasta Nostra.** Tucked away behind the chic Les Arcades and a new environmental art gallery is an informal place we like a lot. Printed on the menu is the command "We demand that you have a good time!" and you probably will, if you happen to like good home-style Italian food, fresh ingredients, friendly service, and a modest tab.

One night we were amused for hours as we watched the owner trot from table to table with a collander filled with porcini mushrooms he had picked that afternoon. You'd think he had just delivered a baby. He insisted every customer admire these delicacies and smell them, unconcerned about the fact that the odor of fungus is an acquired taste. It was quite charming.

We proceeded to order the night's special, which, not suprisingly, featured fresh porcini mushrooms. They were prepared in a cream marsala sauce over fresh (not dried) spaghetti, and it was excellent. We also ordered two other specials, the housemade soup (leek and potato) and vegetarian lasagne, and they were as wonderful as we wish we could make at home.

In general, the menu offerings are classic Italian. Entrees include veal cooked in your choice of four styles (scaloppine, Parmigiana, piccatta, or Milanese) and chicken baked in one of three styles (Sicilian, scaloppine, or Parmigiana). These entrees are served with side portions of house pasta.

The miracle is that everything is prepared in a teensy kitchen right by the entrance; you can watch the goings on while waiting for your table.

PASTA NOSTRA, *139 East Napa Street; (707) 938-4166. Lunch Friday through Sunday, dinner nightly. Beer and wine only. MC, Visa. Moderate.*

✔ **Peterberry's.** Right across the street from Pasta Nostra is this delightful place that calls itself an Espresso Cafe and Aviation Gallery. Here you can get the best coffee in town plus you can be entertained by the display of vintage model airplanes suspended from the ceiling. To add to the effect, the walls are painted to look like clouds, creating the effect of being high in the air while being high on caffeine—that is, until you look out the rather substantial picture windows and see the familiar storefronts of downtown.

The cafe serves breakfast, lunch, and light dinners, and it's the perfect place to go for an afternoon cappuccino.

The cafe also serves as a gathering place for locals. One time we were there, the place was filled with young ballerinas ordering salads, croissant sandwiches, and hot chocolate following an after-school performance. Additional food items include a variety of breakfast pastries, melted cheese sandwiches, and house-made soups, all very good and inexpensive.

PETERBERRY'S, *140 East Napa Street; (707) 996-5559. Open 8 A.M. to 5 P.M. Monday through Saturday, 10 A.M. to 6 P.M. Sunday. Beer and wine only. MC, Visa, Am Ex. Inexpensive.*

✔ Sonoma Hotel.

In the heat of the summertime, one of the nicest spots for lunch in Sonoma is in the courtyard of the old Sonoma Hotel, on the corner of the town plaza. Even when the temperature is in the nineties, the shaded courtyard is always pleasant. It's a good place to have a salad, light pasta, or a sandwich. Indoor dining is also available, but you might want to save that for an evening visit. Then you can have a drink at the 100-year-old mahogany bar and dine on antique oak tables in a Victorian parlor.

The hotel, which does rent rooms upstairs, features an oyster bar on Wednesdays and Fridays. The dinner menu changes twice a month, and the chefs try to use local ingredients such as Vella's cheese and Sonoma sausages, plus fresh vegetables and herbs from the hotel's own garden.

SONOMA HOTEL, *110 West Spain, on the west side of the square; (707) 996-2996. Lunch daily, dinner Thursday through Tuesday, brunch Sunday. Full bar. MC, Visa, Am Ex. Moderate.*

✔ T.J.'s Grill and Bakery.

An old feed store seems like an appropriate location for a restaurant and bakery. However, you would never guess this place's origin just by looking at it because now it is modern and light and airy, with a spacious dining room and a large patio in back with tables and umbrellas. The bakery is well known for its several varieties of healthful and beautiful loaves of breads, as well as wonderful pies and pastries. Bread lovers, be forewarned: The bread goes fast, and the selection gets pretty slim by ten or eleven in the morning.

The restaurant changes moods as the day progresses. In the mornings the dining room and bakery are bustling with people getting ready to start their day with espresso drinks, egg dishes, and items from the bakery.

Lunchtime attracts a less sleepy crowd, ordering soups, omelets, sandwiches on bakery bread, or one of the nine burgers offered. These half-pound charbroiled specialties are served on a French bun and are accompanied by french fries or homemade potato salad. The salads are large and fresh; a favorite seems to be the chicken taco salad, which features charbroiled chicken breast on hot tortilla chips with guacamole and salsa.

At dinner, the menu is more inventive with several main course selections of beef, pork, seafood, and chicken, plus a minimum of five pasta dishes. Because of the bakery, I suggest you order your main course with dessert in mind.

There are no pretentions here about "gourmet" cuisine; they strive for just good, wholesome food.

T.J.'S GRILL AND BAKERY, *529 First Street West; (707) 938-2122. Breakfast and lunch daily; dinner Tuesday through Friday. Beer and wine only. MC, Visa. Moderate.*

CHAPTER **3** Napa County

There is no shortage of places to eat in Napa County. Restaurants have blossomed along with the development of the boutique wine industry to the point where this small area can boast some of the finest places to eat in the entire Bay Area. We will mention a few of the well-publicized ones but concentrate on lesser known restaurants and cafes, the kinds of places that take advantage of the bounty of locally grown produce and are considerate of your cash supply.

✔ **All Seasons Cafe.**   In what looks like a converted corner grocery store, you can be served a lovely lunch or dinner or you can pick up some food to take out on a picnic. The All Seasons Cafe is part wine and gourmet shop, part restaurant, and part coffeehouse, and all the parts work very well.

The dessert case is a knockout, the wine selection is as large and diverse as that of many fancy restaurants, and the menu offers a surprisingly broad selection to suit many moods and appetites, from salads and sandwiches to grilled meat and fowl. The dinner menu changes nightly and takes advantage of whatever is fresh each day. Owner-chef Mark Dierkhising personally walks through the vegetable beds of the local farm where he buys the vegetables for his two Calistoga restaurants, the All Seasons Cafe and the Silverado Restaurant across the street (see page 46). There in the field he mentally constructs his menus, based on the taste, size, color, and availability of the freshest ingredients possible.

So, a fall evening's fare might include pumpkin ravioli with toasted walnuts and sage butter; warm spinach salad with pancetta, smoked chicken, feta cheese, and whole-grain mustard dressing; pizza with spicy tomato sauce, four cheeses, and "just about every herb we have"; grilled chicken breast with fried polenta; and a fresh fish selection—all of it excellent and moderately priced.

During the week, the cafe is open for continental-style breakfast, featuring good coffee, juice, and their wonderful pastries. Oh, by the way, near the front

CALISTOGA
①

door is the freezer featuring the cafe's housemade ice cream. If you're not ready for an entire meal you can at least get a double scoop to go . . .

ALL SEASONS CAFE, *1400 Lincoln Avenue; (707) 942-9111. Breakfast Monday through Friday, lunch daily, dinner Thursday through Monday, brunch Saturday and Sunday. Open for take-out 9 A.M. to 6 P.M. weekdays in the winter; 9 A.M. to 10 P.M. Thursday through Monday in the summer, 9 A.M. to 10 P.M. weekends in summer and winter. Beer and wine only. No nonsmoking section. MC, Visa. Moderate.*

✔ **Bosko's.** This is an unusual Italian restaurant offering basically pasta and large salads. The place is very informal, with sawdust on the floor and lots of noise ricocheting off the walls and ceiling. You order cafeteria-style, choosing from a large selection of hot pasta dishes of many shapes, sizes, and colors accompanied by a variety of sauces. One day a crew of four of us ordered linguine with pesto, lasagne with meat sauce, fettuccine Alfredo, and tortellini; it was a long time before any of us was hungry again. The pasta was freshly made on the premises and cooked to order, the sauces were all delicious, and the check was easy to digest. You can also get meatball sandwiches, an Italian club (turkey, pancetta, lettuce, and tomato on a French roll) or tuna with provolone and Italian dressing. They have an espresso machine, and you can get everything to go.

BOSKO'S, *1403 Lincoln Avenue; (707) 942-9088. Lunch and dinner daily. Beer and wine only. No nonsmoking section. No credit cards. Inexpensive to Moderate.*

✔ **Cafe Pacifico.** As you enter the main part of town you'll come to the very inviting Cafe Pacifico. This is a spacious, airy, and inviting nouvelle Mexican restaurant, featuring creative chicken, fish, and meat dishes in addition to the more traditional tacos, enchiladas, and burritos. Most dishes are accompanied by excellent black beans and rice. The fajitas and grilled chicken are especially good, and the portions are huge.

CAFE PACIFICO, *1237 Lincoln Avenue; (707) 942-4400. Breakfast, lunch, and dinner daily, and brunch Saturday and Sunday. Full bar. MC, Visa. Moderate.*

✔ **Checkers.** Are you looking for a spiffy cafe with black and white decor and modern furnishings? How about a club sandwich, pepperoni calzone, or salad composed of roasted chicken, avocado, gorgonzola cheese, and roasted pine nuts? On a diet and looking for something light, like frozen yogurt or a protein shake?

All the above are available at an informal spot called Checkers, located on Calistoga's main street. This place is trendy to the max, so whatever's hot

Napa

Calistoga
29
St. Helena
4
3
128
Yountville
5
29
2 Napa
12

they've got and they manage to pull it off with reasonable grace. Lunch tends to be a quick affair, with many people stopping in to take food out. Dinners are more leisurely, and the menu expands to include pasta dishes such as gnocchi Florentine, rigatoni sautéed in garlic, and spaghetti with meatballs. Pizza is served all day, and lunch specials include a half sandwich with housemade soup ($3.95) or a minipizza with salad ($4.75). And yes, you can be served fine local wines, espresso drinks, and herb teas. You will probably not get the most memorable meal of your lifetime, but you will get decent food without spending much money. Also, this is a completely nonsmoking establishment.

CHECKERS, *1414 Lincoln Avenue; (707) 942-9300. Lunch and dinner 11:30 A.M. to 10 P.M. daily. Beer and wine only. All nonsmoking. MC, Visa. Inexpensive.*

✔ **Jamee's Restaurant.**   Jamee's is a little jewel box of a restaurant located just off the main drag of town and serving the kind of home-cooked meals you wish you could cook at home. You can order a light supper or a complete dinner, with entrees like poached salmon, pasta with fresh scallops, chicken and apple sausages, marinated grilled pork chops, and filet mignon with madeira sauce. The menu changes often, based on what is available and good that week. Though it is an informal place it is also a special-occasion place, very intimate, sweet, and romantic. This is a tiny spot, so reservations are advised.

JAMEE'S RESTAURANT, *1226-B Washington Street, off Lincoln; (707) 942-0979. Dinner Tuesday through Sunday in summer, Tuesday through Saturday in winter. Beer and wine only. All nonsmoking. No credit cards. Moderate.*

✔ **Silverado Restaurant.**   This is the more midwestern-style version of the All Seasons Cafe across the street. Owned by the same folks, the Silverado Restaurant has the air of a family dining room, with its light wood paneling and green leatherette booths. The food is less ambitious here than across the street, but it is just as good.

The menu classifies the food as Creative American Cooking, which is accurate. This is not "cuisine" or "gourmet," nor is the food described in esoteric terms. At lunch you can get a variety of burgers, salads, a quiche of the day, pasta, and fresh fish specials. One time we ate here, we had a baked halibut with lime and tarragon served simply with rice, fresh carrots, and snow peas plus the pasta special of the day, which was fettuccine with rock shrimp and chorizo in spicy tomato sauce. Both dishes were just fine—good enough to encourage us to come back.

At dinnertime, there is a wider selection, including grilled leg of lamb, roast pork loin with homemade apple chutney, and herb-roasted chicken with a sauce of olive oil, parsley, capers, and shallots. Appetizers include mussels and oysters and the house pasta served in a smaller portion than the entree version.

Like the All Seasons Cafe, there's a huge wine list here, wonderful desserts, and homemade ice cream.

SILVERADO RESTAURANT, *1374 Lincoln Avenue; (707) 942-6725. Breakfast, lunch, and dinner daily. Full bar. No nonsmoking section. MC, Visa. Moderate.*

✔ **Blue Plate Diner.**   Were the fifties really that long ago? Now it seems that every burg has a retro fifties diner. Napa is no exception, and the Blue Plate Diner is it. You'll find all the expected items on the menu, plus a selection of items unheard of forty years ago in the American heartland, including clams and prawns over Japanese noodles, sushi, and lumpia (Filipino egg roll).

However, you are best advised to stick to items that match the decor. A burger, shake, and fries make for a fine and moderately priced meal.

If you must heed the call of nature while dining here, be sure to brush up on your hairdo lingo. You might rush to the restrooms only to be confronted by the doors labeled DUCKTAILS and BEEHIVES. We encountered the sorry spectacle of a sweet elderly lady frantically trying to decide which door to open.

BLUE PLATE DINER, *811 Coombs Street; (707) 226-BLUE. Breakfast, lunch, and dinner daily. Full bar. No nonsmoking section. MC, Visa. Inexpensive.*

✔ **Cafe Kinyon!**   In the location on old Main Street that used to be the very casual Aron's Cafe, there is now a more formal-looking establishment called Cafe Kinyon! (The exclamation point is theirs.) Now, there are white cloths on the tables and real cloth napkins sticking up from the wine glasses, but the menu is still offering good fresh food at moderate prices. Sandwiches are the main fare, but not your common everyday items. You might find a grilled chicken with melted jack cheese and peppers, or roast turkey with cranberry sauce. There are salads, like the shredded chicken with spicy peanut sauce. There's also a soup of the day, such as Portuguese black bean, and a daily quiche. Kinyon is an elegant little spot for a wholesome lunch.

CAFE KINYON!, *823 Main Street; (707) 224-9000. Breakfast daily, lunch Monday through Friday, dinner Thursday through Saturday, brunch Saturday and Sunday. Beer and wine only. All nonsmoking. No credit cards. Moderate.*

✔ **Chanterelle.**   This restaurant proves again the old proverb about not judging a book by its cover. From the outside, you might think the building is a converted chain operation. In truth, it used to be a place called Riccardo's. When Karl Rashash took it over in late 1988, he changed the name to Chanterelle. Rashash had been involved with some of Sonoma's successful French restaurants, such as L'Esperance, Sharl's, and Le Relais, but this is his best place yet.

Chanterelle became an immediate hit. It offers two large, attractive, and comfortable dining rooms, a bar and snack room, and delicious food at bargain prices. The decor is upscale, so that those business people having lunch in suits and ties and executive dresses look right at home. There are large comfortable chairs, with arms and red velvet backs that match the red tablecloths. Everything is done in muted tones, including the subtle indirect lighting. This is where you lunch when you want more than a sandwich, and where you take out-of-town guests for dinner.

The food is continental, mostly French, with an emphasis on lightness. There are items such as sole sautéed with sesame and green onions, served with crisp seasonal vegetables and a rice pilaf. Another popular entree is the chicken breast stuffed with mozzarella and leeks, then grilled and topped with a roasted garlic sauce. Or you could have prawns with ginger, garlic, and wild mushrooms, presumably chanterelles. With selections of pasta, salads, beef, seafood, and poultry entrees, the menu covers just about every conceivable taste and need. If requested, the chef will also prepare your order without salt or butter.

CHANTERELLE, *804 First Street; (707) 253-7300. Lunch Monday through Saturday, dinner nightly. Full bar. MC, Visa. Moderate.*

✔ **Hi-Way 29 Diner.** This is a real truck stop kind of place, and it's not hard to figure out why. Even a truck driver's appetite is challenged here, particularly on Mondays, when the house special is two T-bone steaks for $5.95. No kidding, I've seen them, but was never hungry enough to order the special. Customers told me they were great.

The rest of the menu is what you would expect in a highway diner—burgers and meat-and-potatoes items. A place like this may be the norm in many parts of the country, but in the Napa Valley it's downright exotic.

HI-WAY 29 DINER, *117 Kelly Road, off Highway 29 between Vallejo and Napa; (707) 224-6303. Breakfast and lunch daily. Beer and wine only. MC, Visa. Inexpensive.*

RUTHERFORD ③

✔ **Auberge du Soleil.** Even though the interior design has always reminded Catherine of "The Flintstones," Auberge du Soleil is one of her favorite places to dine on those rare occasions when Jerry is willing to drop a bundle. At lunch and at sunset, you can't beat the view. The restaurant and inn (see Lodging section, page 180) are located on thirty-three acres of pristine Napa Valley countryside; the windows from the restaurant overlook the olive groves, vineyards, and mountains that attract visitors from around the world.

The kitchen gained its reputation for imaginative cuisine from the original chef, the late Masa Kobayashi, legendary for combining the principles of French and Japanese cooking and presentation. The current chef, Albert Tordjman, has carried on the tradition of beautifully presented food, each plate arranged like a work of art. If your seafood salad is accompanied by potato salad, the warm, creamy pommes des terres will be wrapped in a transparent ribbon of cucumber. Fresh edible flowers are inserted just so. Just watching the plates arrive at neighboring tables can be the afternoon's or evening's entertainment.

Though expensive, we would classify the food as perhaps looking better than it tastes. Lunch is chic casual (wear your cleanest Reeboks) with menu items offered à la carte. At dinner the atmosphere is formal and the menu prix fixe. The service is impeccable; plenty of staff people are on hand but not hovering; the waitpersons are very knowledgeable about wines and seem anxious to promote local products. The menu is geared to feature the best available local products, and the place is a Napa Valley institution to be experienced at least once. If eating there is too expensive, you might consider coming up for a drink in the bar.

AUBERGE DU SOLEIL, *180 Rutherford Hill Road; (707) 963-1211. Lunch and dinner daily. Full bar. MC, Visa. Expensive.*

✓ **Fairway Grill.** The Meadowood Resort complex is one of the plushest spreads in the Napa Valley, offering luxury accommodations (see Lodging section, page 183). It is an expensive place to spend the night, but you can have a taste— figuratively and literally—of the good life for the price of breakfast or lunch at the Grill.

In essence, this is the resort coffee shop. You can dine indoors or out, overlooking the lush croquet and golf courses and the beautiful surrounding countryside. The menu is standard grill fare, mostly sandwiches augmented by daily specials that include fresh fish and pasta dishes. Some unusual appetizers, like corn pancakes with wild mushrooms, are offered. Everything is tasty and moderately priced.

You can also splurge on dinner upstairs at the more expensive Starmont restaurant, which offers California-French cuisine in much more formal surroundings.

FAIRWAY GRILL, *on the grounds of Meadowood Resort, 900 Meadowood Lane; (707) 963-3646. Breakfast and lunch daily. Full bar. MC, Visa, Am Ex, Diners. Moderate.*

✓ **Knickerbocker's.** In many places in America a good rule of thumb when looking for a place to eat is to see where the truck drivers go. However, in the California wine country the rule of thumb is to look for places winery owners go. Of course, they have a vested interest in keeping their labels on the wine list, but at the same time they want their product served in good restaurants.

Knickerbocker's is the kind of place where winery owners eat, which is quite a statement considering the abundance of good restaurants within a ten-mile

ST. HELENA
④

radius. It is an unpretentious and modestly priced establishment a few miles north of the town of St. Helena in the Freemark Abbey Wine complex.

Knickerbocker's began as Tony Knickerbocker's catering company, which became so popular he opened the restaurant in late 1986. It was an immediate hit, thanks partly to its array of appetizers available all afternoon. The food is a mixture of California grill accented by Asian, Italian, and French influences. For example, the menu might offer broiled pork tenderloin Chinois; cheese tortellini on a bed of garden vegetables, and steamed Thai crab sausage dumplings. Menus change seasonally to take advantage of fresh local produce, plus there are daily specials based on what's freshest that day. By the way, at lunch, the hamburger served on a housemade bun was great.

The restaurant itself is in a lovely roadhouse-type building with a high, vaulted ceiling, picture windows, stained glass, a giant stone fireplace (very cozy on cool days), and tables outside on a terrace (very pleasant on warm days). The walls are adorned with cheerful paintings by local artists. The atmosphere is conducive to both businesspeople "doing lunch" and visitors leisurely enjoying the Napa Valley.

From the dining room you can see a very cramped and busy kitchen, which may make you wonder "How do they fix so much good food in that tiny place?" The answer is there's another kitchen downstairs, where all the breads and desserts are baked and where the food for the catering business is prepared.

KNICKERBOCKER'S, *in the Freemark Abbey Wine complex, 3020 St. Helena Highway North (Highway 29); (707) 963-9300. Lunch Tuesday through Saturday, dinner Wednesday through Sunday. Beer and wine only. MC, Visa, Am Ex, Diners. Moderate.*

✔ **The Model Bakery.**   Whenever we pull into a new town, we immediately look for a place to have an afternoon cappuccino and something chocolate. In St. Helena we found The Model Bakery. If nothing else, it's fun to look at the ever-changing and imaginative window display of unusual breads. But better than that is the house specialty: a chocolate espresso cookie not to be believed—large and soft, fudgy like a brownie, with nuts. Also on hand is a variety of muffins and pastries. And, they do know how to make a good cappuccino.

THE MODEL BAKERY, *1357 Main Street; (707) 963-8192. Open 7:30 A.M. to 5:30 P.M. Tuesday through Saturday. All nonsmoking. No credit cards.*

✔ **Spring Street Restaurant.**   Did your mother ever take you to lunch at a "ladies'" restaurant? Maybe the tearoom of a downtown department store? If so, prepare for déjà vu when you walk up the stairs of the lovely old home that is now the Spring Street Restaurant. A charming hostess will greet you, then show you a menu that includes salads and light entrees, plus a few heartier dishes to feed the hungry men who have found the place. There's usually a quiche of the day and sandwiches on bread baked on the premises. They also make their own desserts, such as apple pie and lemon cake, accompanied by a selection of teas. Mind your manners!

SPRING STREET RESTAURANT, *1245 Spring Street; (707) 963-5578. Lunch and dinner daily, brunch Saturday and Sunday. Beer and wine only. MC, Visa. Inexpensive to Moderate.*

✔ **Tra Vigne.** Yet another in the Mustard's–Fog City Diner chain is a Northern Italian restaurant just south of the town of St. Helena. Tra Vigne means "among the vines," and this spacious and lovely restaurant is strategically placed to take advantage of the constant stream of visitors to the boutique wineries of the northern Napa Valley.

The menu here is incredibly diverse, offering many pastas, grilled dishes, salads, as well as inventive and unusual combinations. On one visit, four of us had such items as chilled melon and fig soup, grilled then chilled summer vegetables, roast chicken with balsamic vinegar, grapes, and pine nuts, pasta with smoked salmon in a mascarpone cream, and the special sandwich of the day, which was a gourmet hero on homemade Tuscan-style bread. Items are à la carte, so the size of your tab will depend on how many dishes you order.

A major part of the attraction of Tra Vigne is the decor. Inside, it's large and usually noisy with high ceilings and stylish high-tech furniture, resembling a modern trattoria in Milan. Outside, there's patio seating overlooking a beautiful courtyard, where you are transported to the countryside for more quiet dining. This is a "hot spot," so reservations are strongly advised.

TRA VIGNE, *1050 Charter Oak, corner of Highway 29; (707) 963-4444. Lunch and dinner daily. Full bar. MC, Visa. Moderate to Expensive.*

✔ **Trilogy.** Here's a cozy, intimate place run by a trio of veterans of other high-end Napa Valley restaurants. The atmosphere is casually elegant, with service on terra cotta plates with a ceramic glaze. There are only about a dozen tables, each covered with a white tablecloth.

Not surprisingly, the food is California Cuisine, emphasizing local produce. Thus, the menu changes frequently according to what's available. Lunch might be grilled yellowfin tuna with pistachio-ginger butter, smoked chicken salad with raspberry dressing, or fettuccine with fresh basil pesto. Dinner might begin with a ragout of mushrooms served with a corn-chive crepe. In addition to these à la carte items, a prix fixe menu is also offered. You get a choice of appetizer (can you decide between sautéed quail with macadamia nut sauce or crayfish and artichoke with roasted garlic dressing?) and choice of entree (perhaps roast breast of pheasant with rosemary sauce or sautéed king salmon with brown butter, capers, and lemon), plus dessert. When we encountered this deal in early 1989, the complete dinner was $24.

It's a small place, so reservations are recommended.

TRILOGY, *1234 Main Street (the entrance is around the corner on Hunt Street); (707) 963-5507. Lunch Monday, Tuesday, and Friday, dinner Thursday through Tuesday; closed Wednesday. Beer and wine only. No nonsmoking section. MC, Visa. Moderate.*

YOUNTVILLE
(5)

✔ **The Diner.**   This place is more typical of wine country diners than the Hi-Way 29. Although The Diner is totally unpretentious, the food is closer to cuisine than cookin'. Great culinary skill goes into the hamburgers, sandwiches, and Mexican foods that are featured here. The omelets are stuffed and huge and are accompanied by perfect hash browns; on the weekends, the waffles and berry pancakes can't be beat. Desserts are baked on the premises and are pretty swell, too. This is simply good food. At peak meal times, be prepared to wait.

THE DINER, *6476 Washington Street; (707) 944-2626. Breakfast, lunch, and dinner Tuesday through Sunday; closed Monday. No alcohol served. No credit cards. Inexpensive to Moderate.*

✔ **Piatti.**   Claude Rouas, the proprietor of the very tony and expensive Auberge du Soleil in Rutherford (see page 48), opened a less formal cafe a few years ago and found an instant hit on his hands. Piatti will cost you much less than Auberge, and you can sit outdoors in the sun (albeit without the Auberge's spectacular view of the Napa Valley).

The menu is what you'd expect in a good neighborhood trattoria in Northern Italy as opposed to a more opulent ristorante. Appetizers include carpaccio (thin slices of raw beef), eggplant rolled with goat cheese, arugula, and sun-dried tomatoes, and charcoal-grilled radicchio with bacon. Pasta courses include housemade Venetian spaghetti with duck ragout, angel hair pasta with fresh tomatoes, basil, and garlic, and a black-and-white pasta with fresh seafood. Four or five different pizzas are also offered. Main course items (I Secondi Piatti) are simple: grilled chicken, calf liver, steak, fish of the day, and so on. The menu and prices stay the same at lunch and dinner.

Piatti is a very comfortable restaurant, whether you sit out on the patio or inside the stark dining room surrounding a busy bar. It's all stylishly understated, and it attracts the kind of well-heeled customers who seem to turn up at the "right" places. This is not to imply that it is a clubby place for insiders. You will be comfortable there.

Have we failed to mention that the food is terrific? Well, it is.

PIATTI, *6480 Washington Street; (707) 944-2070. Lunch and dinner daily. Full bar. MC, Visa. Moderate.*

CHAPTER **4** San Mateo County

Restaurant operators in San Mateo County begin with two strikes against them. Because this is the closest county to San Francisco, residents have a long history of heading into the city when they want a special meal. Strike two usually comes when they try to get some recognition in the San Francisco press; reviewers are quick to write about new places in Berkeley or Oakland, but seldom venture to San Mateo County. Still, there are many places worthy of note here, and many chefs who would be media stars elsewhere.

✔ **La Locanda**. La Locanda reminds me of the old-fashioned neighborhood Italian restaurants in New York. The obligatory pictures of the motherland adorn the walls, opera wails through the speakers, and genuine sons of Italy in red jackets and a towel over the arm wait on the tables. This is not a trendy, California version of an Italian restaurant; this is the real fettuccine.

As one would hope, the best thing about La Laconda is the food, which is hearty and plentiful and faithful to the Old Country. At lunch, a choice of nine or ten pasta dishes is offered, including linguine with clams, pasta al pesto, and the wonderful house specialty, gnocchi. Other entrees include such staples as veal scalloppine and calamari saute.

Dinner is a more elaborate affair, with more fish, chicken, and veal dishes to choose from. But the dinner is like lunch in that you'll think you've stepped into a good New York Italian restaurant, circa 1959.

BURLINGAME
①

53

LA LOCANDA, *1136 Broadway; (415) 347-1053. Lunch Tuesday through Friday, dinner Tuesday through Sunday. Beer and wine only. MC, Visa. Moderate.*

✔ **Nathan's.**   Nathan's is a continental restaurant with a Viennese accent. Located in the center of town in a 1906 landmark building that once housed a bank, this is a spacious, attractive place to enjoy a leisurely meal. The owner, Nathan Schmidt, is a gracious and energetic host who bounces around the large dining rooms making sure that everyone is having enough to eat. There's little chance of that being a problem.

The menu offers a good selection of traditional continental dishes; a few French, a few Italian, but the best are likely to be Austrian specialties like weiner schnitzel or roasted duck. Portions are large, and your entree will be accompanied by several side dishes. Save room for dessert, which features wonderful pastries and some of the artfully made truffles created by Nathan's celebrated brother, Joseph Schmidt.

Several years ago, Nathan ran a tiny spot down the street called the Old Country Inn, which developed quite a following as an outpost for European cuisine. Now, in this much larger and more elegant space, he has been able to expand business and serve many more people, all without sacrificing quality or charm.

NATHAN'S, *1100 Burlingame Avenue; (415) 347-1414. Lunch Sunday through Friday; dinner nightly. Full bar. MC, Visa, Am Ex, Diners. Moderate.*

HALF MOON BAY
②

✔ **McCoffee.**   This is the place in town for a quick coffee break. It is also a wonderful place for a fast sandwich or snack and to pick up specialty items like coffee beans, fancy mustards, imported cheeses, chocolate truffles, and great costume jewelry. No kidding; last time we ate here, Catherine ordered a turkey sandwich on squaw bread, a cappuccino with low-fat milk, and two pairs of earrings. Owner Elizabeth McCaughey not only has a good sense of puns (Mc-Coffee, McCaughey—get it?), she has a good sense of fun and carries a small stock of wonderful postcards, old-fashioned toys, and jewelry fashioned from things like dominoes and tiny baby dolls. Her sandwiches are generously huge, and she makes good quesadillas with salsa for the bargain price of $1.75.

The front window is plastered with all types of community announcements, and lots of locals drop by for a quick bite, conversation, and just staring out onto Main Street, watching the small town world go by.

MCCOFFEE, *522 Main Street; (415) 726-6241. Open 9 A.M. to 6 P.M. daily. No alcohol served. No nonsmoking section. No credit cards. Inexpensive.*

✔ **Pasta Moon.**   The first time we had lunch at Pasta Moon, Jerry was recognized by an enthusiastic diner. "Hey, Jerry," he said with a thick New York accent, while thrusting his plate toward our table, "you can't get fresh mozzarella and

San Mateo

San Mateo

Half Moon Bay

Redwood City

Woodside

Palo Alto

sliced tomatoes like this anywhere between here and Brooklyn." He and his companion went on to devour huge plates of pasta, an order of tiramisu, and cappuccinos. Clearly they were in heaven, and so were the local ladies at the next table, though their style involved less gusto and smaller portions.

As one would assume, pasta is the specialty of the house, though the menu begins with a tempting array of appetizers. The menu changes each month, but it might include alio arrosto (roasted garlic served with goat's milk cheese and good bread), insalata di arancie e finocchi (a salad of sweet oranges and fennel), and soups, including clams or mussels simmered in tomatoes and white wine and the classic minestrone.

Pasta choices are twelve to fifteen deep. If you like simply prepared foods, try the linguine al pomodoro e basilico, just olive oil, garlic, tomatoes, and basil. If you like hot spicy foods, try the penne arrabbiata, or "angry pasta," made with tomatoes, pancetta, porcini mushrooms, garlic, and hot red pepper. All the pastas are made on the premises and are available for take-out as well.

This is a small, airy place with a pleasant bustle to it, and the kitchen makes good on the promises made by the extensive menu. Just ask the guy from Brooklyn.

PASTA MOON, *315 Main Street; (415) 726-5125. Lunch and dinner daily. Beer and wine only. All nonsmoking. MC, Visa. Moderate.*

✔ **San Benito House.** The San Benito House is a vintage hotel, saloon, and restaurant, built circa 1904. A former schoolteacher, owner Carol Mickelsen, studied cooking with such celebrity chefs as Jacques Pepin and Giuliano Bugialli and apprenticed with the late Masataka Kobayashi of Masa's. She has created a lovely dining room, which is more or less a gallery for local painters, and a garden; on dry and warm-enough nights a large fire pit is lit so diners and overnight guests (see Lodging section, page 189) can sit outside under the stars and sip wine, coffee, and cognac.

Dinner is a leisurely affair, with selections and prices that change every other day or so. The food is classic California Cuisine; each menu is based on what's freshest at the time. Many of the lettuces, herbs, and other ingredients were grown out in the yard; apples from Carol's own trees are used in the desserts.

A typical dinner begins with a salad (perhaps garden lettuces, kumquats, and goat cheese) and a soup. The price is determined by which of three entrees you choose. There will always be a fish, a meat, and some form of poultry offered— perhaps sautéed Monterey squid in garlic sauce, roasted leg of lamb, and grilled quail. The entree is served in an elegant yet unpretentious manner. Sunday brunch is also an elaborate occasion, and reservations for dinner and brunch are a good idea. Because the menu changes so often, you may want to call ahead to find out the entree choices in advance.

Lunch is another matter entirely. It is dished out at a deli counter in another part of the hotel. The menu is limited: housemade soups, salads, sandwiches on bread baked on the premises, brownies, and other desserts. Then you can take your food out to the garden; or, if the weather is bad, you can sit in the old-fashioned saloon, complete with long, wooden bar and animal heads on the wall.

SAN BENITO HOUSE, *356 Main Street; (415) 726-3425. Lunch Wednesday through Saturday, dinner Wednesday through Sunday, plus Sunday brunch. Full bar. All nonsmoking. MC, Visa, Am Ex. Lunch Inexpensive to Moderate, dinner Moderate to Expensive.*

✔ **Flea Street Cafe.** There are so many virtues to the Flea Street Cafe that it's hard to know where to begin. Okay, let's start with the entrance. Once you step from the busy street into the cafe you are transported into a world of country elegance and charm. It feels as if you've suddenly entered a New England inn or the old South. Floral prints on the wallpaper blend with the fresh flower arrangements that adorn the series of small rooms that make up the cafe. You have a choice of sitting at a table or in a booth that comes equipped with a symphony of pillows, which you can arrange to suit your own personal comfort.

MENLO PARK
③

Now for the food and service. Before you order you'll be greeted with hot biscuits topped with sesame seeds. You'll also be offered something to drink, items like cinnamon-orange iced tea and strong coffee. Each meal is a production with special touches, all adding to the pleasure of eating at the Flea Street Cafe (which gets its name, by the way, from its location on Alameda de las Pulgas, or "avenue of the fleas"). Organic produce is used whenever possible. Vegetarian dishes, plus low-fat and low-sodium meals, are so tasty you might forget they're good for you.

Menu items vary with the seasons, but here's the kind of fare you can choose from. For Sunday breakfast: sweet potato pancakes with cranberry purée; seafood hash; and frittata with garlic, onions, basil, and seasonal vegetables. For lunch: grilled chicken sandwich with carmelized onions, swiss cheese, and lemon chive mayonnaise; wild, wild pasta (fettuccine with wild rice, sun-dried tomatoes, feta cheese, and three kinds of mushrooms); and hot cobb salad, featuring nitrate-free bacon, organic tomatoes and lettuces, and a warm Dijon dressing.

The dinner menu is the most ambitious of all. Try grilled boneless chicken breasts served with a sauce of mustard, honey, port wine, and black peppercorns served over wild rice cakes; or Yucatan fish, which is made with the catch of the day dusted with cumin, thyme, cinnamon, oregano, allspice, and chili powder and served with a cilantro avocado sauce. Dinner includes appetizer or soup and a salad.

Though all the examples given above may sound like someone's parody of California Cuisine, it all works and is quite wonderful.

FLEA STREET CAFE, *3607 Alameda de las Pulgas; (415) 854-1226. Lunch Tuesday through Friday, dinner Tuesday through Saturday, brunch Sunday. Beer and wine only. All nonsmoking, except at the bar. MC, Visa. Moderate.*

✔ **Late for the Train.**   Owned by the same folks who brought us the Flea Street Cafe (see page 57), Late for the Train was one of the Bay Area's first nonsmoking restaurants. For a nonsmoker, nothing is worse than having the smell of cigarette or cigar smoke overwhelm the food. The food here is of the healthy variety, though the menu is quite varied, offering something for every taste. You'll get lots of sprouts on your salad and lots of grain in the homemade bread. The specialty appears to be the omelets, which are thick and fluffy and served with their special tamari-seasoned potatoes (OK, if you count cholesterol and salt, the entire menu is not perfectly virtuous).

The food is good, if not as special as the Flea Street Cafe's. The atmosphere is pleasant, and the place is jammed at lunchtime with the *Sunset* magazine crowd from across the street.

LATE FOR THE TRAIN, *150 Middlefield Road; (415) 321-6124. Breakfast, lunch, and dinner Tuesday through Saturday, brunch Sunday. Beer and wine only. All nonsmoking. MC, Visa, Am Ex. Moderate.*

✔ **Webb Ranch Market.**   This is a place to pack your car with snacks for the road or for taking home. Webb Ranch grows some of the best fruits and vegetables in the area and supplies produce to many of the finest restaurants and food shops in the Bay Area. They sell to the public at a stand located a few minutes off Route 280 north of Palo Alto.

Remember tomatoes? Webb Ranch has the real thing. They also have sweet corn that tastes like the kind you can get in the Midwest, plus those tiny green beans the French call haricots verts. Everything is seasonal and wonderful. You can call ahead for a recording that will tell you what's just been picked.

WEBB RANCH MARKET, *Alpine Road exit off Route 280, on the Bay side of the freeway; (415) 854-5417 for a recording, or 854-0838 for a real person. Open only during the picking season, which usually means April through October, 10 A.M. to 6 P.M. daily. No credit cards.*

MILLBRAE
④

✔ **Hong Kong Flower Lounge Restaurant.**   You know the old cliche about finding a good Chinese restaurant: look for the places where Chinese eat. This is taken to the extreme at the Flower Lounge. Almost every day taxis arrive from nearby San Francisco International Airport carrying Asian travelers to the Lounge. You will also see crowds of Chinese Americans who come on pilgrimages from all over the Bay Area for a taste of real Cantonese cuisine.

The Wong family, who owns the Flower Lounge, has four successful restaurants in Hong Kong. When the Wongs decided to try an American venture, they sent their daughter Alice, who had gone to school at Mills College in Oakland, to be in charge. After looking at many locations, she picked the busy El Camino Real in Millbrae as the ideal spot. Her research was apparently right on the money; the Flower Lounge was jammed with customers from the first day.

The restaurant is very attractive and has impeccable service. But the reason you come here is for the food, which may surprise anyone who grew up eating what is usually called Cantonese. Here you will not find chop suey or egg foo yong—those are American inventions. You will find food of complex subtlety and unusual combinations of ingredients. For example, the most popular dish at the restaurant sounds a bit strange, but tastes wonderful. Are you ready for deep fried prawns, coated in mayonnaise and served with honey-coated fire-roasted walnuts? It's great.

The menu is extensive at lunch and dinner, with at least twenty seafood dishes and ten poultry choices, plus noodle, tofu, and vegetable dishes—some familiar (barbecued duck), others unusual (baked lobster with Chinese wine sauce). This is not the fiery food served in Hunan restaurants; instead the emphasis is on the freshness of the ingredients.

And at lunch there is the addition of wonderful dim sum. This treat involves waiters bringing around to the patrons an endless array of dumplings and other little dishes, most of which cost under two dollars each. You choose whichever dishes you wish, though you will have to eat a lot to spend twenty dollars for two.

HONG KONG FLOWER LOUNGE RESTAURANT, *51 Millbrae (corner El Camino Real); (415) 878-8108. Lunch and dinner daily. Beer and wine only. MC, Visa, Am Ex, Diners accepted for $20 or more. Moderate.*

MOSS BEACH (5)

✔ **Dan's Place.** On a hill overlooking the Fitzgerald Marine Reserve is a somewhat funky Italian restaurant that has been in the same family for several generations. Dan's Place is a tradition in town, and you will feel right at home there.

Dan's serves home-cooked Italian meals. Nothing fancy here, just good spaghetti and ravioli, a few veal dishes, and thick minestrone, all served in huge, family-style portions.

DAN'S PLACE, *818 Etheldore Street, one block above Route 1; you can see the sign from the highway; (415) 728-3343. Lunch and dinner daily. Full bar. MC, Visa. Inexpensive to Moderate.*

PACIFICA (6)

✔ **La Vita Cafe.** If you are just getting underway on a trip south and find yourself in need of a quick lunch or snack, let me recommend La Vita. This is a tiny spot with just a few tables and a rather limited menu. But as Spencer Tracy once said about Katharine Hepburn, "There ain't much meat, but what's there is cherce." At La Vita you will get "cherce" salads, homemade soups, thick sandwiches, good desserts, and an espresso machine that turns out a mighty fine cappuccino.

In an area where it's easier to find franchised food than the real thing, this cafe is a welcome stop.

LA VITA CAFE, *164 Reina del Mar; (415) 359-7927. Open 7:30 A.M. to 4:30 P.M. Monday through Friday, 9 A.M. to 6 P.M. weekends. Beer and wine only. No credit cards. Inexpensive.*

PESCADERO (7)

✔ **Duarte's.**   There's not a whole lot to the charming town of Pescadero, so you might wonder how so many people happen to be at a restaurant called Duarte's. There are several reasons. The food is good, the prices are right, and they serve one item for which they are justifiably famous: artichoke soup.

Yes, people come from all over to try this creamy, rich soup made from the thorny vegetable. Duarte's is located in the heart of artichoke country, and they've made the most of this delicacy. The rest of the menu features fresh fish, omelets, burgers, and items you might find in a lot of roadside cafes. My favorite meal there was one lunch where I skipped an entree and went for the soup, a lightly fried squid appetizer, and a piece of wonderful pecan pie. They bake all their pies daily, and they're great. If it's a beautiful day and there are lots of motorists along the neighboring coastline, be prepared to wait in line; on weekends, reservations are advised.

DUARTE'S, *202 Stage Road, in the center of town; (415) 879-0464. Breakfast, lunch, and dinner daily. Full bar. MC, Visa, Am Ex. Inexpensive to Moderate.*

PRINCETON-BY-THE-SEA (8)

✔ **The Shore Bird.**   Set on a harbor in a lovely village filled with restaurants, The Shore Bird is billed as a bit of "Cape Cod on the California coast." Don't expect lobster or other New England delicacies, though. What you will find is an attractive, busy, tourist-oriented restaurant serving reasonably well-prepared fresh fish and seafood in a Cape Cod–style building. The preparation is more old-fashioned here than in the modern grills. Many of the seafood entrees are fried or sautéed, and cooked for customers who apparently prefer their fish well done. It's the atmosphere, rather than the food, that appears to be the main attraction.

The "find" here is located outside the main dining room, in the bar and cafe called The Seafood Cafe where you can get light meals and appetizers. If you're in the mood or in a hurry, it's possible to have a light lunch or snack there at moderate prices.

This place can get crowded, and they do not accept reservations. However, you can call ahead and get your name on a "preferred seating list"; though you are not guaranteed a table at a particular time, in theory your waiting time will be less.

THE SHORE BIRD, *390 Capistrano Road, overlooking Pillar Point Harbor; (415) 728-5541. Lunch Monday through Saturday, dinner nightly, brunch Sunday. Full bar. All nonsmoking, except for the bar. MC, Visa, Am Ex, Diners, Discovery. Moderate to Expensive.*

✔ **Redwood Cafe and Spice Company.** If you love freshly baked breads and muffins, we've got a place for you to have breakfast or lunch. The Redwood Cafe and Spice Company is located inside a house that was built in 1874 for the foreman of one of the town's big lumber companies. (At one time there really were redwoods in Redwood City.) The house was originally built elsewhere in town; to save it from demolition, the Saier family bought and moved it to its present location. Various members of the family took hammer and saw into hand to fix the place up and open it as a cafe in 1979.

REDWOOD CITY ⑨

It is an informal place that serves one of the great breakfasts and brunches in the Bay Area. You have a choice of from eight to twelve different egg scrambles, plus Swedish oatmeal pancakes, and buttermilk pancakes made from James Beard's recipe. The orange juice is freshly squeezed, and a delicious and strong-brewed coffee of the day is served. Then there are those breads and muffins. A basket of them arrives while you're waiting for the entree. Served warm and with butter, they might include pumpkin bread, cornbread, oat bran muffins, and cardamom buns.

The lunch menu offers a selection of sandwiches, soups, and salads, including something called "Politicians' Soup," featuring a blend of fourteen beans. (There's a joke in there somewhere, but we won't touch it.) Desserts are of the old-fashioned school: pies, fruit cobblers, and bread pudding.

It's a good idea to call ahead for a reservation. But if you must wait for your table, you can browse in their country store or stroll in the Victorian garden that surrounds the house. Gardening enthusiasts may like to look at the antique trees and shrubs on the property, including a pepper tree, elderberry tree, and several rose bushes that date back to 1900.

REDWOOD CAFE AND SPICE COMPANY, *1020 Main Street; (415) 366-1498. Breakfast and lunch Tuesday through Friday, brunch Saturday and Sunday. Beer and wine only. All nonsmoking. MC, Visa. Moderate.*

✔ **Maharaja.** If you like Indian food, we have a real find for you. Right in the center of the very unchic downtown of San Bruno is a nondescript-looking restaurant serving great Indian food. We don't know what Maharaja is doing here, but they do know their way around a curry and a tandoori oven. There are daily luncheon specials, and the à la carte items are all a notch below the going prices for this type of food. We sampled tandoori chicken, spinach with wonderfully pungent cubes of cheese, and a lamb curry, and not only were the portions

SAN BRUNO ⑩

ample, but the dishes were wonderful. The atmosphere is nothing to write home about; there is no decor to speak of, and the waiter was reserved, if not borderline surly. Since we often find this attitude in Indian restaurants, we chalk it up to cultural differences. At least our waiter didn't tell us his name and say, "How you guys doin' today?" Anyway, if you go for the food, you won't be disappointed.

MAHARAJA, *528 San Mateo Avenue; (415) 583-5226. Lunch and dinner daily. Beer and wine only. MC, Visa, Am Ex. Inexpensive to Moderate.*

SAN MATEO

✔ **The Coffee Critic.** As a rule of thumb it is easier to find a great meal on the road than a good cup of coffee. Thus it was a delight to find a great place for a cappuccino on El Camino Real. If the smell of roasting beans isn't enough to tip you off, the inviting art deco building has a rounded glass area that lets you peer in to see that this is a place for serious coffee drinkers. There are a few tables where you can sit and have your freshly brewed coffee or espresso drink, and there are many wonderful dessert choices available. The rest of the operation is devoted to selling varieties of coffee beans, most of which are roasted on the premises. Linda Nederman opened this establishment in 1988 and immediately filled a void in the area. Now she has another branch in nearby Burlingame, and the coffee craze is finally spreading to the peninsula.

By the way, you can have your cappuccino with either regular or nonfat milk. Linda and her crew have learned that the nonfat actually makes better foam . . . a welcome surprise that may allow you to have that double chocolate cake without guilt.

THE COFFEE CRITIC, *106 S. El Camino Real; (415) 342-8558. Open from 7:30 A.M. to 5:30 P.M. Monday through Friday, 8:30 A.M. to 5:00 P.M. Saturday, 10 A.M. to 2 P.M. Sunday. All nonsmoking. No credit cards.*

✔ **Nini's.** Nini's might just as well be called Mom's because that's the feeling of this friendly neighborhood coffee shop whose slogan is "The outskirts of town but the best around." Though the neighborhood has changed over the years, it's not the outskirts anymore. Nini herself will probably be on hand, greeting her regular customers by their first names and making sure you get what you want to eat, whether it's one of her huge breakfast specials or a piece of apple pie she baked that morning. This is not Nouvelle Cuisine, it's very good lunch counter food served with love and in huge portions.

If weather permits, you can sit outside in the garden.

NINI's, *1000 North Idaho; (415) 348-9578. Breakfast and lunch Monday through Saturday. Beer only. No nonsmoking section. No credit cards. Inexpensive.*

✔ **231 Ellsworth.** One of the newest bastions of fine cuisine is on a quiet street near downtown San Mateo. This is an attractive restaurant, decorated in soft pastels with subdued lighting and boasting a first-class kitchen. Using fresh California ingredients, a classically trained chef produces French cuisine, and the results are wonderful.

A particular bargain is the prix fixe lunch, which in the summer of 1989 offered soup, appetizer or salad, and entree for $10.50. If you order à la carte, prices will be comparable to San Francisco restaurants. There are always fresh fish dishes, served with wonderfully subtle sauces. Vegetables are cooked so you can still enjoy their taste and texture. In other words, they are not steamed to a mushy death. Much attention is also given to display and presentation. It's a pleasure to look at your meal as well as eat it. Reservations are advised.

231 ELLSWORTH, *231 S. Ellsworth; (415) 347-7231. Lunch Monday through Friday, dinner Monday through Saturday. MC, Visa, Am Ex, Diners. Moderate to Expensive.*

✔ **Hogan's Cafe.**   This is one of the most unusual restaurants in the Bay Area. For starters, it's only open weekdays from 4 A.M. to 2 P.M. Also, it's located in the most unlikely of places, hidden away in the center of a large fruit and vegetable terminal not far from San Francisco International Airport.

SOUTH SAN FRANCISCO
⑫

Inside you'll find a large and bustling place that resembles a sports bar—the regulars playing liar's dice while businessmen in neckties mingle with the produce handlers in workshirts. The walls are decorated with photos of local sports celebrities. The best thing about this place is that the food is *really* good.

And considering that it's smack dab in the center of the Bay Area's main produce market, no wonder. Hogan's has direct access to the freshest fruits and vegetables, and everything is served in trencherman portions. For breakfast, the omelets are huge and overstuffed with cheese and vegetables and whatever else you might wish the cook pack it with. For lunch, the huge salads are popular, but if you're in the mood for meat and pasta dishes, you are definitely in the right place. The osso buco is as good as you're likely to get around here, and the portion was enormous. Giant burgers and corned beef and cabbage are regular stars on the menu, as are such seasonal specials as sautéed calamari.

If you arrive late in the day (around here, that means noon or so), you may be put off by the location. Most of the unloading has been done, so you'll see the area littered with a lot of empty produce crates, stray heads of lettuce, and bits of fruit splattered here and there. Don't let that discourage you; the food here is wonderful *and* inexpensive. If you're an early bird, come for breakfast when all the action happens.

HOGAN'S CAFE, *125 Terminal Court #44; (415) 583-2293. Open for breakfast and lunch 4 A.M. to 2 P.M. Monday through Friday. Full bar. MC, Visa. Inexpensive.*

✔ Jo Ann's.   You are going to have to look hard to find Jo Ann's. This is one of those hole-in-the-wall places that the locals know about and would just as soon keep to themselves. It is tucked away in a little shopping center, about 100 feet off El Camino Real.

At first, Jo Ann's looks like a midwestern Main Street coffee shop, with a long counter and vinyl booths. But then you might notice that the waitresses and cooks are young and are dressed as though they were working in SoMa—San Francisco's hip South of Market district—not industrial South San Francisco. Then you might notice all the media awards on the wall, evidence that this is one of the area's favorite breakfast spots.

Everything is good here, but the main feature is omelets. You design your own. The menu lists about thirty items—mushrooms, jalapeño peppers, avocado, cheeses, etc.; you choose three and the cook goes to work. The three-egg whopper comes with crispy country fries and choice of toast or housemade muffins. Beware of Jo Ann's chocolate muffin; it's like a fudge brownie and twice as addictive.

Lunch features daily specials, terrific burgers, and all the items on the breakfast menu. On one visit we had a marinated grilled chicken sandwich with pasta salad and a Mexican turkey salad, which was loaded with chunks of freshly roasted bird (not the dreaded turkey roll). All were wonderful and inexpensive. Be prepared to wait for seating during peak hours.

JO ANN'S, *1131 El Camino Real (on a frontage road that runs alongside El Camino, south of Kaiser Hospital); (415) 872-2810. Breakfast and lunch Tuesday through Sunday. Beer and wine only. No credit cards. Inexpensive.*

✔ Max's Fried Chicken Restaurant.   If you have never tried Filipino food, Max's will be a good introduction. Located in a small shopping center, Max's is a cafeteria that appears to be quite a hangout for people who have moved here from the Philippines.

A TV will be blaring, crowds will be chattering, and it may be a bit intimidating to walk up to the cafeteria line to place your order because, despite the name, you might not know anything about the food. The best bet is to try anything "adobo." Whether it is the pork or the chicken, it will have a spicy and flavorful sauce that is a staple in Filipino cooking. The fried chicken, as with other deep-fried foods, tends to be on the greasy side.

Put yourself in the hands of the friendly people behind the counter. Tell them what you like and they'll recommend things to try.

MAX'S FRIED CHICKEN RESTAURANT, *2239 Gellert Boulevard; (415) 878-0610. Lunch and dinner daily. No alcohol. No nonsmoking section. MC, Visa, Am Ex. Inexpensive.*

✔ **Alpine Inn.**   Outside the tony suburb of Woodside is an institution of sorts. The Alpine Inn is a roadside bar and restaurant that used to be a stagecoach stop; in fact, officially it is California Historical Landmark No. 852. It's rather funky inside, but you can get a large grilled hamburger and take it to one of the picnic benches out back, overlooking the beautiful scenery.

ALPINE INN, *3915 Alpine Road; (415) 854-4004. Open 11:30 A.M. to 10 P.M. Monday through Saturday, 11:30 A.M. to 5 P.M. Sunday. Beer and wine only. No nonsmoking section. No credit cards. Inexpensive.*

✔ **Nina's Cafe.**   Nina's is *the* place to eat in the gentrified village of Woodside. This means that the place is usually crowded, but it also means that it's worth the wait.

The decor is charming and in keeping with the upscale country look of the town. The lunch menu offers many light dishes such as salads and quiche, plus imaginative uses of fresh ingredients to serve with chicken, fish, and meat dishes. Dinner is a little more elaborate but still features many of the dishes that have come to mean California Cuisine: fresh fish, pasta, and the best available local ingredients.

NINA'S CAFE, *2991 Woodside Road; (415) 851-4565. Lunch Tuesday through Friday, dinner Tuesday through Saturday, brunch Sunday. Beer and wine only. MC, Visa. Moderate.*

✔ **Robert's Market Deli.**   Every so often, our idea of a meal on the road is a good take-out sandwich or salad that we can eat in the car. And since we don't eat at fast-food chain operations, the challenge is to find the Backroads' equivalent of the ease without the grease and sodium and stuff like that.

Robert's Market in Woodside is a good take-out-food-on-the-road place that could come in handy for you. This is actually a well-equipped upscale grocery store that has a deli counter; in case you're arriving on horseback, there are wrought-iron hitching posts out front so you can park your trusty steed for free (this is gentrified equestrian country). The rather substantial deli counter has all sorts of food to go: roast chicken, prepared salads, sandwiches, and baked goodies. You might even get a little marketing done while you're waiting for your order.

ROBERT'S MARKET DELI, *3015 Woodside Road; (415) 851-1511. Open 8 A.M. to 8 P.M. daily; closed major holidays. No credit cards. Inexpensive to Moderate.*

CHAPTER **5** Santa Clara County

Anyone who has ever heard the term Silicon Valley knows that major changes have taken place in Santa Clara County in the past several years. With the unprecedented growth of new industry and the revitalization of the city of San Jose (now officially larger than San Francisco), it's only natural that there would be a demand for better places to eat. At one time, you could travel this large county in search of a good meal. There were always some fine restaurants in Saratoga, a few places in Palo Alto, and one or two in San Jose, but that was it. Now there are many choices.

One confession: Because of the recent wave of immigrants from Southeast Asia, there are many new Chinese, Vietnamese, and Thai restaurants all over San Jose. Because of time constraints, we have not been able to research them properly, which explains their absence in this section.

CUPERTINO
①

✓ **Just Fresh.** This large and popular restaurant, right across the road from the De Anza College Campus, is designed to cover almost all recent food trends. They have pasta, they have huge salads, grilled dishes, and most of the seasonings that restaurant reviewers are likely to applaud. It's an ambitious undertaking to try to provide so much variety on a menu, but by and large, they do a good job. Salads are indeed fresh and use interesting greens and other vegetables. There does appear to be a certain formula to the place, but it is certainly a cut above the average chain operation.

This is an attractive, bustling place where you can eat well if you order correctly. One of our tricks in deciding how to order is to unashamedly look at the plates of people who have already been served. Jerry is not above going up to a customer and asking what she or he is eating. He can also be seen walking up to the kitchen or the open grill area and snooping around, or asking the cooks what they recommend.

JUST FRESH, 21255 Stevens Creek Boulevard; (408) 252-5311. Lunch and dinner daily, brunch Saturday and Sunday. Full bar. MC, Visa, Am Ex, Diners. Moderate.

GILROY
②

✓ **Digger's Restaurant and Bar.** Here in the garlic capital of the world, we have been hard pressed to find a restaurant that will serve adequate doses of "the stinking rose." At last we found it, in what seemed to be the unlikeliest of places. Formerly a steakhouse called "Digger Dan's," the new owner of Digger's kept half the original name and all the original plastic steakhouse decor, then added better food to the menu.

Santa Clara

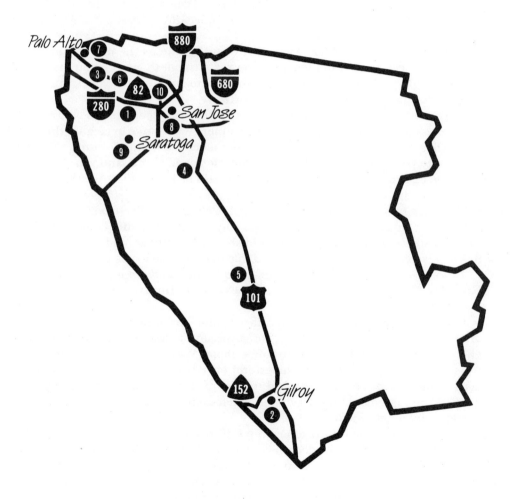

If you like garlic, then order the house salad dressing, a mayonnaise-based concoction that will keep vampires away for the rest of your life. Also, the Gilroy garlic bread, served as an appetizer at dinner, will cure what ails you.

The main menu offerings are a combination of standard Americana (burgers, turkey and swiss at lunch; fish, prime rib, and steak at dinner) plus dishes like stir-fry vegetables, tri-colored pasta with chicken, and chicken teriyaki—standard fare closer to San Francisco, but downright exotic in this part of the world. The aforementioned pasta with chicken is a great dish.

DIGGER'S RESTAURANT AND BAR, *7793 Wren Avenue; (408) 842-0609. Lunch Monday through Friday, dinner nightly. Full bar. MC, Visa, Am Ex. Moderate.*

LOS ALTOS
③

✓ **Arno's.** Main Street in Los Altos always strikes me as the perfect setting for an ad for a "woody" station wagon. There is a timeless, posh suburban look to the place and to the ladies walking from store to store in their Peck and Peck–type skirts and sweaters. Arno's fits in perfectly.

As you enter, you will be greeted by a friendly but proper hostess who does not seem to make a distinction between those diners who arrive in elegant dress and those (like the Backroads crew) in more casual jeans and T-shirts. You'll be ushered to your table, set with a good tablecloth and china, and you will feel as welcome as can be. If it's summer, you will also be happy that Arno's is delightfully air-conditioned.

There are two dining rooms at Arno's, plus a bar area. The food is continental, with an emphasis on fresh ingredients. The menu takes into consideration all tastes, so there are ample selections of fish, chicken, meat, and pasta, and all of it is nicely done. This is the kind of reliable place where locals go every day.

ARNO'S, *397 Main Street; (415) 949-3700. Lunch and dinner Monday through Saturday. Full bar. No smoking section. MC, Visa, Am Ex, Diners. Moderate.*

✓ **Eugene's Polish Restaurant.** California Cuisine has infiltrated restaurants all around the country; nowadays it's not surprising to find goat cheese and radicchio in the most mundane-looking coffee shops. We're all for places that concentrate on low-salt, low-fat, low-cholesterol everything, but once in a while, it's good to push aside the arugula and indulge in an old-fashioned place like Eugene's. The ingredients are fresh and wholesome, but this is not the place you would go for a light meal.

Eugene's takes you off the chic streets of this affluent suburban city and into the Polish countryside. The decor is much like a hunter's lodge, with dark wood and antlers on the wall. The food is authentic and excellent. One lunchtime we tried the white borscht, which was a wonderful and slightly sour potato soup, followed by a combination plate, which arrived brimming with stuffed cabbage, Polish sausage, hunter goulash (hearty beef stew) and Polish hunter stew (with sauerkraut), and three kinds of pierogi. In June 1989, this giant combination plate cost only $7.75.

Along with the traditional Polish dishes listed above, you can also get some good ol' American standbys, like ham sandwiches and chef's salad. Locals come to Eugene's on Thursdays, which is Hamburger Day; the customers swear it's the best burger around.

At dinner, Eugene's lays out the tablecloths, pipes in the Polish music, and dresses the waitresses in peasant outfits. The menu offers the same Polish specials as lunch, plus several additions, including wiener schnitzel, fish filet Baltic style, and veal rouladen. Prices are about one third higher at night.

There's a full bar and a good selection of imported and domestic beers, plus Eugene's Polish hospitality includes a complimentary glass of schnapps at the end of the meal.

EUGENE'S POLISH RESTAURANT, *420 S. San Antonio Road; (415) 941-1222. Lunch and dinner Tuesday through Saturday; closed Sunday and Monday. Full bar. MC, Visa. Inexpensive at lunch, Moderate at dinner.*

✔ **The Peasant Chef.**   This is a family-run restaurant serving food that might well be found in middle-class homes throughout Europe. Specializing in stews and casseroles, it offers a broad selection of items, including vegetarian dishes. You can enjoy items like Russian vegetable pie while your companions eat French crepes and Greek moussaka. Desserts are given special attention here. The service is very friendly.

THE PEASANT CHEF, *368 Village Lane, which is behind the main street in town (Santa Cruz Avenue); (408) 354-8006. Lunch and dinner daily, brunch Sunday. Beer and wine only. MC, Visa. Inexpensive to Moderate.*

LOS GATOS
④

✔ **Super Taqueria.**   Like so many small towns, Morgan Hill has its share of franchised eateries. Finding a place that serves food of the more homemade variety is not easy. But a friend told us about the Super Taqueria, and it's a good thing he did. It would have been easy to overlook.

From the outside it doesn't look like much, sort of like a franchised restaurant without the gloss. The decor doesn't improve much inside, but the food is another story. Inside the Taqueria, you get in line to place your order, which you eat at one of the booths or outside at one of the picnic tables overlooking the town's main drag. You can probably guess the menu selection: tacos, burritos, and so on. But this is not Taco Bell. Meats are nicely cooked, the chicken is very flavorful, and even the beans are delicious. It's all done with top ingredients and good spices.

SUPER TAQUERIA, *16873 Monterey Boulevard; (408) 778-3730. Lunch and dinner daily. Beer only. No nonsmoking section. No credit cards. Inexpensive.*

MORGAN HILL
⑤

✔ **Macheesmo Mouse.** Once upon a time, a group of Stanford MBAs working in the fast-food business got to talking about Mexican food. "We love to eat it," they said, "but the lard and frying and salt could kill us by the time we're fifty." From that came a plan to open a Mexican food joint, fast enough to appeal to the person on the go, cheap enough to be affordable by just about everybody, snazzy-looking enough to make it a fun place to be, and "healthy so that we won't be indicted for manslaughter." Thus, Macheesmo Mouse opened on University Avenue in Palo Alto in March of 1988 (see Palo Alto location, page 73).

Since then, these enterprising entrepreneurs have opened several Macheesmo Mice in the Bay Area and Pacific Northwest. In each place the idea is the same. You get your food within three minutes of ordering, no animal fat is used, and, with the exception of corn chips, nothing is fried; all food is baked or boiled. Prices are really cheap and the atmosphere is very jazzy, decorated in bright colors with neon sculptures, jukeboxes, and with a high noise level.

What can you get in three minutes or less? How about chicken breast, served without the skin and basted in a tangy concoction called Boss Sauce, with brown rice and black beans for $3.85. Slimming? The skinless chicken served with a green salad instead of the rice and beans costs $2.75. Burritos are the specialty of the house: vegetarian or chicken, whole-wheat tortilla optional.

This is an ideal place for anyone concerned about eating healthy food, trying to save money, and/or with little kids. The menu is posted on the wall, and you stand in line to place your order while the other members of your party grab a table. You'll see the American Heart Association red heart symbol next to many of the menu items, signifying their approval. Calorie count is also included. And if you're really on the move, all items can be ordered to go.

Did we mention the totally nonsmoking environment?

MACHEESMO MOUSE, *1910 El Camino (corner Esquela); (415) 964-5558. Lunch and dinner daily. Beer only. All nonsmoking. No credit cards. Inexpensive.*

✔ **Cafe Verona.** This is one of many attractive, stylish new cafes in town, and they did it right. Cafe Verona is modeled after the kind of place where Italians sit for hours, read the paper, drink espresso, and argue politics. With its red brick walls, long coffee bar, huge glass windows, and arty posters, it would not look out of place in the heart of Verona. In Palo Alto, with a major university to provide artists, radicals, studious professors, and computer wizards, the crowd becomes part of the show.

This is a lot more than just a coffeehouse. There is one large glass case in the corner, filled with interesting salads, sandwiches, and pasta items, plus many enticing desserts. Folks stop by for pastries in the morning, for light lunches, or for dinners, which are served hot or cold. All of the food is good, and you are welcome to stay as long as you like.

There are those who think places like Cafe Verona are the singles bars of the nineties. This is an ideal place for one for the road—a cappuccino before heading home after a long day's work. It's also a comfortable place for people to meet and chat.

CAFE VERONA, *236 Hamilton Avenue; (415) 326-9942. Breakfast, lunch, and dinner Monday through Saturday; closed Sunday. Beer and wine only. MC, Visa. Inexpensive to Moderate.*

✔ **Cenzo.** There are several chic and attractive Northern Italian restaurants that have sprung up in Palo Alto in the last year or two. In all honesty, Cenzo doesn't exactly fit into either of those categories. It's still popular and worth recommending, however, because of the value and quality of food. Not that this is an unattractive place, it just doesn't have that "in" look of a stylish Florentine trattoria. It looks more like a typical downtown restaurant that has gone through a few changes of ownership and personality before finding a formula that works.

Fresh pasta, served in many forms, is the main feature at Cenzo. There are also other typical dishes, built around chicken, veal, and fish, but the pasta appears to dominate most of the busy tables of diners.

For those of you in the computer industry, this appears to be a hangout for busy Silicon Valley executives. At lunch, we couldn't help eavesdropping on a nearby table with four attractive, well-dressed workaholics. After their long discussion about mainframes, peripherals, and networking, they decided to set up another meeting later in the day. After consulting portable computers, cell phones, and old-fashioned pocket diaries, they agreed that the next available time for a session would be ten o'clock that night. And you thought you worked long hours.

CENZO, *233 University Avenue; (415) 322-1846. Lunch Sunday through Friday, dinner nightly. Beer and wine only. MC, Visa, Am Ex. Inexpensive to Moderate.*

✔ **Cowper Corner.** There is another version of the fast-food restaurant springing up in the Bay Area that offers good, homemade-style food for the person in a hurry. You stand at the counter and order such items as soup, special salads (like chicken with cashews and curry mayonnaise), and freshly baked breads and pastries, which you carry to one of the tables. In other words, this is a good place for a quick breakfast, a light lunch, or an early dinner without a lot of fuss. There's also an espresso machine.

COWPER CORNER, *498 University Avenue, at Cowper Street; (415) 322-4242. Breakfast and lunch daily. Beer and wine only. All nonsmoking. No credit cards. Inexpensive.*

✔ **Crouton's.**   There's still another place for folks in a rush. Crouton's specializes in soups and salads. Service is cafeteria-style, featuring a well-stocked salad bar that takes up one entire side of the line. On the other side you'll find four or five soups, including chili. You'll also find a fresh fruit bar and freshly baked bread. And, yes, there is a very large supply of croutons for your soup or salad or both.

CROUTON'S, *379 University Avenue; (415) 325-2001. Lunch and dinner daily. Beer and wine only. All nonsmoking. No credit cards. Inexpensive.*

✔ **Fresco.**   Here you will find a touch of contemporary LA in Palo Alto. Fresco means "fresh," and this bright, busy, high-tech restaurant offers a little of everything for everyone. The emphasis is on California Cuisine, with the freshest ingredients put together in unusual combinations. The menu is extensive, offering many choices, from salads to pasta dishes to grilled items.

Part of the operation is an informal ultramodern diner; the other half is a more subtly decorated dining room featuring the same menu. The food is quite good, and the atmosphere is electric. There's one in Sunnyvale now, too (see page 79).

FRESCO, *3398 El Camino Real; (415) 493-3470. Breakfast, lunch, and dinner daily. Full bar. MC, Visa, Am Ex, Diners. Moderate.*

✔ **The Good Earth.**   There is a chain of Good Earth restaurants, all serving a vegetarian-oriented menu, heavy on the whole grains and sprouts but also offering chicken and fish dishes. We think the best of these is the original in Palo Alto. It is a good place to go when you're in the mood for a huge salad or wanting a virtuous dish featuring lots of vegetables. We've noticed that a lot of families with small children patronize The Good Earth, perhaps because the food strikes the happy medium between Denny's and "Being Good for You."

The baked goods are a special feature, and at the front of the restaurant you can buy breads and cookies and other bakery items to go.

THE GOOD EARTH, *185 University Avenue, at Emerson; (415) 321-9449. Breakfast, lunch, and dinner daily. Beer and wine only. All nonsmoking. MC, Visa, Am Ex, Diners. Inexpensive to Moderate.*

✔ **Gordon-Biersch Brewery/Restaurant.**   It would be misleading to pigeonhole this brewery/restaurant as just another brewpub. Sure, the fresh beer is brewed on the premises, and you'll see gleaming equipment in full view behind glass walls, just like the other microbreweries that seem to crop up everywhere nowadays. But Gordon-Biersch could stand on its own as a fine restaurant. The food is California-continental, with the emphasis on German-style foods to go along with the German-style beer.

This is a menu that offers great diversity, including a dozen different appetizers that range from Thai chicken to quesadillas with goat cheese to Maui onion rings, to Italian calamari. Entrees are no less diverse, running the gamut from grilled chicken breast on black beans with salsa to sweet pepper pasta with dried and fresh tomatoes, olive oil, and basil, to jaegerschnitzel with roasted new potatoes and braised cabbage. Interesting sandwiches, salads, and soups are also on hand, as are wonderful desserts.

Special mention must be made about the dense, dark sourdough bread that is made for the restaurant by a small bakery in Santa Cruz. It's the color of the dark beer and is positively addictive.

For those of you who knew Palo Alto way back when, you may be interested to know that Gordon-Biersch is located in what used to be the Bijou Theatre, an art house that went out of business a few years back. When the current owners took over, they inherited a shambles. Now it's a bright, spacious restaurant with enormously high ceilings, lots of wood and white walls, high-tech lighting, and decorated with beautiful photographs of European towns—very attractive and inviting.

GORDON-BIERSCH BREWERY/RESTAURANT, *640 Emerson; (415) 323-7723. Lunch and dinner daily. Beer and wine only. All nonsmoking. MC, Visa, Am Ex, Diners. Moderate.*

✔ **Macheesmo Mouse.**   See Mountain View location, page 70.

MACHEESMO MOUSE, *271 University Avenue; (415) 570-0518. Lunch and dinner daily. Beer and wine only. No credit cards. Inexpensive.*

✔ **Osteria.**   Our first experience with this restaurant revealed much about the place. Every year, Catherine and one of her dear friends treat each other to a birthday dinner. Usually the person who is paying takes the other to a favorite place. Well, one year, Catherine found herself in a deadline crunch and decided to kill two birds with one stone: to take her friend to dinner and to research a restaurant she had heard we should try. They agreed to meet at the Osteria.

It turned out to be a wonderful evening. First of all, Catherine's friend is habitually late, and Catherine sat alone at the table for a long time. The maître d' and waiters were very gracious, in spite of the fact that she was tying up a table while lots of other customers were waiting to be seated.

Finally the friend arrived, and they ordered course after course, each better than the next, ending with a wonderful chocolate and amaretto mousse.

The cuisine and decor are typically Northern Italian. Design is understated, with subdued colors and lighting, and with a touch of class. Most of the food is simply prepared pasta dishes and grilled items, and it is the excellence of simplicity that makes this place so good. Of particular note are the grilled veal and the raviolilike "pillows" stuffed with ricotta and pancetta in a fresh tomato sauce.

OSTERIA, *247 Hamilton, at Ramona; (415) 328-5700. Lunch Monday through Friday, dinner Monday through Saturday. Beer and wine only. MC, Visa, Am Ex. Moderate.*

✔ **Peninsula Fountain and Grill.**   The Peninsula Creamery is one of the last holdouts, a dairy that delivers milk with the cream on top, and it comes in real glass bottles. This old-fashioned touch carries over to their soda fountain and luncheonette in the heart of Palo Alto, which has recently changed its name to the Peninsula Fountain and Grill. Here you can sit at the counter or at booths and have that authentic grilled cheese or tuna-melt sandwich that seems impossible to find anymore, even in this day and age of the diner revival. But no matter what you eat, be sure to have a milkshake. It will be thick and filled with ice cream, and you get the entire stainless-steel container to finish off.

PENINSULA FOUNTAIN AND GRILL, *566 Emerson, at Hamilton; (415) 323-3131. Open 7:30 A.M. to 5 P.M. Monday through Friday, 8 A.M. to 5 P.M. Saturday, 8 A.M. to 3 P.M. Sunday. No alcohol served. No credit cards. Inexpensive.*

✔ **Theo's.**   It wasn't that long ago that Theo's was the new kid in town, a place that served California Cuisine items like fresh fish, grilled chicken, and pasta. Now there are several places that have picked up on this healthful trend. We are happy to report that Theo's is still as good as when it opened, and is still faithful to the concept. Your vegetables will be fresh and flavorful, not cooked until they become mushy. Salads are bountiful and use interesting ingredients, and the atmosphere is still bright and modern.

THEO'S, *546 University Avenue; (415) 322-1272. Lunch Monday through Friday, dinner daily. Full bar. MC, Visa, Am Ex, Diners. Moderate to Expensive.*

SAN JOSE
⑧

✔ **Eulipia.**   This is a very inviting, airy space that symbolizes the "new" San Jose. Serving continental and California cuisines, Eulipia would be a very good restaurant in any metropolitan area. A very complete menu is offered with many interesting fish and chicken dishes, as well as red meat dishes such as blackened New York steak with Cajun spices. There are also pasta and vegetarian dishes. Service is friendly and efficient.

EULIPIA, *374 South First Street; (408) 280-6161. Lunch Monday through Friday, dinner nightly. Full bar. MC, Visa, Am Ex, Diners. Moderate to Expensive.*

✔ **Gervais.**   Just down the street from San Jose's Rosicrucian Museum is a charming French restaurant, tucked away in a nondescript shopping center.

Gervais and Mary Lou Henric run the operation themselves; he's the chef, she's the friendly greeter, and they serve very good French food. The entrees cover the range of fish, chicken, and meat, but it's the sauces that make each dish stand out.

GERVAIS, *1798 Park Avenue at Naglee; (408) 275-8631. Lunch Tuesday through Friday, dinner Tuesday through Saturday. Full Bar. MC, Visa, Am Ex, Diners. Moderate to Expensive.*

✔ **Leaf's.** This restaurant provides another look into the future of American culture. First of all, the place is located in the heart of San Jose's new downtown center, on the second floor of a glitzy modern urban mall, and has large picture windows overlooking the city's light-rail system and ritzy Fairmont Hotel. Inside you'll encounter a cross section of city residents: businesspeople in their neckties and bow blouses, ladies after a day of shopping, young people in Reeboks discussing "relationships" and "commitment," and older folks being nostalgically reminded of the all-you-can-eat places of yesteryear.

Leaf's is an all-you-can-eat establishment, and most of what you can eat here is good for you. All items are served cafeteria style (one of the many gimmicks here is no tipping); the major attraction is the humongous salad bar. There's a separate section where hot items are served, and this includes a choice of freshly made soups and pasta and casserole-type entrees. As you push your tray nearer and nearer to the cashier you pass the desserts, which can be fresh fruit and yogurt (included in the price of the salad bar) or a piece of cake or pie (at an extra charge—they make you pay for your sins here).

You can go through the line as often as dignity allows, or you can order your items to go. If you have access to a FAX machine you can FAX your order ahead of time. (FAX forms are available at the cash register.)

The interior is as slick and modern as you can imagine, all turquoise and pink, with neon flourishes in the window. The food is good, though not as cheap as the all-you-can-eat places we remember from our Indiana childhoods. But then again, those places didn't offer bok choy, jicama, radicchio, and kiwi.

LEAF'S, *1950 South First Street, in the Pavillion mall; (408) 286-0766. Lunch and dinner daily. Beer and wine only. All nonsmoking. Visa, Am Ex. Moderate.*

✔ **Original Joe's.** If you've ever been to a "Joe's" in the Bay Area, you know that several claim to be the "original" and that they all offer huge portions of Italian food, plus steaks, chicken, and calves liver smothered in onions. The food is wholesome and tasty, and there's enough on each plate to feed a family of four.

One of the best Original Joe's is in downtown San Jose. As soon as you walk in the door and take a deep breath, the smell of the food will tell you that you are in for a treat. What's more, the decor is original forties, not a re-creation. This is the kind of place your parents may have taken you to for Sunday dinner. And it's one of the few places in the area where you can get a full meal after midnight.

ORIGINAL JOE'S, *301 South First Street; (408) 292-7030. Lunch and dinner daily (open to 1:30 A.M.). Full bar. No credit cards. Moderate.*

✔ Phoenix Books and Espresso Cafe.   How's this for an only-in-Silicon-Valley scene: Imagine the typical coffee shop poet, the type that ties up a table for five hours with one cup of coffee, a stern expression, and his journal. Now imagine that guy with a Macintosh computer instead of pen and ink. We actually saw this scene at the Phoenix.

Phoenix Books and Espresso Cafe is located in an interesting historic neighborhood in downtown San Jose. Once upon a time the building was the mayor's office. Today it's a very nice bookstore with an excellent cafe featuring a seating and serving counter downstairs by the books and additional seating upstairs overlooking the action in the bookshop below. In addition, the Phoenix has a separate room in back that is used for jazz concerts.

As users of our guidebooks may already know, we have a certain fondness for bookshop-cafes. In some ways, they're all the same. They serve good coffee (very important), housemade soups, salads, sandwiches, and light entrees (very nice), and a selection of sweet things (no comment necessary). This place is especially good because they make their espresso drinks with Illy Caffe, some of the finest coffee available, and because the menu items change according to what's freshest, and they're open late. The upstairs seating area also functions as an art gallery, so there's an always-changing display of photographs and paintings by local talent. Anyway, it's nice to be in an environment surrounded by books; maybe someday all the knowledge between those covers will seep into us by osmosis.

PHOENIX BOOKS AND ESPRESSO CAFE, *17 N. Pedro Street; (408) 292-9277. Open 7 A.M. to midnight Monday through Thursday, 7 A.M. to 1 A.M. Friday and Saturday, 9 A.M. to midnight Sunday. Beer and wine only. No credit cards. Inexpensive.*

✔ Red Sea.   Ethiopian food has come to San Jose, and while we have never been to Ethiopia, we can at least say that Red Sea is as good as its counterparts in Oakland and San Francisco. This is a very lovely spot, run by folks from East Africa and serving dishes from home. That means spicy stews and purées arranged on a large platter and designed to be scooped up by hand. You don't actually eat with your fingers. Instead of a fork or spoon, you use a piece of injera: a spongy, slightly soured bread that looks like a large tortilla. It may sound a bit sloppy, but it's actually a very comfortable and sensual way to eat.

Unlike many ethnic restaurants that open in the United States, there is no attempt to Americanize the decor. African masks, paintings, and posters are everywhere, turning this typical neighborhood home into an exotic refuge from the constantly modernizing city. Just outside the door on First Street, there is the contrast of San Jose's sparkling light-rail system.

If this is your introduction to Ethiopian food, try the combination platters, which will let you taste the roasted chicken, lamb, ground beef, and many vegetables. And for those who are not ready for Ethiopian food, there are a few Italian dishes on the menu, but we have not tried them.

RED SEA, *684 N. First Street; (408) 993-1990. Lunch and dinner daily. MC, Visa, Am Ex, Diners. Inexpensive.*

✔ **Le Mouton Noir.**   Le Mouton Noir ("The Black Sheep") is the Saratoga home of the new California-French style of cooking. This means the atmosphere, though elegant, is less stuffy, the sauces tend to be lighter than the traditional French, and the menu emphasizes seasonal ingredients grown by local producers and served in unusual combinations. Appetizers offered at lunch include steamed mussels in a tomato and herb sauce, cassoulet of escargot in garlic butter sauce, plus a selection of housemade pâtés and terrines. Entrees include fresh spinach salad with sautéed prawns, mango chutney and sesame dressing, a pasta du jour, grilled lamb chops with fresh rosemary, or sautéed chicken breast.

SARATOGA ⑨

Dinner is a more elaborate and expensive production. The number of menu items expands to include an appetizer of red pepper pancakes with smoked salmon in a sweet corn sauce; scallop ceviche, and house-cured gravlax; and entrees such as steamed petrale sole and salmon served with ginger orange buerre blanc sauce; mixed grill; and wild or domestic fresh game du jour.

As for dessert—Le Mouton Noir serves a delicious chocolate silk pie that is not to be believed.

The setting is a 125-year-old Victorian decorated with Laura Ashley prints. Though people do dress up to eat here, Jerry felt fine in his usual Backroads attire (i.e., jeans and plaid shirt), at least at lunch when menu prices are nearly half that of dinner.

LE MOUTON NOIR, *14560 Big Basin Way; (408) 867-7017. Lunch Tuesday through Saturday, dinner nightly. Beer and wine, plus limited bar. MC, Visa, Am Ex, Diners. Lunch Moderate; dinner Expensive.*

✔ **The Trattoria.**   Whenever we are in Saratoga we try to get to The Trattoria. All the pasta is made on the premises and is served in a variety of ways. They also feature chicken, beef, veal, and seafood dishes. Our main reason to stop, though, is to get the appetizers called arancini. These are deep-fried rice balls, held together with mozzarella cheese. You can find them on many street corners in Italy, but for some reason, they are hard to find on the West Coast. The Trattoria makes them just right.

This is a large, informal place, and if it's crowded you can relax with a drink in the courtyard, which separates the restaurant from its take-out pasta shop.

THE TRATTORIA, *14510 Big Basin Way; (408) 741-1802. Lunch Monday through Saturday, dinner nightly. Beer and wine only. MC, Visa, Am Ex. Moderate.*

✔ **Village Rendezvous.** With so many chic continental restaurants in town, you might be in the mood for a good old American hamburger or some scrambled eggs. This place looks like the kind of lunch counter hangout that every town used to have. At breakfast and lunch you can get eggs or burgers, plus items like pancakes and grilled cheese sandwiches served in an informal atmosphere. But the tablecloths come out for dinner, and the cafe competes with the higher priced neighbors down the street with specialties like chicken sauté, New York pepper steak, and lots of pasta dishes. The food here is good, wholesome, and very American.

VILLAGE RENDEZVOUS, *14420 Big Basin Way; (408) 867-2932. Breakfast and lunch daily, dinner Tuesday through Saturday. Beer and wine only. MC, Visa, Am Ex. Moderate.*

SUNNYVALE
(10)

✔ **Dahlak Restaurant.** It wasn't that long ago that ethnic food could only be found in America in the big cities. Now, at least in the Bay Area, it is not unusual to find exotic cuisines in small towns and suburban shopping centers. Take Sunnyvale, for example. Here you'll find some of the best African food around, in a spot that used to be occupied by The Armenian Gourmet and is next door to an Italian restaurant. The place is called Dahlak, and it is run by two delightful sisters who serve the foods of Eritrea and other parts of North East Africa.

Why open in Sunnyvale? Well, the owners lived nearby and wanted to run what they call a "part-time restaurant," one that wouldn't consume their lives. They took this small space and now offer lunch during the week and dinners three nights only. Since they are more or less the entire staff, they can control their hours and expenses pretty well.

Lunch happens to be one of the great bargains in the Bay Area. It's a buffet, offering several stews, chicken and beef dishes, many vegetables, rice, bulgar wheat, several lentil dishes, salad with flax seed dressing, and sour injera, which is a flat spongy bread that you use to scoop up your food. (Knives, forks, and spoons are also available.) The food is wonderful, spiced with lots of herbs, red chiles, and pepper sauce. You can eat as much as you want.

At dinner, the service is a bit more formal, with waitresses to help you choose from a variety of menu choices, including such unusual offerings as lamb tripe and liver tartare. This is a good place for vegetarians, too, since so many spicy and flavorful vegetable dishes are offered. Most of the main courses are stews. Though this food resembles Ethiopian cuisine (both use stews and injera bread), the food at Dahlak is lighter (less butter and ginger). You will experience a variety of exotic and pleasant tastes.

DAHLAK RESTAURANT, *921 Duane Avenue; (408) 732-8444. Lunch Monday through Saturday, dinner Thursday through Saturday. Beer and wine only. No nonsmoking section. MC, Visa, Am Ex. Inexpensive.*

✔ **Fresco II.** See Palo Alto, Fresco, page 72.

FRESCO II, *1103 East El Camino Real; (408) 984-7474. Lunch Monday through Saturday, dinner nightly. Full bar. MC, Visa, Am Ex, Diners. Moderate to Expensive.*

CHAPTER **6** Santa Cruz County

It's hard to think of anything to do with Santa Cruz that doesn't somehow tie in to the beach. Food is usually an afterthought, something you grab on the run, like the fare you'll find on the Boardwalk. Fortunately, there are other options in Santa Cruz and the surrounding area, and new places keep cropping up all the time. In this section, we try to cover all the bases: places where you can pick up a quick snack or get something to take to the beach, informal cafes that are popular with the locals, and restaurants where you wouldn't mind dressing up a bit and having someone serve you a special meal.

This was the area hardest hit by the big earthquake of October 1989. Thankfully for all concerned, none of the eateries in this section were affected for more than a week or so. All the businesses in this area have worked hard to get things back to normal, and as tourism is a major part of the local economy, you will be doing the merchants a great service by patronizing them.

✔ **Book Cafe.** As you may have noticed, we have a soft spot for cafes located inside bookstores. Perhaps it's because the concept is so civilized. Or maybe it's the fact that these places tend to serve nice soups and salads. All right, maybe it's just the mere presence of a cappuccino machine that makes us all gooshy

CAPITOLA

①

inside. Anyway, here's one of several bookshop cafes we will recommend in this book.

The Book Cafe is operated by the same folks who run the Pontiac Grill in Santa Cruz and the local chain of pizza places called The Pizza Company. They know a thing or two about producing good food for cheap in interesting locales (the Pontiac Grill is a former car showroom; see Santa Cruz, page 87). The fare in the bookshop cafe is what's to be expected: the aforementioned soups and salads, plus very good sandwiches and housemade desserts. It's a friendly place, open late, and the bookstore itself is excellent.

BOOK CAFE, *1475 Forty-first Avenue, in the King's Plaza Shopping Center; (408) 462-4415. Open 10 A.M. to 11 P.M. weeknights; 10 A.M. to midnight weekends. No alcohol served. All nonsmoking. MC, Visa, Am Ex. Inexpensive to Moderate.*

✔ **The Chocolate Bar.**   How can anyone resist a place that has a facade festooned with giant chocolate truffles? We certainly couldn't, and were not disappointed once we got inside. It's a tiny place, the kind that defines the cliche "hole in the wall." Really, if there's more than one person inside the aisle they have to stand side by side.

The joint is stocked to the rafters. You can get fancy imported chocolate bars and locally made truffles the size of baseballs. You can get chocolate molded into the shape of cars, flowers, and, for reasons unknown, calculators. You can get freshly made chocolate cake, by the slice or the whole shebang. The Chocolate Bar also serves gelato, brewed coffee, and espresso. There are no tables, but if you don't mind getting bumped you can have your cake and eat it, too, there at the bar. Or have it wrapped to go.

THE CHOCOLATE BAR, *205 Capitola Avenue; (408) 476-1396. Open 10 A.M. to 11 P.M. Sunday through Thursday; 10 A.M. to midnight Friday and Saturday. No alcohol served. No credit cards.*

✔ **Country Court Tea Room.**   The Santa Cruz beach and mountain region is hardly the place one would expect to find a quaint and cozy tearoom, but here one is. Nestled in back of a blooming garden in the town of Capitola, this sweet little place looks like it would be right at home in the English countryside.

Breakfast and lunch are served daily, but the treat is the very civilized afternoon tea. Catherine loves the idea of spending the day at the beach, taking a shower, and at teatime pigging out on little cucumber sandwiches, pastries, and a nice pot of Earl Grey. Teatime is from 2 to 4 P.M. Lunch is light fare such as salads and quiche.

COUNTRY COURT TEA ROOM, *911 Capitola Avenue; (408) 462-2498. Breakfast*

Santa Cruz

Santa Cruz

Watsonville

Monday through Friday, lunch and afternoon tea daily, brunch Saturday and Sunday. Beer and wine only. No credit cards. Inexpensive to Moderate.

✔ **Gayle's Deli and Bakery.**   Tucked away in a cute little shopping center, this is a very pleasant deli and bakery. You can order items to go or eat there for breakfast, lunch, and early dinner. When the weather is clear, most folks take their food outside and eat on the benches in the sun. There are only a few tables inside, in the bakery section. The accent is Italian, and selections include chicken roasted over an oak fire, pasta, sandwiches served on focaccia bread, seasonal vegetables fixed in creative and delicious ways, plus a selection of desserts made on the premises. Gayle's bakery items are excellent, especially the wholesome whole-grain breads and not-so-wholesome breakfast Danishes. There are plenty of cold soft drinks available, and Gayle and her staff brew a fine cup of strong coffee.

GAYLE'S DELI AND BAKERY, *504 Bay Avenue; (408) 462-4747. Open 7 A.M. to 7 P.M. daily. Beer and wine only. All nonsmoking. No credit cards. Inexpensive to Moderate.*

✔ **Mr. Toots.**   When we're visiting the beach at Capitola, Mr. Toots is the place we go for a caffeine injection. It's located right on the main drag by the beach, up a set of stairs lined on both sides with notices of political rallies and various services offered by body workers. This is the sort of place that made the sixties great. Politically correct publications lie on tables for all to peruse, and the establishment (no pun intended) has its own poetry and creative writing newsletter, which publishes the work of local writers, announces upcoming art and music events, and functions as the menu.

Mr. Toots serves a variety of espresso and brewed coffee drinks, including a cafe cinnamon (French roast or espresso coffee with whipped cream, steamed milk, hot chocolate, and grated cinnamon) plus teas, hot cider, and a limited menu of soup, bagels, muffins, knishes, quiche, cakes, and pies. If we're lucky, one of the tables by the window will be unoccupied. Better yet, the weather will be really nice, one of the tables on the tiny terrace overlooking the beach will be free, and life will be grand.

MR. TOOTS, *221 Esplanade; (408) 475-3679. Open 8 A.M. to midnight weekdays, to 1 A.M. Friday and Saturday. No alcohol. No credit cards.*

✔ **Seafood Mama.**   One of the hip sayings of the 1940s was "Give me some seafood, Mama," and Pat and Ted Durkee were listening. They created a fish restaurant that's a nice place to go when you don't feel like getting dressed up or paying lots of money for dinner.

It's a little hard to find, upstairs in a modern business complex. Outside the front door is a blackboard with a long list of what's fresh, and you can have it cooked any number of ways—lightly sautéed, mesquite grilled, burned to a crisp if you want. Once you are seated inside you are immediately served a beer mug filled with ice and celery and carrot sticks. Now for the entree. The gimmick here is that they offer two sizes—eight ounces of fish for hearty eaters, four ounces for smaller appetites and waist-watchers. Then you get your pick of five different side dishes: marinated vegetables, cole slaw, steamed veggies, Spanish rice, or noodles with garlic and Parmesan. If you are watching your weight, beware of the whole-grain sourdough that arrives to the table warm; it's better than you want to know. The rest of the food is not great, but not bad, either. It's just that the concept holds more promise than they can deliver.

The atmosphere is beach informal; that means you must wear shirt and shoes, but if you wear a tie you will feel stupid. The walls are decorated with photographs of old Santa Cruz, creating a nostalgic effect, true to the era of the namesake song.

SEAFOOD MAMA, *820 Bay Avenue (in the Crossroads Center, second level); (408) 476-5976. Dinner nightly. Beer and wine only. MC, Visa, Am Ex. Moderate.*

✔ **Trattoria Primizia.** This is our Italian entry for this section. When it opened several years ago, next to Gayle's Deli and Bakery, it was the first place in the area to serve Northern Italian cuisine, specializing in pasta and veal and seafood dishes with light sauces. They're still at it, and it's still good eating. Though the restaurant does not serve alcohol, diners may bring their own vino.

TRATTORIA PRIMIZIA, *502 Bay Avenue; (408) 479-1112. Dinner nightly. No alcohol served. MC, Visa. Moderate.*

✔ **Corralitos Market and Sausage Company.** Even though this was one of the first places we covered on the "Bay Area Backroads" TV show, more than four years ago, we still get calls asking for the address. I don't know what to make of this. Maybe people in the Bay Area are addicted to sausage; perhaps they're simply fascinated by the idea of a town where the main attraction is a combination grocery store and smokehouse.

The Corralitos Market is tucked away in a small town called Corralitos in the Santa Cruz Mountains. It is a family-run business, an all-purpose community store with bread and milk in front and a terrific smokehouse in back. The owner, Joe Cutler, produces slabs of bacon and miles of sausages smoked slowly over applewood from his own orchard. There's also smoked chicken and a variety of other items, all smoked the old-fashioned way, without any artificial ingredients

CORRALITOS
②

or shortcuts. Several times a day, items are moved out of the smokehouse and into the market's meat counter.

CORRALITOS MARKET AND SAUSAGE COMPANY, *569 Corralitos Road; (408) 722-2633. Open 9 A.M. to 6 P.M. Monday through Saturday, 9 A.M. to 5 P.M. Sunday. No credit cards. Inexpensive.*

DAVENPORT
③

✔ **New Davenport Cash Store.**   From the highway the Cash Store looks like an old-fashioned general store, but it's actually a lovely arts and crafts gallery, shop, restaurant, and bed-and-breakfast inn (see Lodging, page 200). The food is on the health-food side, with whole-grain breads, chunky soups, big salads, and sandwiches to match. Lately the menu has become more sophisticated and interesting, adding main course dishes like fish in mandarin orange sauce and sautéed chicken with wild mushrooms. You will still get locally grown produce, in season, and old standbys like burgers, thick soups, and Mexican dishes. Everything is well prepared, and the atmosphere is relaxed and pleasant. You can even see the ocean across the road from the window seats.

You enter into the gift shop which is right off Route 1. Temptation hits you right in the face if you are a dessert or pastry fan. A coffee counter and an array of wonderful baked goods is impossible to ignore. Try the giant chocolate chip cookies, which are as good as the best homemade cookies of childhood. Also recommended without hesitation: the huge brownies and the various muffins. You can also order food to go and head across the road to the bluffs high above the Pacific. This is a great spot for watching whales when they head south in the summer and fall and return north from December through May.

NEW DAVENPORT CASH STORE, *right on Highway 1, about 15 minutes north of Santa Cruz; (408) 426-4122. Breakfast and lunch daily, dinner Friday, Saturday, and Sunday. Beer and wine only. All nonsmoking. MC, Visa, Am Ex. Inexpensive.*

FELTON
④

✔ **Heavenly Cafe.**   There are very few places to eat in the small town of Felton. If you're looking for dinner, head to Santa Cruz. But if you want to get a sample of local color at breakfast or lunch, stop in at the Heavenly Cafe, right on the main drag.

The posters and notices on the wall will let you know what's going on around town, or you can simply sit there and listen. It appears that delegates from all the various groups that populate Felton drop in on a daily basis. There are the folks who look like sixties hippies, the guys who run the gas station, and the nice ladies from the historical society, all mingling with whoever else happens to drop by. Everybody seems to know the people cooking and serving, and you have whatever it is they offer that day.

At breakfast, this means there is usually some interesting muffins or pancakes to go with the normal selection of eggs and bacon. At lunch, you'll need to know about the day's soup, and maybe there's some goulash or a pot pie. If you prefer a traditional sandwich, that's no problem.

HEAVENLY CAFE, *6250 Highway 9; (408) 335-7311. Breakfast and lunch Wednesday through Sunday; closed Tuesday. Beer and wine only. No credit cards. Inexpensive.*

✔ **The Blue Parrot.**   The Blue Parrot used to be a funky place called the Thunder Deli—which was also quite good, but you wouldn't have wanted to take your Aunt Martha from Des Moines there. However, the place has since been purchased by a charming fellow named Graham (no relation, we swear), who cleaned the place up, sanded the floors, and got his mom to renovate the garden. Now Aunt Martha would be quite comfortable, thank you.

Food is of the healthy variety, with menu items like tofu scramble, sandwiches on whole-grain bread, salads, and housemade soups. Breakfast is a real deal: two eggs (from hens raised without antibiotics, of course), home fries with a crunchy crust, bagel or toast with cream cheese or strawberry preserves for under $4.

The restaurant is quite large, with two dining rooms plus—weather and temperature permitting—seating in the lush and lovely garden. Even on nasty days some people seem to like sitting out there; on a warm Sunday morning it would be an ideal setting for brunch.

You can park in the lot across the street. The restaurant is easy to spot: There's a fetching lady mannequin sitting at a cafe table out front.

THE BLUE PARROT, *1134 Soquel Avenue; (408) 423-2055. Breakfast and lunch daily, dinner Tuesday through Saturday, brunch Saturday and Sunday. Beer and wine only. No credit cards. Inexpensive to Moderate.*

✔ **Casablanca.**   The only thing this restaurant has to do with the Bogart-Bergman classic film is the name. There will be no ceiling fans, no piano player named Sam, and very little intrigue. But it's a good bet the food is better than it was at Rick's Café Américain.

This is the restaurant of a big, white beachfront motel. It is a romantic spot, with a great view of the water.

The menu is updated daily and includes something for almost every taste, from filet mignon to broiled fish to freshly made pasta and vegetarian dishes. There's even a special section of selections for guests under age twelve.

We should mention that even though there is a complete list of appetizers, all dinner entrees include soup or salad, potato or rice, fresh vegetables, and baguette and butter. In other words, they serve a lot of food. This is a very good restaurant, with nicely prepared food and good attention to detail. Reservations are advised.

CASABLANCA, *101 Main Street; (408) 426-9063. Dinner nightly, brunch Sunday. Beer and wine only. MC, Visa, Diners. Moderate to Expensive.*

✔ **Garage Grill.** If you're in the mood for a burger and you also happen to be nostalgic for old service stations, this is the place for you. The Garage Grill is obviously a labor of love, where design is as important as the food. The owners took almost two years to convert an old gas station into a quirky, small diner that serves only lunch. It's sort of a museum of automotive service trivia, with every wall and nook and cranny filled with pictures of gas stations, oil cans, advertising photos and banners, tools, uniforms, mirrors, horns, and what have you. The effect is rather staggering, and it creates a fun atmosphere. This is also a good place to eat alone, offering plenty of counter seats and providing lots of reading material so you don't feel like an absolute jerk just because you're by yourself.

The food is straightforward and well prepared. The boss chuckburger is a half pound of meat, mesquite grilled. It's served on a good bun with crisp wedge fries. Also featured are grilled chicken sandwiches, kabobs of lamb, chicken, beef, or veggies, and Cajun sausages. All food is available for take-out. The owners have taken care to offer quality touches, like their own blend of Sumatra and dark French roast coffee, or locally made Odwalla juices, which are fresh and have no preservatives. They also serve interesting beers and some local wines.

Did we mention that the menu is designed like a parking ticket?

GARAGE GRILL, *2017 North Pacific Avenue; (408) 426-1885. Lunch and dinner Tuesday through Sunday. Beer and wine only. All nonsmoking. MC, Visa. Inexpensive.*

✔ **Hoang Anh.** Here is a genuine find. Hoang Anh is a family-run Vietnamese restaurant that serves wonderful food. It is also one of the great bargains in the area. Don't be misled by the decor, which is totally unremarkable, or the hassled waitress who is trying to service all the tables all at once. What counts is the woman behind the bamboo partition that separates the dining room from the kitchen. She and the rest of her family know how to cook.

It's always a pleasure to find food that's better than you had expected. What made Hoang Anh even more of a surprise was that each dish we ordered was totally different from what we had anticipated. For example, we ordered an appetizer of grilled calamari called cha muc. It turned out to be a huge plate with sliced apples, carrot, cucumber, garlic, lettuce, cilantro, mint, and a type of calamari, or squid, we had never seen before. It had been chopped and processed with spices, tofu, and other ingredients, sliced, and grilled. The idea was to take each of the ingredients, put them inside a delicate rice paper pancake, and then dip it into a hot peanut sauce. Incredible!

Main courses included tender pieces of breast of chicken sautéed with lemon grass and hot pepper, grilled pork and prawns over transparent noodles, tofu and wonderfully crisp fresh vegetables, as well as a wide selection of fish, chicken, beef, and other dishes. Also featured are homemade desserts such as crepes and banana custard cake, which is served warm and tastes like the best bread pudding you've ever had. It's very inexpensive, too.

HOANG ANH, *2019 N. Pacific Avenue; (408) 427-3580. Lunch Tuesday through Friday, dinner Tuesday through Sunday. Beer and wine only. MC, Visa, Am Ex. Inexpensive.*

✔ **India Joze.** This is one of the most eclectic and interesting restaurants we've ever come across on the Backroads. As the name might indicate, India Joze offers many foods from India and other Asian countries. This establishment also serves a variety of fish, chicken, and meat dishes. If you are tempted to order one of the hot spicy dishes, let us give you a warning. When given the option in restaurants, Catherine always orders hot, hot, hot, and it's never been enough for her—except at India Joze, where it was almost too much.

This is a very attractive place, open and airy, with modern art adorning the walls. It is also a very popular place, and during the height of the dinner hour you may have to wait awhile for a table.

One other note on ordering this multi-national food: desserts are sky-high creations that appeal to typical American tastes, especially the range of chocolate specialties.

INDIA JOZE, *1001 Center Street; (408) 427-3554. Lunch Tuesday through Friday, dinner Tuesday through Sunday. MC, Visa, Am Ex. Moderate.*

✔ **Pontiac Grill.** People come here for the decor as much as for the food. This is the ultimate in retro-fifties style, chrome and red vinyl to the max, with little jukeboxes in each booth. The setting is a former Pontiac showroom, and there's a car grill over the food grill.

The other reason people come is that the food is cheap, and considering the price, it's good. Along with a choice of fourteen different kinds of hamburgers, fries, meatloaf, cherry cokes, and other items that match the decor, you can order more modern concoctions such as a pesto quesadilla (a flour tortilla stuffed with cheddar cheese, pesto, and housemade salsa), an avocado and sprout sandwich, and something called a turkey sundae (turkey breast served on top of corn stuffing with mashed potatoes and gravy topped with cranberry relish).

Breakfast is a real bargain: $1.99 for two eggs any style, hash browns, and toast; fifty cents extra gets you a pillowy white biscuit or a hot spicy corn muffin. There's also a cappuccino machine on the premises.

PONTIAC GRILL, *429 Front Street; (408) 427-2290. Breakfast, lunch, and dinner daily. Beer and wine only. All nonsmoking. MC, Visa. Inexpensive.*

✔ **Rebecca's Mighty Muffins.**   Presumably because of the rise of interest in oat bran and other fibers, muffins have replaced chocolate chip cookies as the snack of choice for a lot of people. If you're one of those, try Rebecca's. One hundred percent organic flours are used to create such unusual treats as lemon blueberry, chocolate chocolate chip cheesecake, polenta cheddar, and sweet potato pecan muffins. In season, Rebecca's whips up pumpkin muffins (the pumpkin capital of the world, Half Moon Bay isn't too far away) and we fat-and-cholesterol fighters can feast on oil-free raisin bran, date bran, and oat bran delights. In addition, Rebecca's bakes scones, both sweet and savory (the cheddar jalapeño mushroom is practically a meal in itself), and serves espresso drinks.

Tables are provided for those who care to snack there, or you can ask for your order to go.

REBECCA'S MIGHTY MUFFINS, *514-A Front Street; (408) 429-1940. Open 7 A.M. to 6 P.M. Monday through Saturday, 8 A.M. to 6 P.M. Sunday. No alcohol served. No credit cards. Inexpensive.*

✔ **Sea Cloud Restaurant and Social Club.**   If you have just one mealtime to spend in Santa Cruz, make it at the Sea Cloud. Despite the silly name, this is a terrific place for fresh fish, imaginatively prepared. All of the fish is fresh and prepared perfectly, especially if you like your salmon or tuna on the rare side. They also have wonderful entrees for non–fish eaters. The restaurant is quite attractive, situated on the municipal pier overlooking the Santa Cruz beach and boardwalk. You can drive your car out on the pier and park with relative ease. Just about everything you order will be first-rate, including the luscious desserts. It's a big restaurant, but reservations are advised.

SEA CLOUD RESTAURANT AND SOCIAL CLUB, *Municipal Wharf; (408) 458-9393. Lunch and dinner daily. Full bar. MC, Visa, Am Ex. Moderate to Expensive.*

SOQUEL
(6)

✔ **Greenhouse at the Farm.**   A truly beautiful and relaxing spot for a meal, especially on a nice day, is this restaurant situated on a working farm. The greenhouse is a large Victorian building where you can sit indoors near the salad bar or, weather permitting, outside on a garden patio.

The food features produce grown on the farm, plus items like quiche, omelets, seafood, and housemade soups and breads. The salad bar is well stocked, and you could easily let your salad bar creation become your entire meal. The food is not spectacular, but it is wholesome, and the atmosphere can't be beat.

GREENHOUSE AT THE FARM, *5555 Soquel Drive; (408) 476-5613. Lunch Monday through Saturday, dinner nightly, brunch Sunday. Beer and wine only. MC, Visa, Am Ex, Diners. Moderate.*

WATSONVILLE
⑦

✔ **El Puentito II.** The Bay Area is dotted with little Mexican restaurants out on the Backroads. Unless you have some advance information, it's hard to know if you are going to stumble into a culinary adventure or a mistake. We found out about El Puentito, which means "little bridge," from the sweet ladies at the nearby antique rose nursery, "Roses of Yesterday and Today."

The first signs that El Puentito is not your average dive are the carefully placed plants and fresh flowers around the counter and in the dining room. (Plastic flowers are usually our first signal that we are in the wrong place.) Then there's the counter seating, which lets you see everything that is going on in the kitchen. There's also a corner stove, comforting on a chilly day.

The payoff, of course, is the food. Regulars said to try the chimichangas, which are sort of fried tacos. They were good, but not as impressive as the special that day, chicken fajitas. This was quite a production, involving at least three separate plates loaded with delicious chicken, avocado, fresh vegetables, rice, beans, and fresh tortillas. A veritable feast.

The rest of the menu is traditional Mexican—chile rellenos, chili verde burritos, and the like. The recipes, we were told, are family affairs, handed down from mother to son. The son is Mike Guzman, who also owns and runs another El Puentito in Capitola.

El Puentito is also a neighbor of another favorite destination of ours, the Corralitos Market and Sausage Company (see page 83).

EL PUENTITO, *2904 Freedom Boulevard; (408) 722-3016. Lunch and dinner daily. Beer and wine only. No credit cards. Moderate.*

East Bay

CHAPTER **7** Alameda County

The East Bay cities of Berkeley and Oakland are famous for their restaurants. Some of the finest and best-known places to eat in the entire Bay Area are here, including the world-famous Chez Panisse, where the California Cuisine craze began. These restaurants are highly publicized, easy to find, and are included in all the San Francisco Restaurant guidebooks. So in keeping with the theme of this book, the restaurants recommended here are those off the beaten path, where it's often more difficult to find a good place to eat. We also try to highlight places that rarely, if ever, get public notice.

✓ Beau Rivage. At the end of a road leading to a marina in Alameda stands a rather ornate French restaurant. We can't figure out what it's doing there, except serving very good traditional French food.

ALAMEDA
①

One afternoon I and "Backroads" TV cameraman, Jeff Pierce, both clad in jeans, lunched by candlelight with fine linen and china at a table overlooking the Bay. The waiter didn't flinch as he served us as though we were French royalty. Our chicken and fish dishes were excellent, with delicate sauces and nicely cooked vegetables. The other couple in the room didn't even notice us. Apparently, dinners are more crowded and formal.

This is a traditional French restaurant, run by folks with French accents, as opposed to California French. Be prepared to be charmed.

BEAU RIVAGE, 1042 Ballena Boulevard; (415) 523-1660. Lunch Monday through Friday, dinner Monday through Saturday. Full bar. MC, Visa, Am Ex, Diners. Moderate at lunch, Expensive at dinner.

✔ **The Courtyard.**   One of the most ambitious undertakings we've seen in a while is in the center of the city of Alameda, where Peggy Williams has created The Courtyard. After running a smaller gourmet shop across the street, she took over an historic old building, completely renovated it so that it looks like a Mexican courtyard with stucco walls and beautiful tiles, and installed a cafe, deli, food and gift shop, art gallery, and espresso bar. Less than two weeks after it was opened, it was jammed.

This has become one of the town's unofficial meeting places, where business-people and shoppers gather for lunch and where folks come to hear live music in the evening. In the afternoon, pastries and tea or cappuccinos are the big draw. Finally, there's breakfast served on the weekends.

Lunch features wonderful salads, a variety of sandwiches served on great breads, such as the seeded roll from the Semifreddi bakery in Kensington. There are also daily specials like chicken breast, lightly breaded and pan fried with lemon and topped with avocado and mozzarella cheese. At dinnertime, one might choose between mahi-mahi grilled with pineapple and served with pasta and vegetable, linguini with smoked salmon and lemon dill sauce, or a half pizza with a small salad.

No matter what we describe now, expect things to be different. Peggy is a woman who keeps stirring things up, and her energy makes The Courtyard such an interesting and enjoyable place to visit.

THE COURTYARD, 1349 Park Street; (415) 521-1521. Lunch and dinner daily, breakfasts on weekends. MC and Visa—$15 minimum charge. Inexpensive to Moderate.

EL CERRITO
②

✔ **Fatapple's Restaurant and Bakery.**   For years, Fatapple's has been a popular place for burgers in the East Bay. The original location, in Berkeley, has long been a refuge for college students and families in the mood for a good, inexpensive hamburger, an order of fries, and a piece of homestyle apple pie. Well, a second Fatapple's has opened in El Cerrito, and it offers a much larger operation with a more extensive menu.

This is not to say that you can't get a great burger here; on the contrary, those large, succulent, bargain burgers are still cooked to your degree of doneness, and can be served on either a white or whole-wheat bun. Cheeseburger addicts take note that here the cheddar is grated but not melted. You can also get grilled chicken breast, turkey pot pie, pasta, soup of the day, and wonderful salads. Sandwiches are served on bread baked on the premises; these ovens also supply

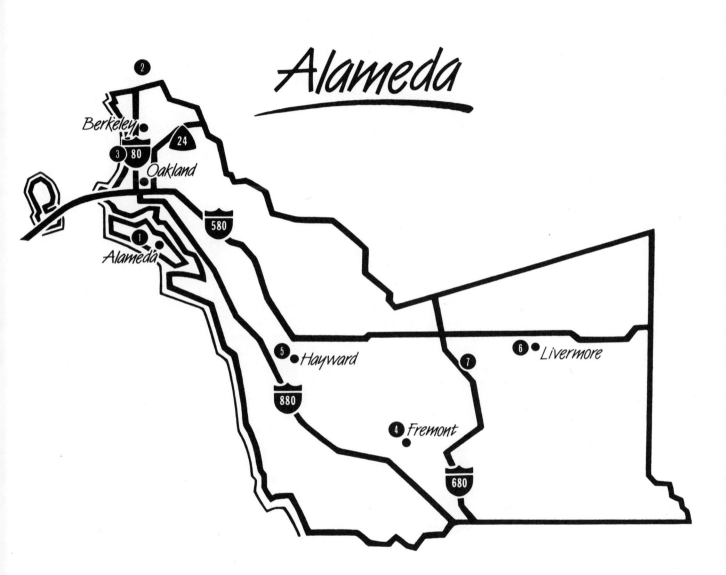

Alameda

Berkeley

80

24

3

Oakland

580

1

Alameda

5 • Hayward

6 • Livermore

7

880

4 • Fremont

680

a large display case with lots of muffins, cakes, and pies that you can take home. They even bottle their own fruit preserves.

Breakfast offerings include egg dishes and griddle items, plus freshly squeezed orange juice and the house blend of Peet's high-octane coffee.

This is a very comfortable and attractive restaurant with a high peaked ceiling, modern metal sculptures, and an open kitchen. Though there's almost always a line, it moves quickly.

FATAPPLE'S RESTAURANT AND BAKERY, *7525 Fairmount Avenue; (415) 528-3433. Breakfast, lunch, and dinner daily. Beer and wine only. All nonsmoking. No credit cards. Inexpensive.*

EMERYVILLE ③

✔ **Bucci's.** The town of Emeryville, which is surrounded by Oakland and Berkeley, used to be a destination only for industrial and warehouse workers or those who wanted to gamble in the legal poker clubs on San Pablo Avenue. But then the artists moved in, got elected into the city government, and made this tiny area the Greenwich Village of the East Bay. In this neighborhood of industrial loading docks and artists' lofts are several fine places to eat. Bucci's has the most dramatic setting in town. Located inside a recently built brick building, the place looks like a stage set. Tall Romanesque columns stretch toward the ceiling, and a giant mirror ascends skyward from behind the bar. Then suddenly the white-wall interior stops, and you can see the exposed wooden beams of the ceiling. Tables are either faux marble or covered with white tablecloths, which lends an elegant flair. Local art adorns the walls.

The food is good, plentiful, and inexpensive. The menu is limited to an ever-changing selection of appetizers, soups, salads, a variety of pizzas (really good pizzas), and three or four light entrees—usually fish, chicken, and pasta. If you stick to a main course and salad-type dinner, two can eat very well for less than $20. If you're alone and just want a light meal, you can eat at the small bar.

One word of caution: It can take a while to get a seat. And since the food is cooked-to-order, you do spend quite a bit of time at your table waiting for your meal—which is fine as long as you're not in a hurry.

BUCCI'S, *6121 Hollis Street; (415) 547-4725. Lunch Monday through Friday, dinner Monday through Saturday, closed Sunday. Beer and wine only. No credit cards. Inexpensive to Moderate.*

✔ **Carrara's Cafe.** In the sixties, there was a cigarette ad that showed a guy with a hole in the sole of his boot and the slogan "I'd walk a mile for a Camel." That's how Catherine feels about the polenta at Carrara's. She can see herself, feet propped up on a chair, hole in the bottom of her aerobics shoes, enjoying this creamy concoction, baked in a ceramic bowl and topped with pesto and Gorgonzola sauce.

This—some salads, housemade soups, desserts, and other snacks—is about it for this coffeehouse's menu. It's a cheerful place to go for an espresso drink, a beer, or something light to eat. Local art for sale covers the walls, and there's a separate nonsmoking gallery in the back. It's a place where locals hang out, so if you want to find out what's happening around town, just engage in conversation someone at a nearby table.

CARRARA'S CAFE, *1290 Powell Street; (415) 547-6763. Open 7 A.M. to midnight Monday through Thursday, 7 A.M. to 1 A.M. Friday, 7 A.M. to midnight Saturday, closed Sunday. Beer and wine only. MC, Visa. Inexpensive.*

✔ **Cajun Jim's.** Although Fremont seems a bit removed from New Orleans, especially when you're in a shopping center called the Fremont Hub, this place manages to give you a feeling of being transported to Louisiana. The decor is nothing special except for some nice posters on the wall, but what does it is the music. Someone has put together a tape of some of the best New Orleans blues and jazz performers, and it sets the mood for a festive meal.

The menu is designed for people who want to try something different, but not too different. Diners are assured their meals will be authentic and spicy, but not too hot. All the traditional Cajun dishes are offered, such as gumbo and red beans and rice, fried catfish and hush puppies, as well as the de rigeur blackened steak, fish, or chicken. Lunches also feature huge sandwiches, several of which are tailored for local tastes; folks down on the bayou would probably get a laugh out of the idea of the "California Cajun," made with vegetables and spicy mustard.

This place will surprise but not overwhelm you. The food is well prepared but scaled down in deference to the neighborhood. Customers in the area have their choice of just about every fast food and franchise known to suburbia, so the folks at Cajun Jim's are playing it safe. Still, it's a place worth trying, with very friendly service and an interesting menu. By the way, Jim really is from Louisiana.

CAJUN JIM'S, *39217 Fremont Boulevard, in the Fremont Hub shopping center off Mowry Street; (415) 794-0409. Lunch and dinner daily. Beer and wine only. MC, Visa, Am Ex. Inexpensive to Moderate.*

✔ **City Park Cafe.** Just around the corner from Cajun Jim's is a touch of San Francisco at the City Park Cafe. Opening in late 1988, this was another gamble in trying to bring new ideas to Fremont. A group of investors from Palo Alto took a former Lyon's Restaurant and transformed it into a very attractive grill and cafe. The decor features a lot of tile, white walls, and fresh flowers, plus an open grill-kitchen area. There's also a separate bar and appetizer area. It's quite an attractive space.

The menu was created by a veteran of the snazzy Fog City Diner in San Francisco, the restaurant that led the way in popularizing the concept of "grazing"—having lots of small tastes of things instead of huge dinners. At the City Park Cafe you can have such large appetizers as fried coconut prawns, crab and corn cakes, and spicy chicken wings. There are several pastas, large and huge salads, smoked meats that have been grilled, and sandwiches. It's the kind of place where you can eat lightly and spend very little, or have several courses and spend a lot. The menu is the same for lunch and dinner.

Beware of the dessert called chocolate, chocolate, chocolate, which is only one of several intriguing desserts offered. Jerry and his cameraman, Jeff Pierce, both gold medalists in the chocolate-eating department, split a single order and couldn't finish it. (Jeff will deny this story.) The dish consists of the fudgiest brownie imaginable, served with chocolate-chip ice cream, and topped with an excellent dark hot fudge sauce. If you are going to end with this, by all means go easy on the rest of the meal. It's a heart stopper.

CITY PARK CAFE, *39001 Fremont Boulevard; (415) 792-7474. Lunch and dinner daily. Full bar. MC, Visa, Am Ex. Moderate to Expensive.*

HAYWARD ⑤ ✓ **"A" Street Cafe and Wine Bar.** The "A" Street Cafe is a very stylish California Cuisine restaurant located in an area more known for its fast-food franchises and Mexican cafes. The menu, which changes monthly, features such items as light pastas, warm chicken salad, and fresh fish. All the food is remarkably fresh and tasty and moderately priced.

The decor is stark white walls with blond wood tables and attractive overhead lamps. Counter service is available for those who hate to occupy a table when eating alone; in the evening the counter doubles as a bar for wine tasting.

"A" STREET CAFE AND WINE BAR, *1213 A Street; (415) 582-2558. Lunch Monday through Friday, dinner Tuesday through Saturday. Beer and wine only. MC, Visa. Moderate.*

✓ **Buffalo Bill's Brewpub.** There's a growing trend in beermaking called the "brewery pub," places that serve beer made right on the premises. You can now find very good brewpubs in just about every city in the Bay Area. Some even have several. One of the first of these is Buffalo Bill's in Hayward. The owner is Bill Owens, who forsook a career as a photographer and now publishes a magazine for brewpub operators and fanciers.

This pub is fashioned after the British concept of a neighborhood place where you can go and feel at home. Simple pub-style food is served, running mostly to stews and soups and good sandwiches. One nice thing about the place is that moderation in drinking is urged. Bill closes early and frowns on "happy hours" and other gimmicks that encourage people to "get loaded."

BUFFALO BILL'S BREWPUB, *1082 B Street; (415) 886-9823. Open 11:30 A.M. to 10:30 P.M. Monday through Thursday, 11:30 A.M. to midnight Friday, noon to midnight Saturday, 1 A.M. to 7 P.M. Sunday. Beer and wine only. Inexpensive.*

✔ **Eden Express.**   This is the sort of place that can help you feel better about the world. Eden Express is a very pleasant coffeehouse that also serves light meals and is staffed by developmentally disabled employees who are learning to interact with society. The food is good and the menu large. Lunch might be a quiche or a housemade soup, breakfasts feature freshly baked pastries, and there is an espresso machine for cappuccino and caffe latte. A wide variety of teas is also available.

Eden Express is also open for banquets, provides catering services, and serves a champagne brunch on Sundays.

EDEN EXPRESS, *799 B Street; (415) 886-8765. Breakfast and lunch daily, brunch Sunday. Beer and wine only. MC, Visa. Inexpensive.*

✔ **The Gazebo.**   Hayward always has lots of surprises when it comes to restaurants, and one of the most pleasant is a tiny French place called The Gazebo. From the location and the exterior, you might expect to find a routine coffee shop. Inside, however, you'll be seated by a gracious hostess at a table with tablecloths and cloth napkins. Soft music will be playing, and the menu offers an impressive selection of fish, chicken, and meat dishes.

Lunch is definitely the bargain here, with many entrees below $8. The sauces are distinctive, and the selection of vegetables and salad greens shows that someone is taking great care to get the best available ingredients.

THE GAZEBO, *1149 B Street; (415) 581-6580. Lunch Monday through Friday, dinner Monday through Saturday; closed Sunday. Beer and wine only. MC, Visa, Am Ex. Lunch Moderate, dinner Moderate to Expensive.*

✔ **Old South Bar-B-Q.**   Barbecue fans can be very discriminating and will argue over which of the many spots in the Bay Area serves the most authentic, best-tasting ribs. Old South always gets a lot of votes.

This is a small place, but they put out a lot of ribs, chicken, and links, all accented by their secret sauce. (All respectable barbecue joints have their own secret sauce.) You have your choice of spiciness, and if you go for the hottest you are likely to shed a tear or two.

OLD SOUTH BAR-B-Q, *27941 Manon Street, at West Tennyson; (415) 782-1163. Lunch and dinner Tuesday through Sunday; closed Monday. Beer and wine only. No nonsmoking section. MC, Visa, Am Ex, Diners. Inexpensive.*

✔ **Val's Burgers.**   This place looks like one of the sets of "Happy Days," except it's the real thing. Val's started in the fifties and never left. The cafe has remained unchanged, except for occasional price hikes. (Nobody can survive selling hamburgers for thirty cents anymore.) This wonderful diner is run by Val and his sons, and you can get huge burgers, fries, and one of the best milkshakes in the world. (We taste-tested three of them on one visit, all in the name of research, you understand.)

VAL'S BURGERS, *2115 Kelly, at B Street; (415) 889-8257. Breakfast, lunch, and dinner Tuesday through Saturday. No alcohol served. No nonsmoking section. No credit cards. Inexpensive.*

LIVERMORE
ⓖ

✔ **El Lorito Restaurant and Taqueria.**   A real surprise in Livermore is El Lorito. Not that it's so surprising to find a good, authentic Mexican restaurant in this area but that it is so well disguised in a nondescript shopping center near the downtown section of town.

When you enter, it appears that this is another quickie place where you place your order and then take your taco or burrito to your table. That's true . . . in the front. But if you go into the rear of the place you'll find a spacious and attractive dining room offering a more varied menu.

Along with the usual Mexican-American dishes, you can have a more complete meal, such as a wonderfully roasted pork, and camarones (shrimp) with a spicy sauce. Even the rice, beans, and tortillas are especially good and are freshly made.

Sunday brunch is served twice a year: Mother's Day and Father's Day.

EL LORITO RESTAURANT AND TAQUERIA, *1316 Railroad Avenue; (415) 455-8226. Lunch Monday through Friday, dinner nightly. Beer and wine only. No credit cards. Taqueria, Inexpensive; restaurant, Moderate.*

✔ **Le Coquelicot.**   Two lovely and ambitious young French women have found their way to Livermore and opened a little cafe specializing in, but not limited to, crepes. It's a breath of fresh Gallic air in a city without a lot of good places to eat.

At breakfast time, you can get their own freshly baked croissants, plain or filled with chocolate. A few egg dishes are also served. Lunch and dinner feature a variety of crepes stuffed with such choices as: shrimps, crabs, scallops and mushrooms in a white wine sauce; or turkey breast, swiss cheese, nuts, sour cream, and spinach, topped with cranberry sauce. A few other entrees are also offered, such as poached filet of sole in champagne sauce and veal scaloppine in a mushroom sauce.

On Tuesday nights, they pull out all the stops and offer a four-course French dinner with two sittings: at 5:30 and 7:30. You are requested to make reservations for "La Soiree du Chef" by the preceding Sunday.

This is a place with a lot of charm, a welcome addition to this neck of the woods.

LE COQUELICOT, *2216 First Street; (415) 373-1123. Lunch Tuesday through Friday, dinner Tuesday through Saturday, brunch Saturday and Sunday. Beer and wine only. All nonsmoking. MC, Visa. Moderate.*

✔ **Wente Brothers Sparkling Wine Cellars Restaurant.** There was a time when once you got beyond Berkeley and Oakland there weren't many places in the county that were new and innovative. Then, about three years ago, along came the new Wente Brothers Sparkling Wine Cellars Restaurant. They spared no expense to make it and the restaurant local showcases.

As for the food, it is quite expensive, but it is also quite good. The chefs do imaginative things with duck, lamb, and fish. They also feature fresh vegetables and often offer such hard-to-get items as stuffed zucchini blossoms. A wide range of California wines is available, but they seem to smile a lot when you order the house brand. Reservations are strongly advised.

WENTE BROTHERS SPARKLING WINE CELLARS RESTAURANT, *5050 Arroyo Road; (415) 447-3696. Lunch and dinner Wednesday through Sunday, brunch Sunday. Wine only. All nonsmoking. MC, Visa, Am Ex. Expensive.*

✔ **Cafe Gourmet.** Happily, this place proved us wrong on two counts. First of all, we assumed that it was impossible to find wonderfully imaginative food, beautifully served, in the center of a corporate business park. Second, we avoid places with the word *gourmet* in the title; usually it's a sure sign that the place is not.

So along comes Cafe Gourmet, an excellent restaurant inside a corporate business park. It's a snazzy-looking small cafe with Italian-style chairs, glass-topped black tables, and stylish dinnerware. The ingredients used are of the highest quality, the food is tasty, and the prices are swell.

One of our favorite selections is the margarita chicken, served either as a sandwich or salad, with tequila-and-lime marinated chicken, pepper cheese, black beans, jicama, tomato, and avocado. Soups are made fresh daily, starting from scratch with housemade stocks, salads are made with crispy seasonal greens and vegetables. Then there's pasta with prawns, scallops, and roasted hot and sweet peppers served in a cilantro cream sauce, or a southwestern lasagne made with chorizo sausage.

A menu of freshly made desserts will be supplied upon request. If you always feel you should skip dessert, you might consider the spa cheesecake, made with low-fat ricotta cheese and yogurt—indulgence without much guilt. Fellow members of the Coffee Addicts Society will be glad to know that espresso drinks are made with beans supplied by Mr. Espresso of Oakland.

Catering as it does to the four or five thousand office workers in the Hacienda

PLEASANTON
⑦

Business Park, Cafe Gourmet currently serves only lunch and afternoon coffee and sweets but has plans to open for dinner on selected nights.

CAFE GOURMET, *5676 Stoneridge Drive, in the Hacienda Business Park; (415) 734-0181. Breakfast and lunch Monday through Friday. Beer and wine only. All nonsmoking. MC, Visa. Inexpensive to Moderate.*

✔ **Pleasanton Hotel.**   Names can sometimes be confusing out on the Backroads. For example, Pleasanton *is* a pleasant town, but the Pleasanton Hotel is not a hotel, it's a restaurant. Well, once it *was* a hotel, as well as a stagecoach stop, a gambling house, a brothel, and the occasional home of the bandit Joaquin Murietta. In fact, the Pleasanton Hotel is the oldest building in the valley, dating back to 1851. All that history enhances the charm of what is now a very good contemporary restaurant.

This is the place to go for a nice, sit-down-and-relax meal. Much has been done to make this a worthwhile stop. Lunch features a series of specials in addition to a regular menu of sandwiches, salads, and hot entrees. Our advice, though, is to stick to the specials, which are likely to feature seasonal ingredients and more creativity than the standard items. The last time we were there they featured Cajun-styled blackened prime rib, fettuccine with shrimp in a scampi cream sauce, grilled mahi-mahi, osso buco, and chicken breast stuffed with tomato salsa and two cheeses.

At dinner the standard menu is more extensive, offering steaks, prime rib, seafood, pasta, and chicken selections; but, again, you can't go wrong choosing from the night's specials.

Those with sweet tooths can rest assured that there is a good selection of desserts, including a fine pecan pie that was filled with nuts from top to bottom. There is also an espresso machine, and they know how to work it.

The wine list features wines from the nearby Livermore Valley, as well as those from Napa and Sonoma. The bar also offers a selection of nonalcoholic cocktails, such as strawberry daiquiris without the booze.

You have a choice of sitting in one of several dining rooms, each decorated in the style of the late 1800s. Weather permitting, dining outside in the courtyard is available.

PLEASANTON HOTEL, *855 Main Street; (415) 846-8106. Lunch Sunday through Friday, dinner nightly, brunch Sunday. Full bar. MC, Visa, Am Ex. Moderate at lunch, Moderate to Expensive at dinner.*

CHAPTER **8** Contra Costa County

Maybe it's because Contra Costa County is so close to Berkeley and Oakland, but we have not come across as many places to write about as we would like. Perhaps it's the lifestyle of the area, which reminds us of Southern California. The weather is much warmer than the cities nearer the Bay, and life seems to center around malls and developments rather than urban-style downtowns. Also, there aren't many visitors, so businesses have to rely on local repeat customers. Franchise joints and fast-food outlets do well in this sprawling area, but restaurants that are fresh and exciting must have a difficult time finding a market. Or, heaven forbid, maybe we have just missed out on some good bets. If so, we apologize to those entrepreneurs who are just waiting for some recognition.

Having said all that, you should know that those restaurants that are good in Contra Costa are very good and easy to visit. You never have to worry about parking, prices are competitive, and there is nothing so pleasurable as being served a great meal when you weren't expecting it.

✔ **Potato Barge.** I don't think I will insult the town of Antioch if I report that there are not a lot of places to eat here. But how could I resist checking out a place called the Potato Barge? If you happen to be visiting the Black Diamond Mines nearby, this is probably your best bet for a bite. Despite the name, this small restaurant doesn't really serve a lot of potato dishes. The name comes from the waterfront location: Barges moving potatoes used to pass by.

ANTIOCH
①

This is a burger and salad bar place, and the food is pretty good. If you stop by and need to use the restroom, be forewarned about the wallpaper in the men's room; it's rated X.

POTATO BARGE, *105 F Street; (415) 757-9585. Lunch and dinner Tuesday through Saturday. Beer and wine only. No nonsmoking section. MC, Visa, Am Ex. Inexpensive.*

✔ **Di Maggio's Sasanami Sushi.** No kidding. There really is such a place and it's in this book because it is such a curiosity. What's more, it's been featured in one of the slickest magazines in Japan and has become something of an attraction for busloads of Japanese tourists. Not because of Joltin' Joe, the Yankee Clipper. Actually, the Di Maggio of this sushi parlor happens to be his distant cousin, who happens to have married a Japanese woman, who happens to be the first woman ever to become a Sushi Master, or Mistress. She hires female sushi chefs; Japanese visitors come to see this believe-it-or-not event—women making sushi.

CONCORD
②

The gimmicks don't end there. Since the Willows Shopping Center, in Concord, is not necessarily a haven for lovers of raw fish and rice, the proprietors have added a railroad track on the ring of a huge, horseshoe-shaped bar. Sushi and sashimi roll by on miniature choo-choos, and the customer can simply take whatever looks good. If you prefer, there is also table service. The food is a bit unpredictable but is mostly on the right track.

DI MAGGIO'S SASANAMI SUSHI, *1975 Diamond Boulevard, in the Willows Shopping Center; (415) 671-7112. Lunch and dinner daily. Beer and wine only. No nonsmoking section. MC, Visa, Diners. Moderate.*

✔ **T.R.'s** T.R. stands for Teddy Roosevelt. We're not sure why, but it really doesn't matter. This is a very large restaurant and bar that serves good food. The menu offers a little something for everybody, from meat-and-potatoes eaters to those who prefer leaner cuisine. You can also get a great burger and fries, grilled chicken or fish, and specials like spinach linguine or a marinated pork sandwich with mustard sauce. Everything is prepared skillfully.

At lunchtime this is a popular spot for nearby businesspeople. At cocktail time the bar is jumping, and there are TV sets everywhere for sports fans.

T.R.'S, *2001 Salvio Street; (415) 827-4660. Lunch daily, dinner Monday through Saturday, brunch Sunday. Full bar. MC, Visa, Am Ex, Diners. Moderate.*

CROCKETT
③

✔ **Nantucket Fish Company.** Sitting out on the Crockett Marina, under the shadow of the Carquinez Bridge, is a bit of New England in the form of a restaurant called the Nantucket Fish Company. To get there, it's almost as difficult as driving to New England, because you have to negotiate a dirt hill and then cross some railroad tracks after you park your car. Once inside you'll think you've stepped into a lost corner of Cape Cod.

The fresh catches of the day are written on a blackboard on a wall. There are also daily seafood entrees, and some dishes for non—fish eaters. If you prefer to avoid fried foods, the best thing to order is whatever is fresh, broiled, without any sauce. In other words, the simpler the better is your best bet. The New England chowder is also quite good.

NANTUCKET FISH COMPANY, *at the foot of Port Street at the pier; (415) 787-2233. Lunch and dinner daily. Full bar. MC, Visa, Am Ex. Moderate.*

DANVILLE
④

✔ **L'Ultima.** Located in a large old house with an inviting front porch, this place bills itself as a "New Mexican" restaurant. That means that L'Ultima serves Mexican food like tacos and enchiladas (dishes in which chile pepper is quite prominent) and southwestern dishes like grilled meats and gourmet stews. It's all quite good.

If you're feeling truly adventurous, have their ultimate dessert: piles of ice

Contra Costa

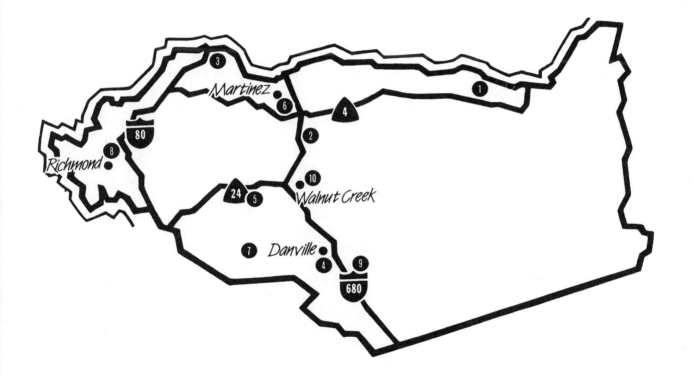

cream and chocolate sauce over pastry, a feast for the eyes as well as the sweet tooth.

L'ULTIMA, *263 South Hartz Avenue; (415) 838-9705. Lunch and dinner daily, brunch Sunday. Beer and wine only. MC, Visa, Am Ex. Moderate.*

✔ **Vally Medlyn's.** This is a diner named after the original proprietor, and it still looks like the typical coffee shop of the forties and fifties. A counter runs the length of the restaurant, plus there are several plastic booths.

As for the food, it, too, is like what you'd find in a typical coffee shop of days past. This is Middle American diner food, and it is prepared faithfully. You'll find soup, tuna salad, grilled cheese, and the perennial hamburger. What's more, the waitresses like to joke with you, and everybody there seems to be having a good time.

VALLY MEDLYN'S, *184 North Hartz Avenue; (415) 837-4040. Breakfast and lunch daily. Beer and wine only. No nonsmoking section. No credit cards. Inexpensive.*

LAFAYETTE
(5)

✔ **Spruzzo!** Being prone to understatement, initially we were turned off by a place that chooses to put an exclamation point after its name. However, in the case of Spruzzo! it's OK. The name is Italian, and it means "flash!" And the restaurant itself is worthy of exclamation.

Located in what is becoming a "gourmet gulch" in Contra Costa County, Spruzzo! is hidden away on a small street off busy Mt. Diablo Boulevard. Weather permitting, which is most times of the year, there is seating in a lovely garden. If it's too wet or too cold, you can relax in a tastefully appointed dining room. The menu offerings are ample and varied, with selections that include pasta, seafood, meats, and poultry, as well as panini (sandwiches) served with a salad or cup of minestrone. Prices do not vary greatly from lunch to dinner.

The idea is to be as authentically Italian as possible, and for the most part they are successful. Each table has its own beaker of virgin olive oil to pour on the freshly baked focaccia bread, like in the trattorias of Tuscany. The waitresses are young, friendly, and cheerful, but generally not the knowledgeable grumpy old man you are likely to encounter in the Italian countryside. (Imagine him saying, "Hi, I'm Luigi and I'll be serving you today.")

SPRUZZO! *210 Lafayette Circle; (415) 284-9709. Lunch Monday through Saturday, dinner Tuesday through Saturday; closed Sunday. Beer and wine only. No nonsmoking section. MC, Visa, Am Ex. Moderate.*

✔ **Tourelle Cafe.** Not far from Spruzzo! is probably the most acclaimed restaurant in Contra Costa County. Tourelle Cafe is situated in a new building that looks as if it were transported from nineteenth-century France. The emphasis is on traditional French and Italian cooking crossed with California Cuisine, using the finest ingredients and offering entrees with wonderful sauces. The menu changes often, determined by what ingredients are freshest. You can always depend on something from the pizza oven, or one of their grilled dishes. Owner Annette Esser also owns the popular Lascaux Restaurant, in downtown San Francisco.

TOURELLE CAFE, *3565 Mount Diablo Boulevard; (415) 284-3565. Lunch and dinner Tuesday through Saturday, brunch Sunday. Full bar. MC, Visa, Am Ex, Diners. Moderate.*

✔ Hot Dog Depot. For a quick bite, the in spot in town is the Hot Dog Depot right across from the railroad station. This place serves many varieties of good, juicy hot dogs, plus items like frozen yogurt, pastries, and an occasional salad. If the weather's right, and the weather is usually warm here, you can sit outside and watch for the train while you look out at the Bay.

HOT DOG DEPOT, *400 Ferry Street; (415) 372-7177. Open 6:30 A.M. to 7 P.M. daily. Beer only. MC, Visa, Am Ex, Diners. Inexpensive.*

✔ La Beau's Bar and Grill. In more ways than one, downtown Martinez is as far from the French Quarter in New Orleans as you can get. That's why it comes as such a surprise to find a place here, only a block or so from the rejuvenated waterfront, that advertises Fine Creole Cuisine. What's more, with its wrought-iron railings and outdoor seating, La Beau's even looks as if it would be at home on Bourbon Street.

This is probably a good time to make it clear that the food here is not the same as the great dishes served at famous places like K-Paul's, but for Martinez it's pretty good.

When you walk into La Beau's, the first thing you will see is the long wooden bar. This is a hangout for locals who are likely to be watching a game on the sports channel or just passing the time of day. Past the bar, La Beau's dining room is quieter, with more of a family atmosphere.

The food is California Cajun: the ever-present blackened dishes, a gumbo and jambalaya, plus something called the French Quarter, which is smoked turkey with avocado and swiss cheese on a croissant. In other words, you'll get the flavor of Louisiana and have the option of ordering more familiar items.

LA BEAU'S BAR AND GRILL, *436 Ferry Street; (415) 372-8941. Lunch and dinner daily. Full bar. MC, Visa, Am Ex. Inexpensive to Moderate.*

✔ Chez Maurice. The little-known area known as Rheem Valley never became the bustling suburb that air-conditioning magnate Donald Rheem envisioned when he developed this neighborhood, but this is a sweet little shopping district

MARTINEZ
⑥

MORAGA
⑦

with a lovely, old-fashioned movie palace (now used for live concerts) and an international collection of restaurants. There's a busy Chinese place, an Italian gem (see Mondello's, below), and an old-line French spot called Chez Maurice.

When you walk through the doorway you know you are in a fifties American version of a French restaurant. The lighting, the booths, the dark interior, all set the mood for a meal that will be classic French rather than Nouvelle or California French. Sauces are the stars of the show here, and your menu choices include traditional dishes like coq au vin and beef bourguignon, all very nicely prepared.

CHEZ MAURICE, *360 Park Street; (415) 376-1655. Lunch Tuesday through Friday, dinner Tuesday through Sunday. Full bar. No nonsmoking section. MC, Visa, Am Ex. Moderate.*

✓ **Mondello's.**   This is a place where you must order dishes made with ricotta and mozzarella. If you think these are the bland, tasteless cheeses found in most supermarkets, you're in for a surprise. It's the difference between a just-picked home-grown tomato and one of those watery, gas-ripened jobs; that is, it's the difference between night and day. The owner's elderly father makes these cheeses the way he was taught back home in Sicily; they're fresh, rich, and full of natural flavor.

Mondello's serves a variety of foods native to Sicily, including fish, chicken, and veal dishes, most notably an excellent cotolettine palermitana—small veal cutlets breaded, pan fried in olive oil, and served with freshly squeezed lemon juice. Another house specialty is pasta con sarde e finocchio: a combination of fresh fennel, sardines, raisins, and pine nuts on housemade pasta.

However, the simplest of dishes are the best. A good antipasto is the slices of fresh mozzarella topped simply with good olive oil. The spaghetti alla Don Vincenzo, named in honor of the cheese-making papa, is an ideal summer dish; the tomatoes and basil are at their peak, topped with a generous portion of Don Vincenzo's ricotta. Any time of year the cannelloni alla Mondello is good; it's made with housemade pasta, dad's ricotta, proscuitto, veal, and spinach, baked in tomato and bechamel sauce. And to top it off, how about the cannoli della Sicilia, the famous dessert of the region made in-house with sweetened ricotta and chocolate chips. Basta!

Mondello's is a small, unpretentious, friendly place; the owner or his wife are likely to wait on you. It's decorated simply, with Sicilian crockery and plates—nothing fancy, no need to dress up.

MONDELLO'S, *337 Rheem Boulevard; (415) 376-2533. Dinner Tuesday through Saturday; closed Sunday and Monday. Beer and wine only. MC, Visa. Moderate.*

✔ **The Baltic.** This comfortable and friendly Italian restaurant is a hangout for many of the folks who work in the Point Richmond area. The Baltic is an informal place, where you can roll up your shirt sleeves and dig into large portions of middle-of-the-road Italian food (such as ravioli and spaghetti with meat sauce), plus sandwiches and soups. The menu is a bit more elaborate at dinner.

THE BALTIC, *135 Park Place; (415) 235-2532. Lunch and dinner daily. Full bar. MC, Visa, Am Ex, Diners. Moderate.*

✔ **Hotel Mac.** The fanciest place in Point Richmond, with prices to match, is the venerable old Hotel Mac dining room. The Mac menu features prime ribs and steaks, fish dishes, and a few items designed to appeal to the gourmet palate. Portions are ample; reservations are advised.

HOTEL MAC, *50 Washington Avenue; (415) 233-0576. Lunch Monday through Friday, dinner Tuesday through Sunday. Full bar. MC, Visa, Am Ex, Diners. Moderate to Expensive.*

✔ **Taj Kesri.** Their ad says, "The best Indian Restaurant in the Bay Area." Maybe that's going too far, but certainly this low-key spot in a little shopping center is worth a visit. First of all, it comes as a great surprise to find such a restaurant in this particular neighborhood because it is surrounded by fast-food franchises and donut shops. Inside, the most Indian part of the decor is the turban worn by the rather stern man at the door. Don't be dismayed. Indian restaurateurs are not generally prone to smiling all that much, but they are still glad you came in.

The menu offers traditional Indian food, starting with appetizers like samosa, which you can have with either chicken, lamb, or vegetable stuffings. They are large and flaky. Curries and tandoori dishes are featured for the main courses. If you're not familiar with tandoori cooking, it's a way of marinating chicken, fish, or meat and then cooking it over intense heat very quickly. The result, particularly with chicken, which is served skinless, is a delicious and low-calorie dish. One luncheon special offers tandoori chicken with an awful-sounding curry dish that turned out to be wonderful. Are you ready for cottage cheese curry? It was actually a spicy melange of vegetables and coconut. All this was topped with a huge slab of nan, which is a flat Indian bread.

The regular menu offers many chicken, lamb, and beef dishes, as well as a few fish choices. There are also many selections for vegetarians.

TAJ KESRI, *12221 San Pablo Avenue; (415) 233-3817. Lunch Sunday through Friday, dinner nightly. Nonsmoking section on weekends. MC, Visa, Am Ex. Inexpensive to Moderate.*

✔ **Chatillon Restaurant.** Good French restaurants are starting to crop up in the suburbs, establishments that would have been found only in San Francisco ten years ago. Presumably, high city rents, parking availability, and the proliferation of suburban industrial parks have created the market. Chatillon fits into this category. Nestled in a small shopping center, it looks like a throwback to an older type of design, the kind of French restaurant you might find in most American cities, with candles, white linen, and waiters in tuxedos flaming dishes in front of your table.

The trick is to go here for lunch, when the no-nonsense waitresses take over and when the prices are almost half the cost of dinner.

As for the food, it's excellent. This is not Nouvelle or California Cuisine, but traditional French and continental cooking with rich and flavorful sauces.

CHATILLON RESTAURANT, *21314-A San Ramon Valley Boulevard; (415) 828-7910. Lunch Monday through Friday, dinner nightly. Full bar. MC, Visa, Am Ex, Diners. Moderate at lunch, Expensive at dinner.*

✔ **Mudd's.** This could be the ultimate California restaurant. They grow their own organic produce and flowers (the restaurant is located on the grounds of the Crow Canyon Institute, a pioneering effort in chemical-free farming), and thus the menu reflects the seasons. The interior design is remarkable, with plants, flowers, and herbs everywhere and a ceiling with a wooden wave design. On nice days you can dine on the patio and stroll out in the gardens where the food is grown.

This is the place to take your children when you want to teach them what freshly picked produce tastes like. It's also an ideal place to take out-of-state relatives when you want to show off the California lifestyle, and just about everybody gets a kick out of walking in the garden.

Best of all the food is terrific. Beef, chicken, fish, and vegetarian dishes are served, and the chef has a very creative flair. For example, appetizers might include garden vegetable soup with wild rice; sautéed scallops with a peach butter sauce; or squash blossoms stuffed with cheeses. Entrees will be along the lines of garden lasagne, with herbs and veggies from outside the door; grilled Petaluma chicken; or roast sugar-cured pork loin served with spicy lentils and tomato chutney.

For dessert, try Mudd's pie: a rich chocolate brownie in a light pastry shell. They also make a wonderful bread pudding with warm bourbon sauce.

MUDD'S, *10 Boardwalk, on the grounds of the Crow Canyon Institute; (415) 837-9387. Lunch Monday through Friday, dinner Tuesday through Sunday, brunch Sunday. Full bar. All nonsmoking. MC, Visa, Am Ex, Diners. Moderate.*

✔ **Max's.** If you see a large restaurant glistening at all hours of the day and night, you have probably found your way to a growing Bay Area institution called Max's. It all started with a little deli south of San Francisco. Then Max's Opera Plaza opened in the city, followed by another in the Gift Center, followed by one near Moscone Center followed by . . . Well, you get the idea.

Max's has finally made it to the Backroads. Like all the other Max's, the Walnut Creek outlet has a snazzy interior and features what is best described as Northern California deli food. You can get such standard deli items as over-stuffed sandwiches of corned beef and turkey, plus enormous salad concoctions with Chinese or Mexican accents. There are also barbecued items, and the house meatloaf is made with veal and turkey. Another feature is the selection of enormous desserts, which are wonderful to look at but tend to be disappointing after you dig in.

Max's is a safe haven; as is with the other Max's restaurants, you know what the food will be like before you order it and it will always be decent. This is not haute cuisine but is a high-quality chain operating with flair. The ambiance is always spirited and fun. There's also a Max's in San Ramon.

MAX'S, *1676 N. California Boulevard; (415) 932-3434. Lunch Monday through Saturday, dinner nightly. Full bar. MC, Visa, Am Ex, Diners. Moderate.*

✔ **Prima Cafe.** Along the shopping district of North Main Street in Walnut Creek is a collection of sidewalk cafes. Some are shaded by large umbrellas, others by trees; all have espresso machines. The busiest of the bunch is called Prima Cafe, which serves Northern Italian–California Cuisine and has a wine-tasting bar and a wine shop in back.

Lunch and dinner begin with focaccia bread served with olive oil instead of butter, in the style of a Tuscan trattoria. At lunch the offerings include a variety of fresh pasta dishes, salads, and sandwiches; the smoked chicken on sourdough is a good bet. At dinner, the menu expands to include such entrees as osso buco. A number of menu items, including pasta dishes and sandwiches, are designed for those on low-sodium, low-cholesterol diets.

The service is very attentive and you're made to feel like you're a guest in someone's home. Though there are tables inside and out, weather permitting you'll want to be out front on the patio, near the sidewalk, watching the world go by—a good way to spend a hot Contra Costa afternoon or evening.

If you have your heart set on one of these outdoor tables, be sure to call ahead for a reservation.

PRIMA CAFE, *1522 North Main Street; (415) 935-7780. Lunch Monday through Saturday, dinner Tuesday through Saturday. Full bar. MC, Visa. Moderate.*

✔ **Spiedini.** The chain that operates the popular San Francisco restaurants Prego and MacArthur Park has a real winner in Walnut Creek. Spiedini is a modern, sleek Italian restaurant offering an extensive menu of interesting dishes. The emphasis is on Northern Italian cooking, along with the ubiquitous pizzas, calzone, and fresh pasta. This is a touch of Milan in Contra Costa County. There's also a touch of Beverly Hills as Spiedini is in a bank building and offers valet parking.

SPIEDINI, *101 Ygnacio Valley Road; (415) 939-2100. Lunch Monday through Friday, dinner nightly. Full bar. MC, Visa, Am Ex, Diners. Moderate.*

✔ **Yogurt Park.** Sometimes we simply don't want a full lunch or dinner, and that's when we head out for frozen yogurt. Our favorite kind is at Yogurt Park. We're not sure if it's the machines they have or the mix they use, but they serve mile-high helpings of soft, creamy yogurt. Six different flavors are available each day; you can call ahead for a recorded message of the day's flavors. These are of the low-fat and nonfat variety, with only sixteen to twenty-five calories per ounce.

YOGURT PARK, *80 Broadway Plaza; (415) 944-4748. Open 10 A.M. to 9 P.M. weekdays, 10 A.M. to 10 P.M. weekends. No credit cards. Inexpensive.*

YOGURT PARK, *1499 N. California Street; (415) 937-2569. Open 11 A.M. to 11 P.M. weekdays, 11 A.M. to midnight weekends. No credit cards. Inexpensive.*

CHAPTER **9** "Yolano" County

Don't try looking for this county on the map; it doesn't exist. "Yolano" is a name created by farmers who put out a map for visitors of Yolo and Solano counties. Both counties are blessed with wide open spaces and few cities. They are much more engaged in growing food here than serving it. Still, in towns like Benicia and even little Suisun City, there are nice Backroads dining surprises.

BENICIA
①

✔ **First Street Foods.** Benicia is an East Bay artists' community. It preceded Emeryville as an affordable spot where artists and craftspeople could rent huge old warehouses and work and live without worrying about daily survival. Because of that community and the city's lovely waterfront setting, there is a good selection of interesting restaurants in town.

Down near the waterfront and antique row is a cozy place for people with light appetites. First Street Foods offers items like pastas, salads, and a pâté or two, served in an atmosphere that is conducive to conversation or just having a cap-

Yolano
(Yolo & Solano)

Woodland ●
● 7

Fairfield
● 3
● 4

RioVista ●

Vallejo

puccino and reading the paper for a while. You order at the counter, during which time you will notice the fabulous antique bar. You take your order to one of several cafe tables, or they will prepare the food to go. Their desserts are good, too, and take-out service is available.

Thursdays and Fridays are Pasta Nights.

FIRST STREET FOODS, *440 First Street; (707) 745-4404. Open 9:30 A.M. to 5 P.M. Tuesday, Wednesday, and Saturday, 9:30 A.M. to 8:30 P.M. Thursday and Friday, 10:30 A.M. to 4 P.M. Sunday, closed Monday. Beer and wine only. All nonsmoking. No credit cards. Inexpensive to Moderate.*

✔ **Mabel's.**   Many hearts were broken a few years ago when a favorite restaurant in Benicia called Dona Francesca was forced to close; hearts were mended when some of the crew opened Mabel's just down the street. This is a fifties diner, complete with booths and a counter. You can get typical diner entrees, such as omelets and burgers, plus daily specials that show some of the imaginative touches of the earlier restaurant. One of the specialties is their version of a Philly cheese steak sandwich, oozing with cheese and peppers. The desserts are wonderful, and you get plenty to eat for your money.

MABEL'S, *635 First Street; (707) 746-7068. Breakfast and lunch Monday through Friday, dinner Monday through Saturday, brunch Sunday. Beer and wine only. No nonsmoking section. MC, Visa. Inexpensive to Moderate.*

✔ **Restaurant at the Union Hotel.**   This is an ambitious restaurant in an historic setting. The hotel was built in 1882; many of the original fixtures are still in place—the lights and pressed-tin walls—complemented by more modern leaded and stained glass, probably the work of local artisans.

Several years ago, chef Judy Rogers made the Union Hotel a culinary destination. The kitchen has since changed hands (Rogers moved to San Francisco), and though the food is not as spectacular as it once was, it is quite good, with an emphasis on seasonal ingredients and creative combinations. Last time we were there, our meal got off to an inauspicious start with a basket of nondescript white bread but recovered with the delivery of the entrees, which were blackened Sonoma lamb chops, poached salmon with ginger and fruit sauce, and a pizzette made with fresh locally made ricotta.

Hamburger eaters take note that the Union Burger is very good, grilled to your idea of doneness and topped with Jarlsberg cheese. Salads are made with baby greens, and, at brunch, the French toast is served with real maple syrup. The menu, which changes every few weeks, offers wine and beer suggestions to accompany each dish.

RESTAURANT AT THE UNION HOTEL, *401 First Street; (707) 746-0100. Lunch Tuesday through Saturday, dinner Tuesday through Sunday, brunch Sunday.*

Full bar. No nonsmoking section. MC, Visa, Am Ex, Diners. Moderate to Expensive.

✔ **Colette.** Small is beautiful in Davis. It's a small city, built around the ever-expanding campus of the University of California at Davis. It is probably the bicycle capital of the world; Davis has 40,000 people and 40,000 bicycles, with adequate lanes and parking provided. Our favorite place to eat is tucked away at the end of Second Street near the Amtrak Station.

It's called Colette, a tiny cafe with nine tables that serves very good and very ambitious food. The style is best described as California French. The California part comes from their emphasis on locally grown fruits and vegetables; the French part is in the sauces and presentation. At lunch this is an informal place; needless to say, most of the local clientele arrives by bicycle. The menu emphasizes light dishes, such as housemade soups, tarts made of onion, squash, and apples, and pasta salads. One intriguing dish we sampled was called Transylvanian goulash, a delicious stew incorporating pork and sauerkraut.

Dinners are full-course affairs, though the atmosphere remains casual. The menu changes each week with such offerings as salmon in blueberry butter sauce; pork tenderloin with ginger mustard, and sea scallops with raspberry vinegar sauce. It's all prepared in a tiny, tiny kitchen by cooks who really know what they're doing.

COLETTE, *802 Second Street; (916) 758-3377. Lunch Monday through Friday, dinner Monday through Saturday. Beer and wine only. All nonsmoking. Am Ex. Lunch Inexpensive, dinner Moderate.*

DAVIS
②

✔ **Fairfield Landing.** Overlooking Route 80 is a strangely nautical-looking place called the Fairfield Landing. This restaurant would look right at home at San Francisco's Fisherman's Wharf, but here it is a long way from the water. Anyway, it is an attractive operation, serving fresh fish plus selections for meat eaters and chicken eaters. The food is not great, but it's adequate, and there are not a lot of choices off the freeway.

FAIRFIELD LANDING, *2440 Martin Road; (707) 429-2370. Lunch and dinner daily, brunch Sunday. Full bar. MC, Visa, Am Ex, Diners, Discover. Moderate.*

FAIRFIELD
③

✔ **Joe's Buffet.** If you want a quick meal or a very good sandwich, try Joe's in downtown Fairfield. This is a friendly, informal spot that has been a Fairfield tradition for years. As you enter you will be greeted by the sight of huge slabs of roast beef and corned beef sitting behind a steam table. There will probably be a pasta dish or two. Place your order and prepare to eat a huge sandwich or platter of pasta accompanied by a salad.

JOE'S BUFFET, *834 Texas Avenue; (707) 425-2317. Open 10 A.M. to 7 P.M.*

weekdays, 10 A.M. to 4 P.M. Saturday; closed Sunday. Beer only. No nonsmoking section. No credit cards. Inexpensive.

SUISUN CITY ④

✔ **Puerto Vallarta.** In one of those polls that newspapers like to conduct every so often, the town of Suisun City was judged the least attractive place to live in the Bay Area. That immediately prompted us to visit and restore the good name of this interesting and attractive little town near Fairfield. And lo and behold, not only did we find a nice main street, and some lovely canals leading to a huge, protected marsh, we also found two terrific ethnic restaurants, right across the street from each other.

Puerto Vallarta is a very good Mexican restaurant. Everything tastes fresh and is prepared with care. The chicken and meats that fill the enchiladas or burritos are cooked with style and seasoning and the sauces are first rate. The rice and beans have texture and taste, as opposed to the countless places where they just lay there in a soggy lump. There is nothing fancy or atmospheric about this restaurant. Just good food, lots of it, and low prices.

PUERTO VALLARTA, *301 Main Street; (707) 429-9384. Lunch and dinner daily. Full bar. No credit cards. Inexpensive.*

✔ **Tasuke.** Tasuke is a little Japanese operation, run by folks who are from the old country. They serve authentic Japanese food, designed for local tastes. Hence, the raw fish will be only the most recognizable and approachable, rather than things like exotic fish livers and exotic clams. Items like sukiyaki and tempura are featured, served on Japanese dishes and bowls, with chopsticks as an option. It's the kind of place that would be good but unremarkable in San Francisco or Berkeley. In Suisun City, it comes as a very pleasant surprise.

TASUKE, *314 Spring Street; Lunch and dinner Monday through Saturday; closed Sunday. Beer and sake only. Visa. Inexpensive to Moderate.*

VACAVILLE ⑤

✔ **Merchant and Main.** If you ask a local where to eat in Vacaville, the answer is unfailingly Merchant and Main. There is a certain civic pride in having a place that is a cut above the many franchise operations in the area. It's a spacious, bustling restaurant with wood paneling and an "old-timey" atmosphere. It's always packed at lunch with local businesspeople.

The menu offers a little bit of everything, spanning the headliners of international cuisine. There's pasta, teriyaki, blackened steak, oysters, fresh fish, and even something called prawns charbroiled Texas style.

Some of the dishes are very good while others don't work at all. The best advice we have to offer is to stick to more traditional items, like the half-pound hamburgers, steaks, and chops. Save room for what they call their Non-Diet desserts.

MERCHANT AND MAIN, *349 Merchant Street, at Main; (707) 446-0368. Lunch and dinner daily, brunch Sunday. Full bar. MC, Visa, Am Ex, Diners. Moderate.*

✔ **City Lights Cafe.** This is a genuine surprise in Vallejo, a town not known for epicurean delights. Situated right in the center of town in an old PG&E building, this spacious and bright cafe offers wonderful California Cuisine at lunchtime. Fresh fish, chicken, pasta, and other staples of light dining are featured, and the chef knows what to do with them. Truly a spot worth going out of your way for.

Dinner is served on special evenings, usually in conjunction with a theater performance.

CITY LIGHTS CAFE, *415 Virginia Street; (707) 557-9200. Lunch Monday through Friday, dinner served occasionally. Full bar. MC, Visa, Am Ex. Inexpensive.*

✔ **House of Soul.** With all the various types of cuisine available in the greater Bay Area, there are surprisingly few soul food restaurants. The House of Soul helps fill that gap nicely.

This is a friendly, rather small spot a few blocks from Highway 80 run by a family that knows the food of the South well. Wonderful fried chicken, chicken-fried steak, greens, and biscuits are usually available. The only item that doesn't measure up is the ribs, only because they have to cook them in a kitchen oven instead of over an open fire. But don't let that keep you away from their other delicious offerings.

HOUSE OF SOUL, *1526 Solano Avenue; (707) 644-3792. Lunch and dinner Monday through Saturday. No alcohol served. No nonsmoking section. No credit cards. Inexpensive.*

✔ **Ray's Burger.** A touch of down-to-earth Americana charm awaits you at Ray's, which is a tiny coffee shop with a counter and a few tables. The jumbo burger is the big news here: a grilled delight of immodest size served with a salad, all for under $4. Ray's also serves Blue Plate Specials like roast chicken for about $4, plus standard breakfast items like eggs, bacon, and white toast, all presented in a very friendly atmosphere.

RAY'S BURGER, *727 Marin Street; (707) 643-6017. Breakfast and lunch Monday through Saturday. No alcohol served. No credit cards. Inexpensive.*

✔ **Jody's Cafe.** On Main Street in Woodland it's hard to miss a pink place called Jody's Cafe. It doesn't look it, but this is the home of very good, authentic Mexican food. Several years ago Jody's Cafe was a typical small-town coffeehouse. Then a Mexican-American family bought it and changed the menu to their homeland cuisine. They just didn't bother to change the name or decor.

Though there are quite a few Mexican restaurants in the area, this appears to be the favorite spot for locals. A woman at the Woodland Opera House (a worthwhile destination) told us that that when her daughter comes to visit from San Francisco, she insists there's not a Mexican place in the big city as good as Jody's. Certainly there are none as inexpensive.

JODY'S CAFE, *1226 East Main Street, to the east of Route 113; (916) 662-9857. Lunch and dinner Monday through Saturday. Beer and wine only. No credit cards. Inexpensive.*

✔ **Morrison's Upstairs.** A culinary surprise is to be found on the third floor of a renovated nineteenth-century luxury apartment building in the town of Woodland. Morrison's Upstairs is a very attractive, cosmopolitan spot for lunch or dinner.

Lunch is a real bargain. The regular menu features fish, chicken, pasta, vegetarian items, and burgers; specials can include swordfish, grilled chicken, and a pasta dish. The chicken turned out to be a grilled boneless breast with a lovely herb sauce on the side, oven-fried potatoes, and fruit. The homemade desserts are also recommended.

MORRISON'S UPSTAIRS, *428½ First Street; (916) 666-0500. Lunch Monday through Friday, dinner nightly, brunch Sunday. Full bar. MC, Visa, Am Ex. Inexpensive to Moderate at lunch; Moderate at dinner.*

CHAPTER **10** Central Valley

The Central Valley may grow more food than any other region in the United States, but this is mass production rather than small farms growing exotic or organic vegetables. That sets the tone for most of the restaurants you'll come across in the valley: more franchise operations than star chefs, and more formula than invention. Still, there are surprises on the Backroads. Every now and then you can stumble onto a place that turns out food exciting and imaginative: for example, the chocolate cream pie at the Coffee Express in Groveland and the grilled chicken at The Milk House in Manteca. Here are the pleasant surprises we have found, starting with the Delta region.

✓ Al's Diner.   Lunch or dinner at Al's is as much a part of visiting this part of the Delta as the historic buildings of Locke. This is not to say that the food is great; instead, think of it as a visit to a local institution.

   Al's is also known as Al the Wop's, a nickname developed before our more enlightened time of ethnic sensitivity, and it seems to have stuck. As you enter the bar you will notice dollar bills hanging from the ceiling. Ask the bartender about them, but be prepared to pay for the answer. The tradition of the joint is that it costs you a buck to find out how the dollars all got up there.

   In the dining room you sit at a table that has not only salt and pepper shakers but also jars of peanut butter and jelly. That's because the specialty of the house is steak or chicken with peanut butter with a side of buttered French bread. What happens with the peanut butter and jelly is up to you.

AL'S DINER, *Main Street, Locke; (916) 776-1800. Lunch and dinner daily. Full bar. No nonsmoking section. No credit cards. Inexpensive.*

✔ **Grand Island Mansion.**   This place serves Sunday brunch only. We're not major brunch eaters—our idea of a wonderful Sunday is to stay home, and anyway the food tends to be too buttery and rich for our taste—but this place sounded so splendid that we dragged ourselves out to the Delta one Sunday morning.

It was worth the trip. First of all, the drive along the canals is one of the nicest in this part of California. We knew we had arrived at our destination when we saw a long driveway edged by giant cypress trees leading up to a four-story, Mediterranean-style mansion. There's nothing like it for miles. This fifty-eight-room mansion had been built in 1917 for an eccentric German financier. The exterior is crumbling a bit—the thirty-foot Corinthian columns on the front porch are cracked and weather-damaged in places—which made the setting all the more wonderful, like arriving on a Real Life set of *Sunset Boulevard*. However, once you walk through the front doorway and into the white marble lobby, the place becomes beautiful. The first floor of the mansion has been lovingly restored, and all the rooms—parlors, sunroom, dining room, and so on—are used as the restaurant.

Brunch is a prix fixe affair: $14.95 for an entree and all the champagne (admittedly cheap champagne) you want. The entree selection includes items like quiche, Italian toast (French toast but with amaretto), and filet Benedict (medallions of pork tenderloin filet topped with poached eggs and hollandaise). We tried the Cajun chicken (pan fried, lightly seasoned with New Orleans–style spices and served with a mint butter sauce) and the coho salmon (served like trout, butterfly filet style and nicely grilled), all attractively served with rice and vegetables and a fresh flower on the plate. The food was quite good, and coupled with the ambiance—the drive, the fire in the marble fireplace next to our table —it made a lovely outing. The price of the meal includes a fresh fruit compote served in a champagne glass, rolls, and sautéed vegetables of the season. Coffee, orange juice, and dessert are extra.

If you decide to visit, be sure to call in advance for a reservation. Allow enough time to look around downstairs (the upstairs is closed off for now) where you'll see the ballroom, a soda fountain, and the game room, with an antique snooker table.

GRAND ISLAND MANSION, *Grand Island Road; (916) 775-1705. Sunday brunch. Beer and wine only. All nonsmoking. MC, Visa. Moderate to Expensive.*

✔ **Henry's.**   Restaurants really are few and far between in this neck of the woods, but at least this one is around seven days a week. Henry's is a standard American diner, serving items like burgers, patty melts, and, for iron stomachs, the Monte Cristo—a deep-fried sandwich with cheese and ham inside; it's tasty, but hardly for the cholesterol-conscious.

Actually, the best things Henry's has going are the cream pies. We can personally vouch for the chocolate and the coconut cream.

HENRY'S, *1000 Highway 12, Rio Vista; (707) 374-6304. Open 6 A.M. to 10 P.M. daily. No alcohol served. MC, Visa. Inexpensive.*

✔ **The Point.** The most attractive restaurant in Rio Vista is called The Point, which overlooks a lovely marina. Again, don't expect great food, but the view is delightful and the options in town are limited. If you put away any comparisons with what you can get in San Francisco, the wine country, or Berkeley, you will enjoy your meal. The menu is standard American fare. Order the simplest, least complicated dishes. Get the point?

THE POINT, *120 Marina Drive, Rio Vista; (707) 374-5400. Lunch Tuesday through Saturday, dinner Tuesday through Sunday, brunch Sunday. Full bar. No nonsmoking section. MC, Visa, Am Ex. Moderate.*

✔ **Rogelio's.** Isleton was once the asparagus capital of the world, or so local legend goes. But the asparagus crop moved south and the canneries that provided employment shut down. For years Isleton was a forgotten little town in the Delta until someone came up with the bright idea to have an annual Crawdad Festival. Today this event draws as many as 70,000 visitors to Isleton every June. Things are picking up again in Isleton.

Our recommendation in this town of less than one thousand residents serves neither asparagus nor crawdads. Rogelio's specializes in Mexican and Chinese food. The combination starts to make sense when you learn that the proprietors are the husband and wife team of Rogelio and Mew Ha Garcia. Thus, the menu offers Mexican fare on one side, Chinese on the other.

Now, we have to level with you. When we were sent to Rogelio's by a local, we were urged to order the chicken fajitas. We started with those, planning to go on to sample some of Mew Ha's specials, too. But the fajitas were so good, and the plate was so loaded with tender hunks of chicken breast in a tangy sauce, refried beans, rice, salsa, guacamole, and housemade tortillas that we couldn't eat another bite. At $7.50 this was the most expensive item on the menu.

Rogelio's is a rather large restaurant, and looks like a Wild West saloon from the outside. There are separate entrances to the long bar on one side and to the family dining room on the other. Diners sit in large wooden booths. The decor is bare bones but comfortable. Since it gets very hot in the summer here in the Delta, you'll be happy to know Rogelio's has a good air-conditioning system.

ROGELIO'S, *Main Street, Isleton; (916) 777-6606. Lunch and dinner daily. Full bar. MC, Visa. Inexpensive.*

FOLSOM

✔ **The Wind Rose.**   Just a few miles before you enter the town of Folsom, you will come to a pleasant restaurant called The Wind Rose. The decor is nothing to write home about, but the food is: well-prepared dishes like seafood pasta or chicken tarragon, with a choice of soup or salad. Desserts are a must at lunch and dinner; these delights are made elsewhere, at a bakery in nearby Placerville, but are worth having; you won't regret having the Mounds Bar, which is coconut cheesecake topped with a crunchy dark-chocolate icing. Lunch is the bargain, since dinners tend to run about three or four dollars more.

THE WIND ROSE, *13407 Folsom Boulevard; (916) 985-6562. Lunch and dinner Monday through Friday, dinner Monday through Saturday. Full bar. MC, Visa, Am Ex, Diners. Moderate.*

GROVELAND

✔ **Coffee Express.**   On the way to or from Yosemite on Route 120, you will pass through the town of Groveland. By all means, plan to have lunch at the Coffee Express. Two delightful ladies opened this small cafe after their children were old enough to take care of themselves, and they offer soups, salads, and sandwiches and home-cooked meals that are wholesome and delicious. Two years passed between our first visit and our most recent stop, and now one of the proprietors has given up on restaurant hours and turned things over to her partner. Still, Edith Wilson keeps making some of the best pies we have ever tasted. So far, we have worked our way through the chocolate, banana, and coconut cream pies, and can't wait to continue the research. On our last visit, Edith was happy to report that a couple from Florida, working from a copy of our first Backroads guide, made a two-hour detour to try the pie and told her it was worth it. The Coffee Express also has an espresso machine, and uses it well.

COFFEE EXPRESS, *18765 Main Street; (209) 962-7393. Open 7 A.M. to 3 P.M. Friday through Wednesday; closed Thursday. No alcohol served. No nonsmoking section. No credit cards. Inexpensive.*

MANTECA

✔ **The Milk House.**   You'd never know it from the outside, but this is a real find. As you pull up to The Milk House, you might think you're entering an old-fashioned dairy store or large ice cream parlor. Inside, you'll be reminded of many a roadside bar room, with some scattered tables. But, someone we met in town suggested we eat here despite the decor, and were we glad. If you are heading to Yosemite, the Gold Country, or the Delta via Manteca, plan a meal at The Milk House.

The regular menu offers steaks, pasta, chicken dishes, and daily specials. We fondly remember a wonderfully fresh king salmon with lemon and capers, a chicken breast amandine, and a great, thick pea soup. Manteca or San Francisco, the food here would stack up favorably anywhere.

THE MILK HOUSE, *1800 West Yosemite Avenue; (209) 239-5221. Lunch Monday through Friday, dinner Monday through Saturday. Full bar. No nonsmoking section. MC, Visa. Moderate.*

✔ Mallards.   On your way to or from Yosemite, you will probably want something to eat. The best place in town to suit all tastes is Mallards, a very large and attractive place on the old Yosemite Road, Route 132.

Surrounded by just about every franchised restaurant you can name, Mallards offers an alternative that caters to every trend. They have an oyster bar, a mesquite grill, and several dishes they say are recommended by the American Heart Association for low-cholesterol diets. My advice is to stick to the most simply prepared grilled dishes and avoid the attempts to be fancy. Also, if you happen to use the restrooms, you will notice they are labeled for DRAKES and HENS. Brush up on your farm terminology before nature calls.

MALLARDS, *1700 McHenry Street (Route 132); (209) 522-DUCK. Lunch and dinner daily, brunch Sunday. Full bar. MC, Visa, Am Ex, Diners. Inexpensive to Moderate.*

MODESTO

✔ Biba.   Biba is the name of the proprietress of this very fine Northern Italian restaurant, and you can feel her influence throughout. As you enter the rather elegant establishment on the fringe of the "hip" section of Sacramento, you'll see Biba's cookbooks for sale, and many articles about her and her TV exploits. Biba is also something of an Italian Julia Child in these parts.

The decor takes you out of the political whirl of the state capital and into a very well-appointed restaurant that could be in any major city in the world. There are white tablecloths and cloth napkins, comfortable chairs, and well-spaced tables: everything sending the message that care is taken to make this a first-rate restaurant. Service is professional and attentive, so you will be at ease whether you are in a business suit or jeans. The menu offers more authentic Northern Italian cuisine than you'll find in most of San Francisco's North Beach establishments. The food is terrific, with a large selection of pasta dishes, fresh fish, and hearty items like osso buco with polenta. This would be a good restaurant anywhere.

BIBA, *2801 Capitol Avenue; (916) 455-BIBA. Lunch Monday through Friday, dinner Monday through Saturday. Full bar. MC, Visa, Am Ex. Moderate.*

SACRAMENTO

✔ Frank Fat's.   Frank Fat's is where the movers and shakers eat in the state capital. Located a few blocks from the Capitol building, this elegant Chinese-American restaurant has probably had more deals written on its napkins and matchbooks than any other place in the state. If you know your politics, you are guaranteed to see at least Somebody there. Because of its popularity, there's a pleasant buzz of activity about Fat's. You feel as if you are part of the action.

Frank Fat's is a narrow restaurant with a huge bar in the center. The decor is rather lavish, with a spectacular tapestry above the bar and a friendly buddha overlooking the main dining room. The back room is the most private, with large padded booths and is more quiet than the main area.

The food is basically Chinese with very good Cantonese, Szechuan, and Hunan items. For American tastes, there are choices such as veal cutlet, steak, and fish. We have only tried the Chinese items, but they were excellent. The selections are more expensive than you normally would pay for a Chinese meal of this type; lunch is less expensive than dinner. The service at Frank Fat's is very good.

FRANK FAT'S, *806 L Street; (916) 442-7092. Lunch Monday through Friday, dinner nightly. Full bar. MC, Visa, Am Ex. Moderate for lunch, Expensive for dinner.*

✔ **Java City.** For coffee fiends like us, it's important to know where to go in any town to get a good jolt of java. If we can find a place that brews a good, strong cup of coffee, that's great; if we locate a place that also roasts its own beans, even better. And if we find a spot that also makes a great cappuccino, all is well with the world.

If you are similarly afflicted, or are simply looking for a good cup of coffee, you will be glad to know that Sacramento has Java City. This is a touch of Berkeley or San Francisco's North Beach within a mile of the state capitol, not only in the quality of the coffee, but also in the atmosphere. Maybe we've found the secret to late-night legislative sessions . . .

The place is a large store where they roast about thirty different kinds of brew and sell beans, coffee mugs, filters, and other java paraphernalia. The place is almost always crowded, often with regulars that locals describe as "Sacramento's colorful characters." They're scattered around at tables inside or, weather permitting, outside on the sidewalk, reading *The Bee*, writing in private journals, or arguing politics.

JAVA CITY, *1800 Capitol Avenue; (916) 444-JAVA. Open 6:30 A.M. to 11 P.M. weekdays, 6:30 A.M. to midnight weekends. No alcohol served. No smoking inside. MC, Visa, Am Ex. Inexpensive.*

✔ **J.R.'s.** Just a few years ago, we had a hard time finding interesting places to eat in the city. Now, there appears to be at least one good new discovery on every visit. One such find is J.R.'s, which is an airy, bright restaurant apparently owned by a movie buff. Either that, or this place got one heck of a deal on pictures of stars of the forties and fifties. Presumably, it's all part of a design to set a mood of nostalgia and informal elegance.

The menu held incredible promise, saying all the right things for our tastes. "J.R.'s menu will rotate on a seasonal basis to give you the finest cuisine possible. The concept is centered around the freshness and quality of ingredients. Many, if not all, of these ingredients are produced here on the premises. (We even make our own vinegar and cheeses.) We refrain from the use of artificial colors and flavors."

Sounds promising, right? Not only that, but the food matched the expectations. There were so many little touches that we appreciated. Fresh tulips were on every table. The salad was filled with good greens. The dressing was served on the side, without our even asking. And the food was very well prepared. Lunch offers a variety of soups and salads, many of which you can order either a whole or half portion. There are unusual sandwiches and specialties, such as the curried chicken in pita bread with walnuts, or fire sticks, which are mesquite-grilled pork, marinated in teriyaki, fire oil, and vinaigrette. There are eight fish entrees, plus daily specials. There are also five daily pasta dishes.

At dinner, there is an even larger selection. Fresh fish is offered either sautéed with lemon butter, grilled with ancho chili sauce, poached in champagne, or baked in parchment. All in all, an incredibly ambitious menu and a kitchen to back it up.

J.R.'S, *2326 J Street; (916) 448-8876. Lunch Monday through Friday, dinner Tuesday through Saturday, brunch Sunday. Full bar. MC, Visa, Am Ex. Inexpensive to Moderate for lunch; Moderate to Expensive for dinner.*

✔ **Pava's.**   One day the lunch special at Pava's was that traditional Italian favorite tortellini with Cajun cream, turkey and peppers. Okay, okay; so Marcella Hazan might not approve, but the combination worked and the dish was wonderful. It's this spirit of culinary adventure that makes Pava's such an interesting place, and the fact that the food is good and the atmosphere very homey and pleasant that makes Pava's a terrific restaurant.

Pava's became a hangout years ago, back in the days when people were starting to dress and eat in ways that shouted ALTERNATIVE LIFESTYLE. As the years have gone by, Pava's has kept step with the times while still holding on to its folksy atmosphere. Today it is a combination New Age–California Cuisine restaurant.

At lunch you can get anything from a hamburger to the pasta of the day to Asian chicken salad with soba noodles to a vegetarian burrito. For dinner the menu features a selection of light supper items plus such heavy artillery as New York steak and grilled chicken or fish. Last but not least, Pava's has an espresso machine, a staff that knows how to use it, and sinful desserts.

PAVA'S, *2330 K Street; (916) 443-2397. Breakfast, lunch, and dinner Monday through Saturday, brunch Sunday. Beer and wine only. MC, Visa. Inexpensive to Moderate.*

✔ **Weatherstone Coffee and Trading Company.**   In contrast to the jumping scene at Java City (see page 122), Weatherstone seems sedate. This tasteful and low-key cafe with tables inside and out is a very friendly place, good for a pick-me-up espresso drink and is a place to keep in mind if you want a light meal: chicken or vegetarian tamales, tabouleh and pasta salads, housemade soups, and small salads. The lovely old brick building that houses Weatherstone is located in the general vicinity of the city's bed-and-breakfast establishments.

WEATHERSTONE COFFEE AND TRADING COMPANY, *812 Twenty-first Street; (916) 443-6340. Open 7 A.M. to 11 P.M. daily. No alcohol served. All nonsmoking. MC, Visa, Am Ex. Inexpensive.*

STOCKTON   ✔ **The Fish Market.**   Overlooking the port of Stockton is a place called The Warehouse, which is a local version of San Francisco's Ghiradelli Square. Indeed, it is an old and large warehouse that has been converted into a shopping center and features a few nice restaurants with a river view. One, The Fish Market, is a large, ambitious restaurant which would look at home near Boston Harbor or San Francisco's Fisherman's Wharf. As you enter, you see an ice case with today's catches on display. There's a large bar, waitpersons in their white shirts and black ties and white aprons, and diners wolfing down portions of fresh fish, rice, and sourdough bread. Again, you can eat either inside a very large and attractive dining room or out on the deck, closer to the water. You should be advised that it gets very hot in Stockton during the summer, and the inside is comfortably air-conditioned.

The menu offers a wide variety of choices, from simply broiled or grilled fish to more elaborate dishes that feature sauces. We advise sticking to simplicity whenever possible and making it clear how you want your fish done. Most places assume the customer wants it cooked well through, which often dries out even the best and freshest piece of fish. At The Fish Market they will cook it "rare" for you if you insist.

THE FISH MARKET, *445 West Weber, in The Warehouse; (209) 946-0991. Lunch and dinner daily, brunch Sunday. Full bar. MC, Visa, Am Ex. Moderate.*

✔ **Ye Olde Hoosier Inn.**   First a confession, or at least a declaration. Both authors of this guidebook are Hoosiers, having grown up in the great state of Indiana. This qualifies us to judge the authenticity of a California establishment that dares to promise Hoosier food. It also makes us wonder why anyone would be drawn to a place promising such cuisine. New Orleans, sure. Hong Kong, Florence, or Paris. How enticing! But Hoosier?

Well, the fact is this is one of the oldest and most successful restaurants in town and was actually started by some folks who were homesick for Indiana and midwestern life. It also happens to be very inexpensive, folksy, and charmingly kitsch, with wonderful waitresses who have been there and back. The food is authentically small-town hoosier, except for the absence of Jell-O salad and lunch meats.

The big seller is the fried chicken, which is an ample portion of heavily battered chicken served with overcooked vegetables and potatoes. There are also other traditional entrees, like ham, chicken-fried steak and pork chops, and biscuits and cream pies to keep you from going away hungry. This is the kind of place you try for the experience and sincere corniness, and even if it would hardly qualify as a great meal, you somehow leave feeling more cheerful than when you went in.

YE OLDE HOOSIER INN, *1537 N. Wilson Way; (209) 463-0271. Breakfast, lunch, and dinner daily. No alcohol. No credit cards. Inexpensive.*

CHAPTER **11** Gold Country

The Gold Rush's gastronomic contributions are rather modest: sourdough bread (in fact, the miners were called "sourdoughs") and the Hangtown Fry. The latter is an omelet with oysters, first concocted in the town of Placerville, where a hangman's noose still decorates Main Street. In other words, in contrast to areas like Napa and Sonoma, food is not the main draw around here.

Once you downgrade your expectations, however, there are surprises to be found. As the Gold Country develops a wine industry, adventurous restaurateurs have begun to crop up here and there. This is particularly true of the Northern Mines area, around Nevada City.

As a general rule, good food in the Gold Country is wholesome and unpretentious rather than innovative or exotic. The best places are those that use local ingredients and cook simply. Our experience is that those restaurants that try to pass as "gourmet" are to be avoided.

✔ **Larry's 4 K's Drive-in.**   Outside Murphys is a small town called Avery, where you'll find a very friendly cafe-diner that's a family operation. There really is a Larry, and the four K's are his wife and three daughters: Karen, Kathryn, Kath-

AVERY

leen, and Karla, I think. They all moved up here from Berkeley a few years ago to set up a dream life in the Gold Country, a dream that included having their own restaurant. This old converted drive-in serves burgers, hot dogs, and milkshakes, but these are really good burgers, hot dogs, and milkshakes, plus homemade fried chicken, a fishwich made from real fish, soup, or spaghetti—whatever they feel like cooking up that day. There are a surprising number of items on the menu, and there's a real family feeling about the place.

LARRY'S 4 K'S DRIVE-IN, *Highway 4; (209) 795-2661. Breakfast, lunch, and dinner daily. Beer and wine only. No credit cards. Inexpensive.*

COLUMBIA ✔ **City Hotel.**   If you're in the southern part of the Gold Country, you should plan on lunch or dinner at the City Hotel. The setting is the dining room of Columbia's original hotel, built in 1856. Both the lodging accommodations and the dining room are staffed by students enrolled in the Hospitality Program at local Columbia College.

The style could be described as Wild West elegant, with Victorian flourishes and china inside this building that could be a set for a western. The service is quite formal, with linen napkins and chilled forks and plates for the salad.

The menu follows suit. Appetizers include escargot bourguignon and French onion soup. At lunch, one can get such modern concoctions as a mesquite-grilled hamburger or club sandwich; or at lunch and dinner one may order such fancy dishes as grilled chicken breast in a champagne mustard seed sauce or pork sautéed in pecans and white wine. The dessert selection is extensive, including a fresh fruit sorbet, soufflés, cherries jubilee, and an assortment of pastries and cakes, all made on the premises by struggling students.

Sometimes a young server will need assistance when opening a bottle of wine, but it only adds to the charm of the place. The service tends to be enthusiastic and attentive as the students learn the ropes of fine dining service. Good places to eat are few and far between in this part of the world, which makes the fact that one can get escargots and a freshly tossed Caesar salad with chilled fork even more appealing. Making reservations at least two weeks in advance is recommended.

CITY HOTEL, *Main Street; (209) 532-1479. Lunch daily Easter through November 1; Wednesday through Sunday the rest of the year. Dinner nightly Memorial Day to Labor Day; closed Mondays the rest of the year. Be sure to call ahead. Full bar. All nonsmoking. MC, Visa, Am Ex. Moderate to Expensive for lunch, Expensive for dinner.*

EL DORADO ✔ **Poor Red's.**   The average visitor to the Gold Country doesn't find a lot of reasons to come to the town of El Dorado, unless the wind is just right. Then maybe you will catch a whiff of strong barbecue. If so, follow your nose, and Route 49 to Poor Red's. This place looks the way a barbecue joint should look. No fancy tables, no decor at all to speak of. There is just a long bar, a tiny dining room, and a huge back room with an oven that takes up one wall, where they smoke some of the best meats this side of Kansas City.

This is one of the few places that hates being included in a book like this or being shown on TV. They say they have enough business and aren't looking for any publicity. Still, we figured we had to tell you about one of the best and cheapest barbecue spots in Northern California. Their ribs and chicken are worth a trip out of the way. At lunch, they serve mainly sandwiches and platters like sliced barbecued pork or beef; then ribs come out in the evening, after they've cooked all day.

POOR RED'S, *Main Street; (916) 622-2901. Lunch Monday through Saturday, dinner nightly. Full bar. No nonsmoking section. MC, Visa. Inexpensive.*

✔ **Tofanelli's.** This spacious downtown cafe is a paradise for vegetarians. The meat eaters in your party can be well fed, too. While one gets a juicy hamburger, the other can have a tofu burger, and the cholesterol-conscious person can have a turkey burger. Several casserole-type vegetarian entrees are also offered, and the huge garden salads are a feast for eyes and palate.

TOFANELLI'S, *302 West Main Street; (916) 273-9927. Breakfast and lunch daily, dinner Monday through Friday. Beer and wine only. MC, Visa. Inexpensive to Moderate.*

GRASS VALLEY

✔ **Theresa's.** This is where the locals eat in the Sutter Creek–Jackson area. Theresa's is a friendly Italian restaurant serving pasta dishes, chicken, veal, and fresh seafood in sizable quantities. Although the family is from Genoa and usually offers a Northern Italian pesto dish or two, the sauces run to the Southern Italian tomato-and-oregano variety.

THERESA'S, *1235 Jackson Gate Road; (209) 223-1786. Dinner Friday through Tuesday. Full bar. No nonsmoking section. MC, Visa. Moderate.*

JACKSON

✔ **Jamestown Hotel**. A favorite among the locals, we find that it runs hot and cold; at a single meal some dishes will be outstanding, others not so great. However, it's still one of the better options in the southern Mother Lode. The dining room is quite lovely, with balloony chintz draperies and floral Victorian wallpaper. Sunday brunch is a big deal here with fancy offerings like sirloin steak and eggs and various daily specials. Lunch features a selection of informal fare, mainly sandwiches and salads and the good old American standby: the cheeseburger.

Dinner is the main meal here. Last time we ate at the Jamestown Hotel, Jerry had the free-range veal in a wild mushroom sauce and it was excellent; Catherine had a Gorgonzola linguine, and it didn't work. What the heck, 50/50 is not bad.

JAMESTOWN

JAMESTOWN HOTEL, *Main Street; (209) 984-3902. Lunch and dinner daily, brunch Sunday. Full bar. All nonsmoking. MC, Visa, Am Ex. Moderate.*

NEVADA CITY ✔ **Jack's Creekside Cafe.**   This used to be a rather unusual place called Jack's for Dinner; you would call ahead for a reservation and Jack would go to the store and shop for the number of folks who called by 5 P.M. Of course, you would be at the mercy of Jack's mood, but you would also get a memorable five-course meal served on fine china, with crystal and silver at the place settings.

Now, Jack and his partner, Jack, have expanded to serve lunch, dinner, and Sunday brunch, and the course selection is up to you. The cuisine is usually continental, but the exact menu will depend on the season. It's a good idea to call ahead for reservations.

In good weather, you may dine outside by the creek.

JACK'S CREEKSIDE CAFE, *101 Sacramento Street; (916) 265-6641. Lunch Tuesday through Saturday, dinner Wednesday through Saturday. Beer and wine only. MC, Visa. Moderate to Expensive.*

✔ **Michael's Garden Restaurant.**   In a small house in the main section of town, Michael's Garden Restaurant serves continental dishes and prepares them quite well. Features of the restaurant include imaginative sandwiches and stir frys at lunch, and elegantly prepared steak, seafood, and pasta dishes at dinner. At lunch or dinner, try the lemony cheesecake, a house specialty. This is a relaxed place with small dining rooms for intimacy.

MICHAEL'S GARDEN RESTAURANT, *216 Main Street; (916) 265-6660. Lunch Tuesday through Friday, dinner Monday through Saturday. Beer and wine only. MC, Visa. Moderate.*

PLACERVILLE ✔ **Cafe Zoe.**   If you happen to be in Placerville, your best bet for a meal is right in the center of town. Zoe's is a charming place featuring housemade soups and freshly baked breads, scrumptious desserts, and an espresso bar. It's a good stop for lunch if you're in the central Gold Country or on the way back from South Tahoe.

CAFE ZOE, *301 Main Street; (916) 622-9681. Lunch Monday through Saturday, dinner Friday through Sunday, plus brunch Sunday. Beer and wine only. MC, Visa. Inexpensive to Moderate.*

SONORA ✔ **Good Heavens—A Restaurant!**   The name gives you an idea of the good humor and exuberance behind this cafe. The decor is sort of flea market Victorian, like dining in a quirky tearoom. The owner and his helpers are so exuberant while extolling the virtues of their housemade quiche, soups, salads, sandwiches, and daily specials that you will want to try everything. Then just wait until they tell you about their cakes . . . Supposedly, *Gourmet* magazine has been trying to coax the recipes out of them. It's a place full of good-natured fun, and the food is good if not spectacular. This is a nice lunch to stop for if you are passing through town and want a light meal.

GOOD HEAVENS—A RESTAURANT!, *49 N. Washington Street; (209) 532-3663. Lunch Monday through Saturday, brunch Sunday. Beer and wine only. No nonsmoking section. No credit cards. Inexpensive to Moderate.*

✔ **Hemingway's.** Even in San Francisco, Hemingway's would be considered a good restaurant; considering it's located in the Gold Country, it's incredible. Hemingway's was started by Robert DeVinck, who had worked in various restaurants around Carmel. Wanting to open his own place, he realized that Carmel needed another restaurant like everybody needs a hole in the head, so he gambled on starting a fine dining—California Cuisine establishment in the southern Mother Lode.

Lucky for us all, his risk panned out, to use the jargon of the region. Nowhere else nearby will you be offered dishes like grilled Astoria sturgeon with orange-jalapeño butter, sweet potato hash browns, and carmelized pears, not to mention fresh linguine with a tequila and lime cream sauce. Last time we stayed in the Gold Country, Hemingway's was the only restaurant we visited that offered a sandwich on whole-grain bread. Even the house vegetarian plate, which usually is the blandest, albeit healthiest, selection one can make, was presented creatively and with a variety of zingy tastes.

Hemingway's makes a fresh soup of the day and offers familiar items like hamburgers and salads along with more exotic selections involving kiwi and unpronounceable sauces. Everything from soup to dessert is made there and is excellent. Also, the wine list is worth noting, with a wide selection of California wines and featuring premium Gold Country product.

The menu changes daily, depending on what's fresh and available. The selection and prices stay constant for the day. The atmosphere is very pleasant, with tablecloths and photographs of the namesake author on the wall plus a shelf of his books displayed with silk roses. Reservations advised, especially for dinner.

HEMINGWAY'S, *362 S. Stewart Street; (209) 532-4900. Lunch Tuesday through Friday, dinner Wednesday through Sunday. Beer and wine only. MC, Visa, Am Ex. Moderate to Expensive.*

✔ **Sonka's Apple Ranch.** As we've mentioned, people do not come to the Gold Country for the primary purpose of finding good food. However, there is one dish that is worth a trip to the Gold Country, and that's the mile high apple pie at Sonka's

Apple Ranch, just outside the town of Sonora. This dish has become so popular that nearly every freezer in the greater southern mines area contains at least one Sonka pie.

These pies are wonderful, and you can watch them being made. For health code reasons you stand behind a plate glass window in the gift shop. You will be spellbound as the ladies turn pie making into a spectacle. They also make other pastries, including mile high strawberry pie (in season, of course), plus a variety of jams and jellies—it's all so darn wholesome.

The usual routine for the visitor is to walk around the gift shop for a while, to watch the pies being made, then to order a slice of pie hot from the oven. You can eat it while seated at one of the many picnic tables located between the ranch house and the gift shop. Then, if the season is right, you can watch apples being picked, sorted, and crushed for cider. Peak apple season is late summer through autumn.

SONKA'S APPLE RANCH, *Cherokee Road; (209) 928-4689. Open 8 A.M. to 5:30 P.M. daily; closed major holidays. No credit cards. Inexpensive.*

CHAPTER **12** Lake Tahoe

This is a region of California people visit for its beauty and recreational opportunities. Because there's a captive audience and real estate is at a premium, chain- and franchise-food operations flourish here. Winter is a particularly grim time for the culinary arts; the location alone makes the shipment of fresh vegetables, etc., difficult if not impossible.

Fortunately, there are a few restaurants that are just about as good as the places you'd find closer to San Francisco, run by proprietors who make the effort to obtain high-quality ingredients. Breakfast is a particularly good bet.

CARNELIAN BAY ✔ **Old Post Office Restaurant.**   Before you hit the slopes or head out on a hike, you might want to stoke up on breakfast at the Old Post Office Restaurant. This place is a North Lake Tahoe tradition, and even if you are not a huge eater, you might enjoy watching others wolfing down stacks of pancakes, biscuits and country gravy, and various egg dishes. The food is pretty good here, but the emphasis is on volume.

OLD POST OFFICE RESTAURANT, *5245 North Lake Boulevard; (916) 546-3205. Breakfast and lunch daily. No alcohol. No credit cards. Inexpensive.*

✔ **Cantina Los Tres Hombres.** If you are looking for a place that is filled with people out for a good time, head for the Cantina. This mammoth Mexican-American restaurant has many rooms and serves enormous portions of decent enchiladas, tacos, and burritos. Atmosphere is king, however, and the big draw seems to be the huge pitchers of margaritas. Many folks never make it past the drinks and appetizers in the lounge. The nachos alone could satisfy a normal appetite.

CANTINA LOS TRES HOMBRES, *765 Emerald Bay Road, at Tenth Street; (916) 544-1233. Lunch and dinner daily. Full bar. No nonsmoking section. MC, Visa, Am Ex, Diners, Discover. Moderate.*

✔ **Sorenson's Country Cafe.** If you happen to be in the vicinity of Markleeville, where people go to soak in Grover Hot Springs, or Kirkwood, where people go to ski, arrange to have breakfast or lunch at Sorenson's. It's right on Route 88, about a half hour south of the lake. This is a resort and conference center (more details about that in our Lodging Section, see page 226) with a very laid-back cafe. How laid back? Well, last time we were there, in the middle of taking an order, the owner-host looked at his watch and said, "Oh, I have to run down the road to meet my kids. I'll be back in about ten minutes." Sure enough, his guests waited, enjoying the roar of the fire and the George Winston music playing, not minding a bit. In other words, this is the sort of place to go when you're not in a hurry.

The dining room consists of three big, rough-hewn tables that you share with others. The tiny kitchen behind the dining room—lodge reception area—lobby produces wonderful stews, soups, quiches, pasta salads, and housemade breads for lunch. We recommend the beef burgundy and the chicken brunswick stews, especially during winter visits.

Breakfast includes a variety of muffins, bagels, and croissants, plus waffles, quiche, and a hearty morning stew.

If you're able to give yourself over to the slow-paced rhythm of the resort, this is the sort of place you leave feeling better than when you walked in.

SORENSON'S CAFE, *Route 88; (916) 694-2203. Breakfast and lunch daily, dinner Thursday through Tuesday. Beer and wine only. All nonsmoking. MC, Visa. Inexpensive.*

✔ **Cafe Fiore.** The tiny restaurants seem to be the best bets for good food in the Lake Tahoe area. There are lots of huge operations with lots of noise and fun seekers downing cocktails and hors d'oeuvres before dinner. This is simply not our style. We prefer quiet, cozy places like the Cafe Fiore, which has about ten tables, a husband-and-wife team in the kitchen, and an efficient waitress navigating the area in between.

Cafe Fiore serves simple Northern Italian cuisine. You will have at least nine pasta selections, three chicken dishes, and several meat or fish entrees to choose from. Although the place doesn't make its own pasta, the sauces are housemade and are quite good and the prices are reasonable. Desserts are made fresh daily and espresso drinks are available.

The restaurant is tucked away in the rear of a small shopping complex along the main road to the busy Heavenly Valley ski area. Cafe Fiore is a great place to carbo-load if you plan to spend the next day on the slopes. It's a small place, so reservations are advised.

CAFE FIORE, *Ski Run at Tamarack; (916) 541-2908. Dinner Monday through Saturday. Beer and wine only. All nonsmoking. MC, Visa. Moderate.*

✔ **Cuckoo's Nest.**   The Cuckoo's Nest is for a special, romantic evening, especially after you've hit the jackpot at one of the local casinos. This is expensive dining, but much, much better food than you will get in the fancy rooftop restaurants in the big hotels.

Anton Zemp, who boasts more than forty years of experience in fine restaurants in Switzerland and the United States, is the show here. He is the owner, chef, maître d', waiter, and probably the chief bottlewasher of this place he calls "the only petite restaurant in Lake Tahoe." The Cuckoo's Nest has but five tables.

Quality ingredients are the gimmick here (remember, we *are* in Tahoe, where things like fresh, crisp vegetables are special). All sauces are based on stock from his stockpot; he uses no MSG or salt and does not use a microwave. Only French roast coffee and loose-leaf tea is served (no instant or tea bags here). Obviously, you should not be in a hurry; all food is made to order.

Anton offers several interesting chicken, veal, fish, and beef dishes on his menu, but more likely than not he will entice you with his nightly specials. One night he featured a fresh morel mushroom sauce on veal fillets—a particularly memorable experience. We have friends who want to return to Tahoe just to eat here again. He's very proud of his personal service. The pace here is leisurely; the check does not arrive until it is asked for.

A word of caution: Be sure to ask the price of the recited specials, as they tend to be more expensive than the standard menu items; an unexpectedly high tab is a lousy way to end a great meal.

CUCKOO'S NEST, *2502 South Lake Tahoe Boulevard; (916) 541-0873. Dinner nightly. Beer and wine only. MC, Visa, Am Ex, Diners. Expensive.*

✔ **Dixie's Cajun and Creole Cafe.**   If this place were located in the heart of New Orleans or even San Francisco, we'd have a hard time recommending it. But considering where it's located, it is certainly a cut above most of the food to be found on the south shore.

At least you can get blackened fish and a good house salad (the house dressing is truly great, a spicy combination of seasonings they won't divulge). Another tip: the corn and crab soup and desserts.

Of course you'll find on the menu signature items: gumbo, jambalaya, red beans and rice, a variety of blackened fish—including catfish, all of it fresh—and blackened chicken. The fish entrees come with pan-fried potatoes, corn on the cob, and sweet cornbread muffins. The kitchen offers five degrees of hotness: mild, medium, one, two, or three stars. As a barometer, Catherine, who can eat very hot spices, ordered the two stars then realized that three would have been no problem. If you play it safe and would like more hotness on your plate, shakers of chili peppers are provided next to the salt and pepper on the table.

This is a very friendly cheery spot with lots of stuff: blackened pans suspended from the rafters, flags, aprons, Tabasco sauce packaging, drawings by school-children decorate the walls. Smoking and nonsmoking sections are in separate rooms, divided by the entryway; smokers can puff away without disturbing any-one, and nonsmokers can have their breathing space.

DIXIE'S CAJUN AND CREOLE CAFE, *681 Emerald Bay Road; (916) 541-0405. Dinner nightly. Beer and wine only. MC, Visa. Moderate.*

✔ **Heidi's Pancake House.** Though decorated to look like a Swiss chalet, Heidi's is a 100 percent American breakfast restaurant that also happens to serve lunch and dinner. You'll recognize the look inside immediately: booths of dark wood with leatherette seats, lamps with gold chains, imitation stained glass, and wait-resses dressed in those nifty brown dresses with the starched pockets and the apron that picks up on the trim of the dress. Before you even order, someone will be around with an insulated container of hot coffee; not strong, but hot.

All of the breakfasts are good and ample, but the pancakes are the winners. So are the waitresses, who love to kid and tease and let their hair down. If you're having breakfast in South Lake Tahoe, you've got to try Heidi's.

HEIDI'S PANCAKE HOUSE, *3485 Highway 50; (916) 544-8113. The breakfast menu is served from 7 A.M. to 5 P.M. all day, dinner is from 5 P.M. to 9 P.M.; open every day. Beer and wine only. MC, Visa. Inexpensive to Moderate.*

✔ **Hot Gossip.** This is where the best hot chocolate and best espresso drinks on the south shore are to be found. It's a tiny place within a small shopping mall, with only a few tables and a couple of counter seats overlooking the parking lot. Caffeine addicts will be pleased to be offered a "coffee of the day" in addition to cappuccino.

Those with a sweet tooth can choose from a variety of freshly baked muffins, brownies, and cookies, including an unusual offering called a Ninja star: a triangular-shaped layered goodie, consisting of shortbread, nuts, with the tips dipped in chocolate.

The coffee bar also has a newsstand with an admirably eclectic selection, including *Time, American Film,* and newspapers from the greater Bay Area.

HOT GOSSIP, *Highway 50 at Ski Run; (916) 541-4823. Open 7 A.M. to 7 P.M. daily. No alcohol. No nonsmoking section. No credit cards. Inexpensive.*

TAHOE CITY

✔ **Lakehouse Pizza.**   Here you have a pizza parlor, Tahoe-style. The jukebox is blaring, everyone is beautifully tanned and in great shape, and the waitresses are incredibly bubbly because they have either just returned from the lake or the slopes or are heading that way.

The food is also geared for active people. They serve enormous portions of pasta, gigantic hero sandwiches, pretty good pizza, and other dishes you can enjoy as you look out on the lake. At lunch, Lakehouse Pizza is a good place to relax; at dinner and into the night, the joint is jumping.

LAKEHOUSE PIZZA, *120 Grove Street, on the lakeside in the center of Tahoe City; (916) 583-2225. Breakfast, lunch, and dinner daily. Full bar. No nonsmoking section. MC, Visa, Am Ex. Inexpensive to Moderate.*

✔ **Rosie's.**   For a meal in Tahoe City that's more substantial than pizza (see Lakehouse Pizza, above), more casual than Wolfdale's (see page 135), Rosie's offers American-style food excellently prepared. This lively spot is right across the road from The Lake. It's decorated like a spiffy roadhouse or lodge, with antler chandeliers, Indian rugs draped over the rafters, a huge stone fireplace, and a collection of antique bicycles, baby carriages, and skis.

The kitchen is a busy place, and they really know how to cook back there. A variety of excellent muffins and breads are baked daily and are served with sandwiches, salads, and egg dishes, or may be purchased to take home. The bran muffins are the best around and are huge; we took one back to the hotel for the next morning and couldn't eat the whole thing.

The breakfast menu is served until three in the afternoon, and you can get three-egg omelets, huevos rancheros, eggs Benedict, the "straight all-American breakfast" (two eggs, three slices of bacon, country potatoes, and choice of toast), waffles, French toast, and Swedish oatmeal or sourdough pancakes.

The lunch includes cheeseburgers, housemade soups, salads, plus a variety of sandwiches served on thick slices of freshly baked bread.

Dinner features entrees from the mesquite grill, including fresh fish, steaks, pork tenderloin, and a variety of chicken dishes, including jerk chicken (the name refers to the hot Caribbean spices, not to you or the chicken herself) and lemon chicken, plus pasta, roast duck, and stir-fried vegetables over wild rice. For the fat and cholesterol-conscious, grilled items are available without butter or oil.

Desserts include New York–style cheesecake, bachelor bait chocolate cake (it's just what you'd imagine it to be), and peanut butter pie.

By the way, the house coffee is excellent, and espresso drinks are also available. The bar attracts a lively bunch in the afternoons and evenings, so if you want some action and something good to eat, this is the place to go. There's live music and dancing at Rosie's every Tuesday night.

And yes, there really is a Rosie.

ROSIE'S, *571 N. Lake Boulevard; (916) 583-8504. Breakfast, lunch, and dinner daily. Full bar. No nonsmoking section. MC, Visa, Am Ex, Diners. Moderate.*

✔ **Wolfdale's.** The most written-about restaurant in the north Tahoe area is Wolfdale's, which offers what it calls "cuisine unique." We call it California Cuisine with a Japanese influence. Every plate is beautifully arranged and presented, the ingredients will be fresh and seasonal, and the food will be perfused with subtle combinations of tastes. This is one of those spots that is on most people's must list, so be sure to plan ahead and have a reservation well in advance of your visit. Also be advised that there is always a built-in danger when you go to places that have had so many rave reviews. It's difficult to live up to advance expectations. Still, this is inventive cooking, using the best available ingredients and with every attempt made to create a memorable meal.

WOLFDALE'S, *640 North Lake Boulevard; (916) 583-5700. Dinner Wednesday through Monday; closed Tuesday. Full bar. All nonsmoking. MC, Visa. Moderate to Expensive.*

✔ **The Left Bank.** The Left Bank couldn't have survived in Truckee ten years ago. This used to be a very blue-collar town with very few tourists. Dining establishments had to cater to the rail and lumber crowd, and that meant lots of burgers and steaks and fries. But now, Truckee is as gentrified as most places in the Bay Area; walk down Commercial Row and you'll have your pick of pasta, pizza, Mexican, Chinese, and other varieties of cuisine, most of it pretty good.

TRUCKEE

But nothing in town can compare to Paula Baudry's cooking at The Left Bank. Taught by her husband, who used to be head chef at Maxim's in Paris, Ms. Baudry creates delightful lunches and dinners that are as good as anything you'll find in the well-known restaurants in San Francisco.

As you enter you are greeted by the peaceful strains of classical music, so peaceful, I might add, that we blissfully missed our Amtrak train (the station is right across the street). Oh, well, we shrugged when we realized our dilemma; anything for a good meal. The decor is simple but elegant, with red brick and stone walls, red carpeting, and well-placed tiers of booths, which offer each party a feeling of privacy.

Lunch is a real bargain, with many of the entrees in the six- and seven-dollar range. The menu is eclectic, offering cheeseburgers, baked brie, huge salads, pasta dishes, and fresh salmon. In addition, there are daily specials. We sampled the osso buco, a seafood pasta, and the jambalaya, and we're pleased to report everything was good. Desserts included chocolate mousse and a rum-raisin cheesecake; both were lavish productions, with swirls of sauces filling the plate.

Dinner offers a choice of entrees, including fresh seafood dishes. Prices are likely to be about double the lunch menu. The Left Bank also has an extensive wine list.

THE LEFT BANK, *1098 Commercial Row; (916) 587-4694. Lunch and dinner Wednesday through Monday; closed Tuesday. Beer and wine only. No nonsmoking section. MC, Visa, Am Ex. Moderate at lunch, Expensive at dinner.*

✔ **Squeeze Inn.**   Okay, we admit it. We can be seduced by names. We couldn't resist having breakfast in a place called the Squeeze Inn. In spite of its name, it's a surprisingly large place. The specialty of the house is omelets. There are more varieties offered than you need to know about now, but suffice it to say they are of the four-egg variety and have a tendency to occupy most of the plate, with very good home fries and wheat-berry toast elbowing in. As the menu states with tongue in cheek, if you must be less adventurous you can get regular stuff like pancakes and hot cereals.

This is a very informal place that will make you glad you didn't settle for a franchise operation breakfast.

SQUEEZE INN, *Commercial Row; (916) 587-9814. Breakfast and lunch daily. Beer and wine only. All nonsmoking. No credit cards. Inexpensive.*

CHAPTER **13** Mendocino County

There are several things to keep in mind before planning to eat out a lot in this county, particularly in the popular tourist village of Mendocino. A lot of the restaurants do not accept credit cards. Bring cash, traveler's checks, and your checkbook to avoid a sticky situation. Also, many places are closed on Monday and Tuesday nights, if not for the entire winter. Plan your trip accordingly. You will find most of the good spots open on the weekends.

With all that in mind, you have some pleasant options in Mendocino County, ranging from typically American, unpretentious fare to restaurants that get notice in national publications.

✔ **Albion River Inn.**   As we mentioned in the introduction, many restaurants are closed on Monday and Tuesday. Thus this is an important restaurant to know about when visiting the Mendocino area. The Albion River Inn is not only a very good restaurant, it's also open seven nights a week.

The menu is ambitious, featuring the hit parade of California Cuisine dishes: grilled fish, fresh pasta, seasonal vegetables. The fish is very good, the pasta often a bit exotic, like linguine blackened with squid ink.

The restaurant is part of a large inn and is situated on the cliffs above Albion Cove. If you can, get there for sunset, because it's a great place to watch the sun go down. After dark you can't see anything but a sea of pitch black outside the window, but the sound of the ocean is lovely.

ALBION RIVER INN, *Coastal Highway One; (707) 937-1919. Dinner nightly. Full bar. MC, Visa. Moderate to Expensive.*

✔ **Boont Berry Farm.**   This place is a real find. Nestled next to the railroad car real estate office (a landmark in town), the Boont Berry Farm is sort of a health-food store—organic produce place that makes salads, soups, and sandwiches, including a burrito du jour, to eat there, or take on the road. You can also get a variety of juices and other healthy drinks. The store portion of the operation carries Bruce Bread, a very substantial loaf made by a legendary baker in town; if you love fresh bread as much as we do you'll want to take some home with you.

BOONT BERRY FARM, *13981 Highway 128; (707) 895-3576. Open 10 A.M. to 6 P.M. daily. Beer and wine only. No credit cards. Inexpensive.*

✔ **The Boonville Hotel.**   This operation will probably always be known as "That place that used to grow its own vegetables before the owners disappeared." Years ago, The New Boonville Hotel was a pilgrimage spot for fine diners all over the Bay Area. Hordes of people who had never heard of Boonville were suddenly invading this little agricultural and logging area to stroll in the garden and eat the perfectly prepared meals served here. When the complex operation got to be too much for the proprietors, they left town, literally in the middle of the night, leaving many unhappy employees and creditors.

So much for the past. The present owners have scaled down the ambitions of the place, which makes The Boonville Hotel (the current owners dropped the "New" from the name) less of a tourist attraction and more of just a plain fine place for lunch or dinner.

The menu changes daily, and there are only a few choices. A typical lunch menu might feature a mixed green salad, a soup of the day, a pizza, a hamburger

ALBION

BOONVILLE

(a truly great hamburger, we might add, with a housemade bun and served with a seasonal relish), a baked ham sandwich, and a quesadilla with chicken or chorizo, plus desserts and coffee. A typical dinner menu might feature salad, corn cakes, pizza of yellow tomatoes and goat cheese, grilled chicken breast, roast pork loin, a risotto, and desserts. With the addition of the wine list, that's the whole shebang.

Despite the size of the menu, we've never been disappointed with the meal.

THE BOONVILLE HOTEL, *corner of Highway 128 and Lambert Lane; (707) 895-2210. Lunch and dinner Wednesday through Sunday; closed Monday and Tuesday. Beer and wine only. All nonsmoking. No credit cards. Moderate to Expensive.*

ELK ✔ **Roadhouse Cafe.** There's not much in this town, just a Shell station, a cemetery, a public park, a bar, several bed-and-breakfast places, and a great place for burgers and omelets. The Roadhouse Cafe is a friendly place, where locals drop by to shoot the breeze and warm up by the fire on cold days; visitors are made to feel welcome.

The cafe's claim to fame is that it serves the best tap water in all of Mendocino County. But when you're hungry you'll probably be more interested in the hearty daily specials like vegetarian black bean chili, homestyle muffins, coffee cakes, cookies, and good brewed coffee. There's also a cappuccino machine on the premises.

ROADHOUSE CAFE, *Highway One, next door to the Shell station; (707) 877-3285. Breakfast and lunch Tuesday through Sunday; closed Monday. Beer and wine only. No nonsmoking section. No credit cards. Inexpensive.*

FORT BRAGG ✔ **North Coast Brewing Company.** There's a new trend developing on the Backroads: pub food. It was born of the proliferation of brewpubs, microbreweries that make and serve their own beer on the premises. The food came as an afterthought to enhance the fresh beer. But often the food is so good that the brewpub is becoming a logical destination for teetotalers who just want to eat well.

The North Coast Brewing Company is one of the best of these places. It's located inside the most modern building on Main Street, and has a huge parking lot in front. The pub itself has two spacious rooms, each on either side of the glass-enclosed brewery equipment. One room is used for dining, the other for lounging and listening to jazz on the weekends.

The menu is designed to complement the beer. Of course there are burgers, chili, sausages, and salads, but also Cajun beans and rice and side dishes like hush puppies with a very garlicky aioli sauce, and church social potato salad. At dinner, additional entrees are on the menu, including a fresh fish catch of the day, broiled chicken, steak, and a pasta special.

It's a nicely run place, with an excellent policy of serving free soft drinks to the designated driver of a group that is there to indulge in the beer.

NORTH COAST BREWING COMPANY, *444 N. Main Street; (707) 964-BREW. Lunch and dinner daily. Beer and Mendocino wines only. No credit cards. Inexpensive to Moderate.*

✔ **The Restaurant.** It may appear a bit presumptuous to name one's business *The Restaurant*, but it turns out to be very appropriate here in Fort Bragg. This was the first spot in town to cater to just about every taste, serving fresh fish, chicken, beef, and vegetarian dishes and doing them all very well. With a fishing harbor nearby, you are likely to find a good choice of seafood. If you prefer simplicity, try the salmon steak, carefully broiled, with crisply cooked vegetables and a good salad. Nothing fancy, just reliably good food.

THE RESTAURANT, *418 North Main Street; (707) 964-9800. Lunch Monday, Tuesday, Thursday, and Friday, dinner Thursday through Tuesday. Beer and wine only. All nonsmoking. MC, Visa. Moderate.*

✔ **The Cheesecake Lady.** If you love desserts, stop in here. You'll find a tempting assortment on display, a few tables where you can sit and relax, and a counter espresso bar. This small cafe is the front section of a huge wholesale bakery operation that provides cheesecakes and other goodies to bakeries and restaurants as far away as San Francisco and Sacramento. We stop here every time we're in the area (solely in the name of research, of course). There are more flavors of cheesecake than we ever dreamed of, and the chocolate mousse cake is too good to be real. At breakfast you can get a croissant or muffin and a good cappuccino.

THE CHEESECAKE LADY, *on Route 101, next door to the Hopland Brewery; (707) 744-1441. Open 7:30 A.M. to 6 P.M. weekdays, 9:30 A.M. to 5 P.M. weekends. No alcohol served. All nonsmoking. No credit cards. Inexpensive.*

✔ **Hopland Brewery, Tavern, Beer Garden, and Restaurant.** For a very good lunch or light dinner, this brewpub puts out a very respectable spread. You can get housemade soups, salads, juicy burgers, and daily specials that are surprisingly tasty and inventive. When the weather is warm, you can sit outside in the beer garden. As the name implies, they make their own beer, and it is very good. Nonbeer drinkers might enjoy the pub's housemade mineral water, and there is a full supply of nonalcoholic beverages.

HOPLAND BREWERY, TAVERN, BEER GARDEN, AND RESTAURANT, *13351 South Highway 101; (707) 744-1015. Lunch and dinner daily. Beer and wine only. No nonsmoking section. MC, Visa. Inexpensive.*

HOPLAND

✔ Sundial Grill.   This is an "uptown" place to dine in the Hopland area, a restaurant in which you won't feel out of place in a tie or nice dress. Located in the Fetzer Winery complex right on Highway 101, the Sundial Grill features California Wine Country Cuisine, which means that most of the ingredients (including the lamb, free-range chicken, specialty cheeses, exotic mushrooms, and edible flowers) were raised or grown within a few miles of the restaurant. In fact, the restaurant is a showcase for the beautiful produce grown by the Fetzer people at their nearby Valley Oaks Food and Wine Center; ask the host or hostess about visiting the garden after lunch (it's nearby and open to the public most of the time).

Tie or no tie, the Sundial Grill is worth going out of your way for. The meal begins with freshly baked focaccio, a dense Italian herb bread to be dipped in extra virgin olive oil. The rest of the menu changes with the seasons, but will always include a daily soup, salad, and items like duck enchilada; seafood cannelloni with Chardonnay cream sauce and caviar; Mendocino lamb; pork tenderloin served in a port reduction sauce; and grilled fish. Even nonvegetarians will enjoy the grilled vegetable and polenta plate (lunch only), served with an elegant and flavorful dipping sauce. And desserts? Well, since you asked, there will be seasonal fruit pies and tarts plus an assortment of year-round favorites, including a sensational peanut butter pie and a heart-stopping chocolate pâté.

SUNDIAL GRILL, *13500 S. Highway 101, in the Fetzer Complex; (707) 744-1328. Lunch and dinner Wednesday through Sunday, brunch Sunday. Wine only. All nonsmoking. MC, Visa, Am Ex. Moderate.*

LITTLE RIVER

✔ Little River Restaurant.   Not to be confused with the Little River Inn across the road, the Little River Restaurant is a teensy, tiny place adjacent to the post office. If you're in the area, this is definitely one place where you should go. There's nothing fancy about it; you'll feel comfortable in jeans, though you would not feel out of place in finery, either. There are two seatings for dinner, at six and at eight-thirty.

If this restaurant does not have the smallest dining room in Mendocino County, it certainly does have the smallest kitchen. It's fun to peek in and watch chef-owner Jeri Barrett, her sous chef, and the waitress practically dance together to get the food onto the plates and out to the customers.

Before she owned this restaurant, Jeri was in the quail-breeding business, and as a result she serves an amazing quail entree. The birds are larger and less gamey than what we usually get. After broiling, she serves them with a port hazelnut sauce that is worth the drive up the coast. The duck, too, is exceptional, served roasted with an apricot-vermouth sauce.

In addition to daily specials, the regular menu includes four appetizers: brie baked in phyllo pastry; steamed mussels; baked escargot, served with garlic butter; and sautéed prawns with a champagne beurre blanc sauce. If duck and quail are not to your liking, other entree items include salmon, snapper, rack of lamb, New York steak, and filet mignon. All entrees come with soup, salad, and fresh bread.

A variety of desserts are offered each night, including the house specialty, a chocolate-amaretto mousse.

LITTLE RIVER RESTAURANT, *7750 North Highway 1; (707) 937-4945. Dinner Friday through Monday; also open Tuesday in summer. Beer and wine only. All nonsmoking. No credit cards. Moderate to Expensive.*

✔ **Cafe Beaujolais.** This homey cafe near the main tourist action in Mendocino is a Bay Area favorite, garnering a lion's share of local and national publicity and the nickname "The Chez Panisse of the North Coast." Most food writers wax ecstatic about the cafe's breakfast, with its offerings of eggs fresh from a local ranch, housemade muffins and pastries, and a cup of coffee as good as you'll find anywhere in San Francisco.

Lunch features salads made with vegetables grown out in back of the restaurant or on nearby farms, plus sandwiches and daily specials. Dinner is a bit more adventurous, but all meals emphasize fresh ingredients prepared skillfully.

Recently the restaurant acquired a brick oven and now serves freshly baked breads and pizzas.

This place is popular with locals and visitors, so be prepared to wait.

CAFE BEAUJOLAIS, *961 Ukiah Street; (707) 937-5614. Breakfast and lunch daily, dinner Thursday through Sunday in spring and summer; call ahead in winter and fall for current schedule. Beer and wine only. No credit cards. Moderate.*

✔ **Chocolate Moosse.** Right in the heart of the village, across the street from a very good bookstore, is a nice little cafe for a late breakfast, light lunch, lovely dinner, or afternoon coffee break. Menu items are light fare along the lines of soups, pasta salad, lasagne, and spanikopita. Sweet things like coffee cake and blackout cake are displayed under glass domes, impossible to avoid. Meanwhile the sound system in the place plays soothing music, from classical music to whale songs (not songs about whales, but actual recordings of whales).

CHOCOLATE MOOSSE, *390 Kasten Street (at Albion); (707) 937-4323. Winter hours: 10 A.M. to 5:30 P.M. Sunday through Thursday, 10 A.M. to 10 P.M. Friday and Saturday. Summer hours: 10 A.M. to 9 P.M. Sunday through Thursday, 10 A.M. to 11 P.M. Friday and Saturday. Beer and wine only. All nonsmoking. No credit cards. Inexpensive.*

✔ **Mendocino Bakery and Cafe.** Though they do serve soup and salad here, the emphasis is on items that come out of the oven. The breads, pizzas, lasagnes, cakes, pies, muffins, and cookies lean to the healthy side, with the use of whole-wheat and organic flours, and sandwiches with contents like tofu. It's all very good and fresh, served to go or to consume in the attractive cafe setting. An espresso machine is also on the premises.

MENDOCINO BAKERY AND CAFE, *10455 Lansing Street; (707) 937-0836. Breakfast and lunch daily. No alcohol served. All nonsmoking. No credit cards. Inexpensive.*

✔ **Mendocino Cafe.** If you're hungry and not in a hurry, the Mendocino Cafe is a place to have a real Mendocino experience. At lunch, your waitress may arrive at your table carrying a baby on her hip. At dinner, one person's entree may arrive at the table twenty minutes before everyone else's. If you're going to eat here, you have to get into the spirit of the place, and if you can you will have a delicious, healthful, and inexpensive meal.

At breakfast, the more unusual offerings include blue cornmeal waffles and the breakfast burrito (eggs, salsa, and cheese wrapped in a tortilla). At lunch and dinner, the extensive menu includes at least one soup, barbecued chicken wings, pork ribs or chicken, smoked on the premises, and fresh fish. No lard or animal fat is used in preparing the food, and requests to cool it on the salt and additional oil are honored by the chef.

Weather permitting, you can dine outside on a patio that overlooks the ocean, which is at the end of the block.

MENDOCINO CAFE, *44980 Albion Street, at Lansing; (707) 937-2422. Breakfast, lunch, and dinner daily. Beer and wine only. All nonsmoking. No credit cards. Inexpensive.*

NOYO HARBOR ✔ **Carine's Fish Grotto.** Just south of Fort Bragg, and about twenty minutes north of Mendocino, is a little fishing harbor with several seafood restaurants. Our favorite is Carine's, though we've never tried any of their fish. We go to Carine's for the hamburger, an entire pound of good ground beef on a huge bun, accompanied by a sky-high mound of french fries—all for $6.50 (in 1989). You can sit inside or, weather permitting, outside at picnic tables on a dock overlooking the harbor, where working fishing boats putt out and in.

Carine's posts outrageous-looking prices for their dinners, but don't be discouraged. When I asked Mama Carine about an entree with a $35 price tag, she assured me it is enough to feed a party of five or six.

CARINE'S FISH GROTTO, *32430 North Harbor Drive; (707) 964-2429. Lunch and dinner daily. Beer and wine only. No credit cards. Inexpensive to Moderate.*

✔ **The Broiler Steak House.** We seldom eat steak at a restaurant, or at home for that matter. Most of the reasons have to do with avoiding fat, but we can also be put off by steakhouse prices in the San Francisco area. What a surprise to find The Broiler, which is on a backroad about seven miles north of Ukiah.

The restaurant sits all alone at night, across from a school. It looks like a roadhouse from the forties, the kind of place where you expect to see Ida Lupino behind a counter and Humphrey Bogart sitting in a booth. Everything is wood-paneled and homey. You know you are not entering into the domain of the trendy. This is the type of American cuisine most of us grew up eating.

Once you step inside you will know that this is where the locals hang out, at least those who want good red meat. And this is the place where I was glad to break out of my abstinence and try a steak for a change. Not only was it one of the best steaks I have ever had, but how do you like the sound of a giant top sirloin with potato, salad, and vegetable for $10.50?

As you can imagine, you dress informally in this rustic roadhouse. Jeans and a plaid shirt will do, for members of either sex. The waitresses are all efficient and friendly, and there is rarely a tourist in sight. There are other items on the menu, but the reason to come here is for a huge steak.

THE BROILER STEAK HOUSE, *8400 Uva Drive; (707) 485-7301. Dinner nightly. Full bar. MC, Visa, Am Ex. Inexpensive to Moderate.*

CHAPTER **14** Redwood Empire

Most of our dining experiences in this part of Northern California have been centered around Eureka and its neighboring communities. This is a long way from the Bay Area, as much as five hours by car, and the styles of restaurants are generally more similar to the Midwest than to San Francisco. Here are a few exceptions.

✔ **Carter Hotel.** In an attempt (and a successful one, we might add) to bring fine dining to this region of the Redwood Empire, the chic Carter Hotel serves dinner three nights a week. In the tradition of fine California restaurants, the menu changes frequently and is designed around the best ingredients available at the time. At least three entrees are offered, usually a fish, a meat, and a chicken dish, plus soups, salads, and pasta dishes. Breads and desserts are made on the premises. You may order à la carte or a complete dinner; the latter includes an entree, soup, after-dinner coffee, and cordial and is priced at $19.95—quite a bargain, when you think about it. Seating by advance reservations only.

CARTER HOTEL, *301 L Street; (707) 445-1390. Dinner Thursday through Saturday. Beer and wine only. All nonsmoking. MC, Visa, Am Ex. Moderate.*

✔ **Ramone's Cafe.** Ramone's is the spot for imaginative cuisine in the city of Eureka. Located in a tiny alley in the Old Town section, it's a charming little place succeeding in its attempts to present good food that is out of the ordinary.

For example, on one visit, two in our crew had to try the special of the evening called "chicken mamoo," which was advertised as being very spicy. We all tasted it and agreed it was the hottest dish any of us had ever eaten. It was also excellent. Other specials included an unusual stuffed steak, some more traditional veal and chicken dishes, and fresh fish. Everything was good and plentiful. Ramone's Cafe is probably your best bet in town for a place that's open regularly.

RAMONE'S CAFE, *409 Opera Alley, corner of Third and E streets; (707) 444-3339. Lunch Tuesday through Friday, dinner Tuesday through Saturday. Beer and wine only. MC, Visa, Am Ex, Diners. Moderate.*

✔ **Samoa Cookhouse.** Everybody who comes to the Eureka area must cross the bridge to the village of Samoa to eat in the historic cookhouse. Once the commissary for lumberjacks before they headed out into the forest, the cookhouse still serves up Paul Bunyon–size meals for hearty appetites. Part of the building is now a museum of the early logging industry, but there is still room to serve hundreds of people simultaneously.

Everything is served family style, and you get what they happen to be serving that day. Breakfast might be as many eggs as you can eat, potatoes, sausages, biscuits, juice, and coffee, with maybe a few pancakes thrown in. Lunch might feature endless plates of fried chicken, mashed potatoes, vegetables, rolls—you get the idea. The food is not what you would call Nouvelle Cuisine, but it's a real value.

Sunday dinner begins at noon. Though no alcohol is served, it's OK to bring your own.

SAMOA COOKHOUSE, *across the Samoa Bridge from Eureka; (707) 442-1659. Breakfast, lunch, and dinner daily; closed Thanksgiving and Christmas. MC, Visa, Am Ex, Diners, Discover. Inexpensive.*

FERNDALE ✔ **Becker's Pool Hall.** This is a real hangout for the citizens of Ferndale. In the front part of the room there's a lunch counter, a few tables, and some books and magazines. In the back there's always a card game in progress and a group of kibitzers huddled around the action. The only thing missing at Becker's Pool Hall is a pool table.

Lunch consists of sandwiches and whatever the cook happens to make that day; it might be chili, an elaborate casserole, or good old spaghetti. It really doesn't matter because the real reason to come here is the atmosphere and the chance to meet the townspeople, who are very devoted to and opinionated about their town. For what it's worth, the phone listing for the Pool Hall is under "Greek Investment Company."

BECKER'S POOL HALL, *409 Main Street; (707) 786-4180. Open 7 A.M. to 3 P.M. Monday through Saturday. No credit cards. Inexpensive.*

✔ **Ferndale Meats.**   For a wonderful and wonderfully huge sandwich sliced from big slabs of beef or ham right before your eyes, stop in at this butcher shop downtown. You can eat it there or take it on a picnic.

FERNDALE MEATS, *376 Main Street; (707) 786-4501. Open 8 A.M. to 5:30 P.M. Monday through Saturday. No alcohol. No credit cards. Inexpensive.*

✔ **Larrupin' Cafe.**   About a half hour north of Eureka out in the woods near the towns of McKinleyville and Trinidad is a very popular restaurant run by a woman named Dixie. That ought to be a clue to what you'll get here. *Larrupin'* is a southern term for good eating, and that's what Dixie offers at her cafe, although it is not what you might expect.

The menu is more along continental lines, offering a variety of steak, chicken, and other dishes. There are special touches, like the plank of appetizers and vegetables that are delivered to every table. Depending on the night, you might also find barbecue and Louisiana dishes. Dixie even bottles her secret sauces and sells them around the area. Larrupin' has a real following, so be sure to call ahead; reservations are a must.

LARRUPIN'S CAFE, *1668 Patrick's Point Drive; (707) 677-0230. In winter, dinner Friday, Saturday, and Sunday only; in summer, Wednesday through Monday. Beer and wine only. No nonsmoking section. No credit cards. Moderate.*

MCKINLEYVILLE

CHAPTER **15** Monterey, Carmel, and Big Sur

Because this is such a busy tourist center, there are almost as many restaurants on the Monterey Peninsula as there are in the San Francisco area. Unfortunately, there aren't nearly as many good ones.

Keep in mind that most of the huge fish houses near the wharf in Monterey are overpriced and tend to overcook their fish. In Carmel, the difficulty is often in getting into places (both restaurants and parking places) because of the crowds, which again results in high prices. We will limit our recommendations to the few out-of-the-way places we think are special, meaning they offer good food or an unusual only-in-the-area experience—and preferably both.

BIG SUR

✓ **Deetjen's Big Sur Inn.**   This is a very rustic, homey dining room in an equally rustic, even funky, inn next door to the Henry Miller Library. The food is house-made, with a limited menu offering steak, a vegetarian plate, and daily specials. The food is very fresh and wholesome. There's likely to be a fire in the fireplace, adding to the woodsy charm of the place. There are two seatings each night for dinner, and reservations are advised.

DEETJEN'S BIG SUR INN, *Route 1, 19 miles north of Lucia Lodge, one-half mile south of Nepenthe; (408) 667-2377. Breakfast and dinner daily. Beer and wine only. No credit cards. Moderate.*

✓ **Nepenthe.**   Nepenthe is a must stop for visitors in the area. In a dramatic setting overlooking the ocean, you can have burgers and housemade soup, baked chicken, steak, or vegetarian specialties. The food is simple and good, but that's not the main reason for stopping here. This is the only spot we can think of where you can be a tourist and get the genuine experience of Big Sur at the same time. The architecture is derivative of Frank Lloyd Wright, so the buildings become part of the landscape and enhance the feeling of the mountain. Folks come here just to walk around and see the spot where Orson Welles thought he and Rita Hayworth would live in paradise. They had an argument, early in their stormy marriage, and never moved in, but the story adds somehow to the pleasure of the visit.

If the wait for a Nepenthe table is too long, go down the outdoor steps to the smaller Cafe Amphora and have a light snack or a great dessert with cappuccino. The view is the best part of the visit anyway.

Guests park at road level and walk up a long, winding stairway to the restaurant. There is a smaller lot on the restaurant level for the staff and for disabled patrons.

NEPENTHE, *Route 1, 1 mile south of the Ventana Inn; (408) 667-2345. Lunch and dinner daily. Full bar. MC, Visa, Am Ex. Moderate.*

CARMEL

✓ **La Boheme.**   If the line is not too intimidating, you might like the adventure of eating in this small cafe. The menu changes daily, and the diner is not given a choice: what they cook, you eat, all served family style. The cuisine is European peasant food, and I should add that the peasants seem to eat better than the royalty. I suggest calling first to find out what's being served; unfortunately, they don't take reservations at the same time.

LA BOHEME, *Dolores at Seventh Street; (408) 624-7500. Dinner nightly. Beer and wine only. MC, Visa. Moderate.*

✓ **Thunderbird Bookshop Cafe.** This is a very nice family-owned-and-operated book-store and cafe, located in a large shopping mall. The cafe itself is in the back of the shop, among the shelves of history books, en route to the room where meta-physical literature is on display. At lunch you get your food by going through a cafeteria line. You begin by placing an order for soup or a sandwich (the smoked chicken sandwich is highly recommended, by the way, made with chicken cooked in the wood-burning stove and mixed with nuts and raisins). Then you and your tray head down to the salad bar section, where you can construct a giant concoction of assorted greens, garlicky croutons, curried rice, and pasta. You will also find a tempting array of desserts. By the time you reach the cash register, your sandwich will be ready.

Dinner is a more formal affair, with waiter and waitress service. The menu consists of such items as prime rib, rack of lamb, chicken cooked in Dijon mus-tard sauce, pasta, and nightly specials.

Afternoon tea and dessert are served in the cafe daily between 3:30 and 5:30. This is an almost entirely nonsmoking establishment.

THUNDERBIRD BOOKSHOP CAFE, *in The Barnyard Shopping Center, Highway One and Carmel Valley Road; (408) 624-9414. Lunch daily, dinner Tuesday through Sunday. Beer and wine only. MC, Visa. Inexpensive to Moderate.*

✓ **Rio Grill.** Owned by the group that brought us Mustard's in the Napa Valley and the Fog City Diner in San Francisco, the Rio Cafe is our favorite of the bunch. This is the kind of menu many places copy when they want to offer California Cuisine. Here you will get wonderful salads, fresh pasta, grilled fish and chicken, and a great burger, all served with imaginative sauces and made from the freshest ingredients. Unfortunately, you will also get a lot of company, as this is a very popular place.

CARMEL VALLEY

The decor is simple, with blond wood tables set against white walls, and the atmosphere is calm. This is quite an accomplishment, since the Rio Grill is in the center of a busy shopping center off the main highway. Reservations are advised.

RIO GRILL, *101 Crossroads Boulevard, in the Crossroads Shopping Center; (408) 625-5436. Lunch and dinner daily. Full bar. MC, Visa. Moderate to Expen-sive.*

MONTEREY ✔ **Nick's Oceanside Cafe.** Tourist areas like Cannery Row have more captive audiences; it's a rare treat to find a little cafe that's as good as a place locals might go to, which is the case with Nick's Oceanside Cafe. Open for breakfast and lunch only, Nick's has a salmon-colored dining room with tablecloths to match in what looks like a former warehouse or canning operation. Here you can get fresh squeezed orange juice, freshly ground French Roast coffee, traditional breakfast fare (eggs any style, a bread basket of toast, biscuits and muffins, and hash browns called Nick's Spuds) plus not-so-traditional fare (omelets made with low-cholesterol egg substitute, breakfast burritos), and a lunch menu of sandwiches, hamburgers, and Mexican dishes. Portions are large and the daily specials can be a bargain. Lunch is served until 4:30 P.M.

NICK'S OCEANSIDE CAFE, *700-H Cannery Row; (408) 649-1430. Breakfast and lunch daily. No alcohol. No nonsmoking section. No credit cards. Inexpensive to Moderate.*

MOSS LANDING ✔ **Moss Landing Oyster Bar.** Moss Landing is a commercial fishing town, and the Oyster Bar takes advantage of the location. You can start with such appetizers as fresh clams, crabs, and oysters, or Boston-style clam chowder, all served with a basket of slightly sweet brown bread and spongy sourdough. Lunch entrees feature pasta and more seafood; the dinner menu expands to include filet mignon and other beef dishes. Pay attention to the daily specials, because these feature the freshest catches from Monterey Bay. Most of the fish dishes are grilled and are served with imaginative sauces. Last time we were there, sand dabs were in season, and it was lots of fun to pick out the tiny bones to get at the sweet meat. The Monterey Bay salmon was less work but just as delicious, cooked just right with the outside bearing marks from the grill, the inside moist and tender.

A gentleman, obviously a regular customer, sat at the table next to us and asked the waitress if berry shortcake was available that day. When she said yes, he simply ordered the clam chowder as an entree, saving room for dessert. Being astute culinary detectives, we followed this guy's lead and ordered the shortcake. It was the best we'd had in ages, smothered in fresh strawberries and served on top of a cinnamon-y yellow cake with real (not canned) whipped cream.

The building looks like it might have once been a house. It's located right on the main drag of town, just off Highway 1.

MOSS LANDING OYSTER BAR, *413 Moss Landing Road; (408) 633-5302. Lunch and dinner Tuesday through Sunday. Beer and wine only. Nonsmoking section available. MC, Visa, Am Ex. Moderate at lunch, Expensive at dinner.*

✔ **The Whole Enchilada.** As you might expect, this place serves Mexican food. As you might not expect, it is a rather attractive and ambitious place that also offers jazz concerts on Sunday afternoons.

The Whole Enchilada is right off the highway, so it attracts many of the tourists driving by, along with a good mix of locals. It's apt to be jumping. The food is fairly standard Mexican-American fare, with good-size portions. The house specialty is seafood, most of it caught by local fishermen.

THE WHOLE ENCHILADA, *Highway 1; (408) 633-3038. Open 11:30 A.M. to 9 P.M. Wednesday through Monday; closed Tuesday. Full bar. MC, Visa. Inexpensive to Moderate.*

✔ **Fishwife Restaurant.**   While tourists shell out the bucks to eat in one of the many fancy-smancy restaurants in Carmel or on Monterey's Fisherman's Wharf, locals line up to eat at the Fishwife. Located near Asilomar Beach and attached to the BeachComber motel, this inexpensive, informal restaurant serves homestyle fish and pasta dishes. We're not going to say this is the best restaurant in the world, but it is very good and it is a bargain. It's also a great place for persons on restricted diets; most dishes can be prepared in a low-fat, low-sodium manner. Only vegetable oils are used—in other words, no artery-clogging animal fats will darken your plate—and fried fish is breaded with cornmeal (which supposedly absorbs less oil than bread crumbs). One of the specialties of the house is "air-fried potatoes"—basically strips of potatoes roasted without oil.

It's an attractive place and the service is very friendly. Expect to wait; this is a popular spot and reservations are accepted for only one-third of the tables.

FISHWIFE RESTAURANT, *1996½ Sunset Drive; (408) 375-7107. Lunch and dinner Wednesday through Monday; closed Tuesday. Beer and wine only. All non-smoking, except bar. MC, Visa, Diners. Inexpensive to Moderate.*

PACIFIC GROVE

✔ **Dona Esther.**   Backroads cameraman, triathelete, and world-class eater Jeff Pierce has been known to travel an hour out of his way to eat at Dona Esther. He claims they have the finest enchiladas he's ever eaten, and trust us, Jeff has eaten a lot of enchiladas. Jeff has also been known to have a weakness for the margaritas at Dona Esther.

Jeff is not alone in his passion for the place. The first time he took us there, we started a conversation with the man at the next table who said he had driven from San Francisco just to have lunch there.

I don't want to oversell the place, but Dona Esther is very good. The menu runs along traditional lines with tacos, flautas, and, of course, enchiladas, and the portions are very large. A nice added touch: the courtyard for eating outdoors on warm days and nights.

DONA ESTHER, *25 Franklin Street; (408) 623-2518. Breakfast, lunch, and dinner daily. Full bar. MC, Visa, Am Ex, Diners, Discover. Inexpensive to Moderate.*

SAN JUAN BAUTISTA

✔ **Felipe's.**   Although this may look like yet another Mexican restaurant, there is a difference. This is a Salvadoran-Mexican restaurant, so in addition to the tacos and so on, you can get pork stews and other dishes native to El Salvador. All the food is quite good, and the owner will be thrilled if you experiment with the Salvadoran specialties.

FELIPE'S, *313 Third Street; (408) 623-2161. Lunch and dinner Wednesday through Sunday. Beer and wine only. No credit cards. Inexpensive.*

✔ **Jardines de San Juan.**   As you can see, you will have no trouble finding Mexican food in San Juan Bautista. One of the most popular spots in town is just down the street from Dona Esther, and the food is quite similar. As suggested by the name Jardines, or gardens, you sit under the shade trees in a protected courtyard, and between courses you can wander through their impressive collection of cacti.

JARDINES DE SAN JUAN, *115 Third Street; (408) 623-4466. Lunch and dinner daily. Full bar. No nonsmoking section. MC, Visa. Inexpensive to Moderate.*

✔ **Mariposa House.**   If you're in San Juan Bautista and are in the mood for lighter fare than Mexican food, you can get quiche, pastas, salads, and sautés at the Mariposa House. The setting really is a house, a block off the main street. The food here is as close as you can get to California Cuisine anywhere in town.

MARIPOSA HOUSE, *37 Mariposa Street; (408) 623-4666. Lunch and dinner Tuesday through Sunday; closed Monday. No nonsmoking section. MC, Visa. Moderate.*

Backroads LODGING

"Do you know of a great bed and breakfast in the wine country that's not crowded, serves great food, is inexpensive, takes kids and pets, has a hot tub, and is out in the woods?" In one form or another, we get asked that question at least once a week. This part of the guide is designed to give you a lot of those kinds of places, depending on your particular needs. Please notice this is not a comprehensive guide to all accommodations in the Bay Area. We are concentrating on those places that have the feeling of the Backroads and getting away from it all. Therefore, we offer very few large hotels or chain operations. They usually locate where there is high traffic. This is a selective list of special places that struck our fancy. Be advised, however, that one person's cozy bed-and-breakfast inn is another person's Nightmare on Elm Street.

An example: In a resort town that shall remain unnamed, we checked into a place that sounded great—a Victorian mansion in a picture book setting. The first peculiar thing we noticed was the house dog, a really ugly, half dead–looking hellhound chained out back in the weedy parking lot. We were willing to pass over that first impression as we walked around to the front of the inn until we rang the doorbell, and the innkeeper who answered was this hollow-eyed, slightly stooped-over guy dressed sort of like a mortician. From there on in, the place seemed to us like a bad joke; we kept expecting Allen Funt to step out from behind a curtain to tell us this experience was being staged for "Candid Camera."

151

But no, this was the real thing. Everything in the place—the furnishings, the wife of the innkeeper, everything, to put it delicately—gave us the creeps. The bureau drawers were lined with dime store Christmas wrapping; the *tsatskes* (Yiddish for *schmutz*) used to decorate the room were like rejects from Woolworths. There was a feeling to the place that made us wonder if somebody with an axe was going to get us in the hallway.

And yet . . . at breakfast the next morning the other guests were chattering away, obviously enjoying the place and having a lovely time. A journal left for guests to write their impression of the place was filled with glowing descriptions of the wonderful accommodations and charming hosts.

So keep our likes and dislikes in mind when judging if one of our recommendations is really for you. For example, Jerry cares more about having a good feather pillow than whether there is room service. Catherine loves room service, but is more interested in an inn that does not allow smoking. Neither of us cares much about a hot tub. You may prefer a bed and breakfast where you can get really chummy with the proprietors; we would rather be ignored until we ask for something. As a general rule, we like to stay in places that offer private bathrooms; however, we have found lovely places that were such bargains that it would have been wrong not to include them just because of the plumbing (and if your timing is right, you will have that bathroom to yourself anyway). We like a full, cooked breakfast, but business permits in some areas forbid the innkeeper from supplying one. At some bed and breakfasts, continental means coffee and a roll, but at others, it means fresh fruit, cereal, hard-boiled eggs, freshly baked fruit tarts and pastries, and everything else that can keep them within their license.

The inns and hotels listed in this book are places we would choose to spend the night. They are clean, comfortable, unusual, and/or ambitious. We will try to supply as much objective information—TV or no TV, cutesy country charm or sophisticated elegance, etc.—for you to decide whether this place is for you.

An important thing to keep in mind is that if you choose an inn, or to stay in a spare cottage or room in someone's home, you will want to get to know the person running the place first. Phone or write the inn and ask questions that will satisfy you. Is there a two-night minimum? What about a cancellation policy? Also keep in mind that a really great innkeeper will spell everything out for you, anticipating your questions. In fact, a good rule of thumb is: If you like the innkeeper you'll like the inn. And vice versa.

Since it is impossible to pin down a price that will be the same by the time you read this, please use the range of prices as a basic guideline rather than gospel. Most of these prices are for single or double occupancy and do not include tax. In addition to phone numbers, we have also listed mailing addresses, so you can send away for brochures.

To help you to do some additional research, here are some services you might find useful:

✔ **American Family Inn/Bed and Breakfast.** This service makes arrangements for visitors to stay in private houses around San Francisco, the wine country, and the Monterey Peninsula. For an informational brochure, write P.O. Box 349, San Francisco, CA 94101, or call (415) 931-3083.

✔ **Bed and Breakfast International.** This service arranges lodging in private homes and apartments up and down the West Coast (and in Hawaii, Chicago, Las Vegas, Seattle, and New York City). For more information write to 151 Ardmore Road, Kensington, CA 94707, or call (415) 525-4569.

✔ **Bed and Breakfast Innkeepers of Northern California (BBINC).** This organization of innkeepers was founded in 1982 when it seemed like every other Victorian house was hanging out a bed-and-breakfast shingle. The idea was to establish a standard of comfort, cleanliness, and courtesy; each member inn is regularly inspected by other innkeepers to be sure the group standards are being maintained.

In our experience the concept works most of the time. Many of the inns recommended in this book are BBINC members, but others we would not recommend (including the House of Horrors described above) are also BBINC members. BBINC publishes an annual travel guide that lists all their member inns; if you use this guide, nine times out of ten you will find a good place to stay, and on the road those are pretty good odds. For a brochure write to P.O. Box 7150, Chico, CA 95927, or call 1-800-284-INNS.

One final note for those of you who require disabled access. Please phone ahead to make sure the access is really what you require. We have limited our listings for lodging quarters with wheelchair access to those that have state certification.

North Bay

CHAPTER **16** Marin County

The location of Marin County dictates that most of the places for getting away from it all at a special inn are in the western part of the county. Sure, there are hotels in Sausalito and San Rafael, but one is a bustling tourist town and the other is the business center of the county, and both are right off Highway 101. Besides, they are also so close to San Francisco that most visitors spend the night in the city to enjoy the best of both locations.

We will concentrate on lodging that is away from the crowds, which often means out toward the coast and the areas of Muir Beach, Inverness, and Point Reyes.

You may find it handy to know about two organizations out in the Inverness–Point Reyes area. Inns of Point Reyes and Bed and Breakfast Cottages of Point Reyes are the cooperative efforts of innkeepers and one-room cottagekeepers in the area who have formed a network and can provide referral services for you. If you would like the brochures of these member establishments, you can contact: Inns of Point Reyes at (415) 663-1420; and Bed and Breakfast Cottages of Point Reyes at (415) 927-9445.

✔ **Golden Hinde Motel.**   The dominant choice of accommodations in this inviting town is the bed-and-breakfast inn, but since our listings are alphabetical, we start with an alternative.

(See map on page 5.)

INVERNESS

155

If you're not in the mood for the chumminess and close quarters of bed-and-breakfast places and would prefer the anonymity that motel rooms can offer, check out this place. It's right on the main drag of the lovely little town of Inverness. Rooms vary greatly from some very large quarters to some rather small units, and in either case accommodations are hardly lavish; it's more like spending the night in someone's beach cabin. But there is a swimming pool for all and a fireplace and plenty of wood in most rooms. Many units have little patios overlooking Tomales Bay. There is a certain funky charm to the place, and the motel's restaurant, Barnaby's, has a pleasant and airy dining room.

GOLDEN HINDE MOTEL, *12938 Sir Francis Drake Boulevard (mailing address: P.O. Box 295, Inverness, CA 94937); (415) 669-1389, or toll-free in California 1-800-443-7575. Thirty-five-guestroom motel, some rooms with kitchens and/or fireplaces. Parking provided. TV but not phone in rooms. Pool. No pets. Children welcome. Nonsmoking rooms available. Rate range: Sunday through Thursday $50 to $80, weekends $65 to $95, plus 8% tax. MC, Visa. No minimum stay.*

✔ **MacLean House.**   As noted above, the wee town of Inverness has several well-run bed-and-breakfast establishments. By calling Inns of Point Reyes, you will learn about the elegant Blackthorne Inn and Ten Inverness Way, both fine inns in Inverness. If your top priorities are value and privacy, however, our first choice is the MacLean House. Located on a hill in a residential neighborhood only a few minutes from the center of town, this intimate inn has only two rooms for rent. These rooms are good-size, large enough to include a sleeping loft. They are below the main house and have separate entrances, if you really want to get away from the rest of the world. And in addition to being attractively decorated, each room has its own private bath. Guests have a choice of feather or the other kind of pillow. There is neither telephone nor television in the rooms.

The town of Inverness was named after a place in Scotland, so it seems fitting to stay in a place called MacLean that serves scones and shortbread at breakfast. On nice mornings breakfast is served out on the patio, which has a spectacular view of Tomales Bay. But if you're stuck indoors, the view is still nice from inside the dining room.

Reserve your room well in advance; with only two rooms it's not surprising this place gets booked up.

MACLEAN HOUSE, *122 Hawthornden Way, Inverness, CA 94937; (415) 669-7392. Two-bedroom bed-and-breakfast inn, both with private bath. Continental breakfast. No phone or TV in rooms; down pillow optional. No pets. Children "negotiable." No smoking in rooms. Both rooms priced at $85 (plus $10 for a third person) plus 8% tax. No credit cards. Two-night minimum stay on weekends.*

✔ Mountain Home Inn.   This is a place with a legacy. The original Mountain Home
Inn was built in 1912, a way station for the steam trains that used to run up
Mount Tamalpais. Over the years the inn became a favorite place for hikers and
other outdoorsy types to meet before tackling the trails near the inn or as a place
to finish a vigorous outing with refreshments from the bar and restaurant. The
original structure burned in 1983 and was rebuilt.

The design of the new Mountain Home Inn was inspired by the grand lodges
in Yosemite, Glacier Park, and Mt. Hood but was built on a smaller scale. When
you enter the lobby you're greeted by lots of wood paneling and an impressive set
of pillars that are tree trunks with the bark left on. On this lobby level is the bar
and an intimate twelve-seat dining room, complete with wood-burning fireplace.
The overnight accommodations are downstairs.

If you're looking for a special-occasion getaway and don't mind paying nearly
$200 a night, ask for the deluxe rooms. They feature vaulted ceilings, Jacuzzi
tubs, wood-burning fireplaces, comfortable sitting-reading areas, and king-size
beds; most have private decks.

The more modest so-called Standard Rooms and Standard Rooms with View
are very small but do have their own bathrooms (some with shower only) and
most have a little private terrace. You would not want to spend much time in the
room.

Most people who stay here have come to spend time outdoors and to get away
from it all, therefore none of the rooms has television or telephones, though, if
you insist, arrangements can be made for a portable black and white set and a
cordless phone. The inn is located at the junction of several popular hiking trails;
the front desk can equip you with a list of these and other places in the area to
hike.

MOUNTAIN HOME INN, *810 Panoramic Highway, Mill Valley, CA 94941; (415)*
381-9000. Ten-bedroom lodge. All rooms with private bath; four rooms have
Jacuzzis. Continental breakfast. No phone or TV in rooms. No pets. Children
welcome. Smoking allowed in rooms. Rate range: $108 to $178, plus 8% local
tax. MC, Visa. No minimum stay.

✔ Pelican Inn.   We will never forget the day we drove in a pea soup fog along the
snakey, clifflike section of Highway 1 between Mill Valley and Muir Beach; the
mist was so thick that the only thing we could see was a few feet at a time of the
dividing line painted on the highway. As we descended down the mountain
below the fog line our first sign of civilization was remarkable: a Tudor-style
inn, surrounded by a manicured lawn and cottage garden. Smoke from a fireplace billowed out the chimney as if to signal that our treacherous journey had
come to an end.

This port in the storm was the Pelican Inn, built to be a re-creation of a sixteenth-century English farmhouse and pub. The effect is something like a Tudor version of Disneyland. Inside and out are the traditional white plaster walls and dark, exposed beams. Guests enter the inn through the atmospherically (i.e., dimly) lit pub, where most likely a boisterous dart game will be in progress. Upstairs the sleeping quarters carry on the Anglican fantasy—heavy brocade curtains adorn the windows, paintings of hunting scenes and other sights of the English countryside decorate the walls. All the rooms have queen-size beds. The guest rooms are very attractive but small, so if you're planning to hang around the inn for any length of time you'll probably find yourself using the "snug" (a cozy common room) provided for guests; here you can lounge around, legs outstretched, in a roomy armchair by the fireplace and read, play the piano, or meet the other guests.

The posted announcement regarding breakfast typifies the sense of whimsy with which the inn is run: "It is humbly requested your breakfast be consumed between 8:15 and 10 A.M., since management is intimidated by a ferocious cook who commences luncheon preparation at that time." The breakfast is English and hardy: bangers and eggs, toast, marmalade, coffee and tea; cold cereals are also available for those wishing to adhere to a more American diet.

THE PELICAN INN, *on Shoreline Highway (Highway 1), Muir Beach, CA 94965; (415) 383-6000. Seven-bedroom bed-and-breakfast inn. All rooms with private bath. Full breakfast. No phone or TV in rooms; down pillows optional. No pets. Children welcome. Smoking allowed in rooms. Rate range: $110 to $135, plus 8% tax. MC, Visa. No minimum stay.*

OLEMA

✓ **Olema Inn.**   Once upon a time, Olema was a rough-and-tumble logging town. The Olema Inn opened in 1876 as a stagecoach stop, saloon, and heaven knows what else. In 1988, the place was restored into a fine restaurant and wine bar (see Dining section, page 14) with four bed-and-breakfast rooms upstairs. The setting is ideal for a getaway weekend: located right near the entrance to the Pt. Reyes National Seashore, with a good restaurant downstairs. A full breakfast is included in the room rate, and after a day at the seashore you can have an elegant dinner without getting into the car again. The rooms are small, but they are tastefully decorated, with a combination of antique furniture and modern fabrics and fixtures.

You should be aware that the Inn is at the intersection of Route 1 and Sir Francis Drake Boulevard. In the busy summer season that could mean noise from the traffic.

OLEMA INN, *10000 Sir Francis Drake Boulevard, Olema, CA 94950; (415) 663-9559. Four-bedroom bed-and-breakfast inn. All rooms with private bath. Full breakfast. No phone or TV in rooms. No pets. No smoking in rooms. Rate range: $95 to $105, plus 8% tax. MC, Visa, Am Ex. No minimum stay.*

✔ Point Reyes Seashore Lodge. Sometimes the charm of lodging on the Backroads is the opportunity to stay in a historic building. But other times it is nice to have more modern accommodations. If you prefer the latter, check out the Point Reyes Seashore Lodge.

Built in 1988 from lots and lots of blond wood, this is a cross between a lodge and a luxury motel. Special care was taken to provide extra details of craftsmanship. From the outside you will notice pretty little windows made of opalescent glass; from the inside, these windows allow filtered light to enter the room while providing privacy from the outside.

All rooms have private baths with a view from the tub, telephones, down comforters, and feather pillows; many have fireplaces and some have whirlpool baths. The top-of-the-line rooms are two-story suites with a sitting area, wet bar, and bathroom with whirlpool tub downstairs, sleeping loft with feather bed upstairs. Downstairs a fireplace and pool table are provided for the evening's entertainment.

Like the Olema Inn across the road, the Lodge is located right on the coast highway. Though the luxury suites are set back far enough so that road noise isn't a problem, others are little more than a parking space's distance from the road. Even though Highway 1 isn't heavily traveled at night, if the sound of an occasional car or truck disturbs your sleep, you will want to be sure the room you reserve is set back from the highway.

Handicapped facilities are available.

POINT REYES SEASHORE LODGE, *10021 Coastal Highway 1, Olema, CA 94950; (415) 663-9000. Twenty-one-bedroom lodge. All rooms with private bath, phone, and radio; no TV. Down pillows optional. Eleven rooms have private Jacuzzis. Continental breakfast. No pets. Children welcome. Smoking in rooms "discouraged." Rate range: $85 to $120 for a regular room, $140–$160 for suite, plus 8% tax. MC, Visa, Am Ex. No minimum stay.*

✔ Ferrando's Hideaway. As we indicated at the beginning of the Inverness listings, several entrepreneurial women in the Point Reyes area have developed an alternative to bed-and-breakfast inns; they run bed-and-breakfast cottages, one-unit retreats with the privacy of renting a private house and the benefit of someone else providing breakfast. There are at least eight such cottages in the Point Reyes area, but we were particularly enchanted by Ferrando's Hideaway. The cottage itself is separated from the main house by a garden and has its own private walkway entrance; other than the business of checking in you don't have to see anyone else during the length of your stay. The cottage has a sleeping loft upstairs; downstairs is a little kitchen with ministove and refrigerator. When you arrive your hostess has stocked the kitchen with fruit, homemade baked goods, fresh coffee beans, and eggs from her chickens.

POINT REYES

Cottage guests also have use of the Ferrando family hot tub.

FERRANDO'S HIDEAWAY, *12010 Highway 1 (mailing address: P.O. Box 688, Point Reyes, CA 94956); (415) 663-1916. One-room cottage with sleeping loft and kitchenette. Ingredients for breakfast provided. No phone or TV; radio, stereo, and down pillows provided. Hot tub on premises. No pets. Children welcome. No smoking in cottage. Rate range: $90 midweek, $100 weekends, plus 8% tax. No credit cards. Two-night minimum stay on weekends.*

✔ **Holly Tree Inn.**   Of all of the country inns in this section, the Holly Tree is the most country-fied. Built in 1939 as a vacation getaway, it is set off the road, nestled in a nineteen-acre estate. In the morning before breakfast it's nice to stroll around the grounds; you'll find holly trees, mountain laurel, lilacs, and a creek with a little wooden bridge.

The four guest rooms are upstairs, on the same level as the common sitting room with a fireplace. The rooms are decorated in gentrified country style, the bedspreads and curtains fashioned from Laura Ashley prints. The two large rooms have king-size beds and a small sitting area; one other has a queen-size bed, and the smallest has a double.

Breakfast is served on the weekends at 9:30 A.M., during the week at 9 A.M. This might be bad news for those inclined to get up early and get moving, or to sleep in, or who are in an antisocial mood until noon or so. The good news is breakfast is a major production and the inn is known for its homemade poppy seed bread.

In addition to the four guest rooms, the Holly Tree also has a private cottage separate from the main house. It has its own kitchenette; breakfast supplies are delivered the night before so you won't be disturbed in the morning. Sometimes during midweek in the winter the price is reduced and this place becomes a real bargain.

HOLLY TREE INN, *3 Silver Hill, Inverness Park (mailing address: Box 642, Point Reyes Station, CA 94956); (415) 663-1554. Four bedrooms in main house plus one private cottage; all with private bath. Full breakfast. No phone or TV in rooms; down pillows optional. No pets. Children welcome. No smoking inside. Rate range: $90 to $130, plus 8% tax. MC, Visa. Two-night minimum stay on weekends.*

✔ **Point Reyes Youth Hostel.**   Those who do not require luxury overnight accommodations might want to check out the Point Reyes Youth Hostel, a part of the American Youth Hostel system. There is no age limit for guests. "Youth Hostel" is a bit of a misnomer; it is open to all ages. For $6.50 a night you can stay near Limantour Beach if you do not mind sleeping on a bunk and sharing the bathrooms, kitchen, and chores.

The positive side is that the accommodations offer a chance to meet people from all over the world, and you will probably eat very well (guests tend to pitch in to create wonderful communal meals). You will stay within walking distance of the beach and can watch the sunset from the lodge room.

Clearly, hosteling is not for everyone, but the facility at Point Reyes is particularly inviting.

POINT REYES YOUTH HOSTEL, *Point Reyes National Seashore (mailing address: P.O. Box 247, Point Reyes Station, CA 94956); (415) 663-8811 from 7:30 A.M. to 9 A.M. and from 4:30 P.M. to 9:30 P.M. Main information number for Point Reyes Seashore: (415) 663-1092. Forty-four-bed hostel. No private baths. No pets. Children welcome. Rate: $6.50 per adult, $3.25 per child. Three-night maximum stay.*

CHAPTER **17** Sonoma County

As we've stated in our other books, Sonoma County is the most fertile Backroads country in the Bay Area. It offers coastline, vineyards, farms, Russian River recreation, and history, and lots of good places to eat and stay. We will concentrate on places to stay in each of the separate regions of the county: the Valley of the Moon area around the town of Sonoma, the Russian River, the Alexander Valley, Santa Rosa, Petaluma, and the coast. There are many choices, ranging in price from bargains to splurges.

(*See map on page* 23.)

✔ **Schoolhouse Inn.** Bodega is a quiet farm community a few miles from the ocean. In 1963, Alfred Hitchcock picked this as the perfect setting for thousands of winged creatures to attack unsuspecting citizens in the movie *The Birds*. Remember the schoolhouse where Tippi Hedren's hair got all pecked and messed up? Well, now it's a bed-and-breakfast inn, and would be an interesting place to visit even if it hadn't been used as a movie set.

The original Potter School was built in 1873 and remained in operation until 1961. The upstairs of the schoolhouse was used as the town's community center. But it's never quite been the same since Mr. Hitchcock and gang moved into town to make the famous movie.

The school building was purchased in 1965 by Tom Taylor, who has used the place as his home, an art gallery, a restaurant, a community gathering place and, now, a bed-and-breakfast inn.

Okay, okay, so the place isn't a five-star establishment. The rooms and bath-

BODEGA

room facilities are comfortable but not lavish. This is a country inn with wooden floors and a farmhouse feel to it. But there is a definite charm to the place. In addition, the rates are good, the breakfast lavish, the original school blackboards (as seen in the movie) are still on the walls, and forevermore you can tell your friends, family, and anybody who'll listen that you stayed at the place where *The Birds* was filmed.

We should note that because this is a converted schoolhouse, the school rooms–bedrooms do not all have adjoining bathrooms. The guests of two of the rooms must travel down the hall to get to their respective private baths. One of the guest rooms is adorned by the Bodega town quilt—the handiwork of a group of citizens who made it to raise money for some worthy cause.

Guests seem to hang out upstairs in the old community center. There a full breakfast is served. That's also where you'll find a television, a VCR (only one movie available, though—guess which one), and a life-size cut-out of Sir Alfred.

SCHOOLHOUSE INN, *17110 Bodega Lane (mailing address: P.O. Box 136, Bodega, CA 94922); (707) 876-3257. Four-bedroom bed-and-breakfast inn. All rooms with private bath. Full breakfast. No phone or TV in rooms. No pets. Children "not encouraged." No smoking in rooms. Rate range: $52 to $64 midweek, $65 to $80 on weekends, plus 8% tax. MC, Visa. Two-night minimum stay on holidays.*

BODEGA BAY   ✓ **Bodega Bay Lodge.**   There is a bit of a tourist boom in this picturesque and busy fishing village right on the coast highway. Presumably because of the ocean location, considerable sums of money have been spent to build large hostelries. The two we recommend are similar in appearance and style, and the price range is basically the same.

The Bodega Bay Lodge is like a modern, deluxe motel. Rooms are grouped together into a collection of "lodges." Each room is quite spacious, many with vaulted ceilings. Some have fireplaces; all have minirefrigerators, private decks, and views of Bodega Bay. Communal facilities include a swimming pool, sauna, and exercise room. The lodge is located at the southern end of town, nestled on grassy dunes that overlook beaches. The Lodge is part of a well-run group of hotels that includes Lafayette Park Hotel (see Contra Costa, page 207).

BODEGA BAY LODGE, *Coast Highway 1, Bodega Bay, CA 94923; (707) 875-3525. Seventy-eight-bedroom lodge-motel. All rooms with private baths, phone, TV. Pool, hot tub, sauna, and fitness room on premises. No pets. Children welcome. Rate range: Sunday through Thursday, $85 to $165, weekends $96 to $176, plus 8% tax. MC, Visa, Am Ex, Diners, and Discover. Two-night minimum stay on weekends.*

✓ **The Inn at the Tides.**   The Tides is a busy tourist complex right on the water, centered around a very busy seafood restaurant. (See Dining section, page 22.) The Inn is across the highway, perched on the hillside overlooking The Tides and the fishing boats of Bodega Bay. The rooms are located on various levels of the terraced hillside so that everyone has a view of the water and of the wonderful sunsets. The Inn is attractively designed and filled with the kinds of touches you expect at upscale hotels, such as good soaps and shampoo, fluffy towels, remote control TV, etc.

The rate schedule here is rather complicated. Rates vary from room to room (with fireplace and/or king-size bed is more expensive than without), on weekends, and higher summer rates apply to winter holidays. For example, a room with a king-size bed and fireplace costs $160 a night in the summer; the same room is $135 in the winter. However, all year round you can get a break on midweek and multiple-night stays.

So it's not cheap, but the rooms are very nice, large enough to spend some time in admiring the view, relaxing by the fire, or maybe catching up on some letter writing.

THE INN AT THE TIDES, *800 Coast Highway 1 (mailing address: P.O. Box 640, Bodega Bay, CA 94923); (707) 875-2751 or toll-free within California 1-800-541-7788. Eighty-six motel rooms grouped into two-story "lodges." Continental breakfast. All rooms have private baths, phone, TV, and radio. Pool, hot tub, and sauna on premises. No pets. Children welcome. Nonsmoking rooms available. Price range: $110 to $185 (see explanation in description), plus 8% tax. Lower rates for multiple-night stays. MC, Visa, Am Ex. Two-night minimum stay on holidays.*

✔ **Sonoma Mission Inn.**   There's been a health resort in one form or another in this location since the mid 1800s, taking advantage of the natural hot springs that run under the property. The current inn was constructed in 1927, built to architecturally re-create a California mission, complete with arcade and bell towers. In 1980 the main building was restored, a new building with additional guestrooms was built, and a European-style spa was added to attract visitors from around the world.

The reputation of Sonoma Mission Inn is that of an upscale resort, the kind that shows up in magazines like *Vogue*. Even though many of the rooms are on the small side, there is a style to the place and to the people who come here. We are including it in this humble Backroads book because of the bargains that are available in winter. For the past two years, the Inn offered a midweek deal: a double occupancy room for $70, and that included use of their terrific coed spa, tennis courts, and two swimming pools (services such as massage, facials, and aerobics classes do cost extra, however). If you can get that rate, plus one of the larger new rooms in the new building, that's some deal.

BOYES HOT SPRINGS

For those on low-fat or low-sodium diets, the Inn is one of the pioneers in Spa Cuisine; it's featured in The Grille, off the large and comfortable hotel lobby.

SONOMA MISSION INN, *18140 Sonoma Highway (Highway 12) (mailing address: P.O. Box 1447, Sonoma, CA 95476); (707) 938-9000. One-hundred-seventy-bedroom hotel and spa resort. All rooms with private baths, phone, TV, and radio; down pillows optional. Two pools, hot tubs, tennis courts, plus full spa facility on premises. Valet parking optional. No pets, though boarding arrangements can be made. Children welcome. Smoking allowed in rooms. Rate range: rooms, $95 to $275; suites, $300 to $525. Rates lower in winter and during occasional weekday specials. Add 6% tax all year. MC, Visa, Am Ex, Diners, Discover. Two-night minimum stay on summer weekends.*

GEYSERVILLE ✔ **Campbell Ranch Inn.** The town of Geyserville, located in the northern part of Sonoma wine country, offers a distinct variety of places to stay. If you have—or wish you could have—fond memories of staying out in the country with a kindly aunt and uncle, the Campbell Ranch Inn should bring back some memories. Mary Jane and Jerry Campbell have a lovely spread on thirty-five acres overlooking rolling hills, vineyards, and olive groves. Even if you never left the place you could have an action-packed weekend of swimming in a pool, hot tubbing, playing tennis, basketball, horseshoes, and Ping-Pong. When you do go out in the evening, a freshly baked pie or cake will be waiting for you when you return.

One feature the relatives never offered: You get a breakfast menu that you leave outside your door, specifying the time you'd like to eat and choices that include juices, fresh fruit, omelets, potatoes, white toast, zucchini bread, bran muffins, blueberry muffins, sour cream coffee cake, plus beverages.

The inn is the Campbell's ranch-style house; guestrooms are the bedrooms in the home, once occupied by the Campbell's now-grown children. All rooms have private baths, king-size beds, great views, and books (including a collection of Christian literature); terry bathrobes and big towels are provided for the pool and hot tub.

The decor reminds us of the old "Dick Van Dyke Show"—early sixties-era furnishings, easy chairs, shag wall-to-wall carpeting—making for the kind of homey place where you feel it would be okay to put your feet up on the furniture. Guests are welcome to play with Mr. Campbell's elaborate model train set.

CAMPBELL RANCH INN, *1475 Canyon Road, Geyserville, CA 95441; (707) 857-3476. Five-bedroom bed-and-breakfast inn. All rooms with private bath. Full breakfast. No phones in rooms; down pillow optional. One room with TV; one room with radio. Pool, hot tub, tennis courts, basketball hoop on premises. No pets. Children "not encouraged." No smoking in rooms. Rate range: $80 to $100, plus 8% tax. MC, Visa. Minimum stay: two nights on weekends; three nights on holidays.*

✓ Hope-Merrill and Hope-Bosworth houses. Two of the most stunning Victorian inns in the Sonoma wine country are in the town of Geyserville and are run by the Hope family. They have converted two mansions, the old Merrill and Bosworth homes, into lovely bed-and-breakfast inns across the street from each other. They also offer an unusual feature called Stage-a-Picnic—horse-drawn stage-coach rides to nearby wineries where you have a lavish picnic lunch.

The Merrill House is the more lavish of the two. Originally built in 1870, it is Victorian to the max, each room a veritable explosion of design, color, and period artifacts. The wallpaper alone is worth a trip to Geyserville (this awe-inspiring silk-screened wallpaper was designed and made by Benicia artist Bruce Bradbury). The Peacock Room, located downstairs, is the showpiece room of the house. It features a fireplace, whirlpool bath, and some of the finest antique furniture in the house.

A new addition with two rooms was added several years ago and made to look as though it had always been there. One room overlooks the house swimming pool, the other a vineyard. All rooms in the Merrill House have private baths.

Across the street is the more modest, folksy Hope-Bosworth House. The original owner, George M. Bosworth, was the town mortician. When the wealthy Merrills suffered the tragic deaths of several children, Mr. Bosworth got the property across the street as payment for his services. He built his home in 1904.

It is more understated than the mansion across the street but is still quite lovely and comfortable and less expensive. Two of the five guestrooms have private baths. Downstairs, the Sun Porch Room has its own private entrance.

Breakfast in both houses is a lavish affair, featuring housemade breads and pastries, egg dishes, fresh fruit, and Rosalie Hope's jams and jellies. Her husband, Bob Hope (who has, no doubt, heard every joke in the world about his name), offers his housemade wine to guests in the afternoon. Guests of both houses have access to the pool behind the Merrill House.

HOPE-MERRILL HOUSE, *21253 Geyserville Avenue (mailing address: P.O. Box 42, Geyserville, CA 95441); (707) 857-3356. Seven-bedroom bed-and-breakfast inn. All rooms with private baths; two rooms with Jacuzzis, three with fireplaces; two with showers-for-two. Full breakfast served. No phone or TV in rooms. Pool on premises. No pets allowed. Children "not encouraged" on weekends. No smoking in rooms. Rate range: $85 to $115, plus 8% tax. MC, Visa, Am Ex. Two-night minimum stay on weekends.*

HOPE-BOSWORTH HOUSE, *21238 Geyserville Avenue (mailing address: P.O. Box 42, Geyserville, CA 95441); (707) 857-3356. Five-guestroom bed and breakfast. One room with half-bath; two rooms share a bath. Full breakfast. No phone or TV in rooms. Pool across the street at Merrill House. No pets. Children "not* *encouraged" on weekends. No smoking in rooms. Rate range: $60 to $80, plus 8% tax. MC, Visa, Am Ex. Two-night minimum stay on weekends.*

✔ **Isis Oasis Lodge and Cultural Center.** This is probably the most far-out place we will recommend in this book. By "far-out" we're not talking geography; we're talking concept. Certainly the sign that greets you at Isis Oasis will explain what we mean. It advertises bed and breakfast, with therapy, massage, tarot reading, past-life excursions, dance, theater, and the availability of various spiritual and corporeal experiences.

The "oasis" was founded by Lora Vigne, who calls herself an artist, New Age minister, and tarot reader. She wears her hair à la Elizabeth Taylor in Cleopatra and wears clothes that evoke the feeling of Egypt. She is particularly devoted to the Egyptian goddess Isis, goddess of fertility. She has created "a retreat for body and spirit" on eight and a half acres of woods and meadows where exotic animals (including an ocelot, a llama, and an emu) mingle with artists, New Age spiritualists, and curious visitors.

Folks who spend the night or a week here have a choice of accommodations. The main lodge has several common rooms and individual bedrooms; guests share a large bathroom with showers. There are also tepees; the wine barrel room, which is a tiny bedroom in an actual barrel; and last but not least, yurts. (At the risk of underestimating your housing knowledge, I will explain that a yurt is a large, round Afghan structure, similar to a tepee.)

Breakfast is a full country-style affair, including such items as fruit, juices, French toast, pancakes, eggs, and muffins.

The Center is often rented to groups on retreats or seminars, and there is usually a lot of activity. Still, it is also a very quiet and peaceful place. You can be part of a group or be by yourself. You can spend all your time alone by the swimming pool or hot tub or just take part in the activities that appeal to you.

ISIS OASIS LODGE AND CULTURAL CENTER, *20889 Geyserville Avenue, Geyserville, CA 95441; (707) 857-3524. Guest accommodations include: twelve-room lodge, towerhouse, honeymoon cottage, tepee, farmhouse for groups up to five, three yurts, and a room made from a wine barrel. Full breakfast. Pool, three hot tubs, spa, sauna, and massage rooms on premises. Pets allowed in yurts, tepee, and barrel room. Children welcome with prior arrangement. No smoking in rooms. Rate range: $35 to $90 ($18 per person group rate); tax included. MC, Visa. No minimum stay.*

GLEN ELLEN ✔ **Beltane Ranch.** In the 1890s, this two-story wooden structure served as a ranch bunkhouse. Then the owners of the land lived in the place for many years, using only the downstairs. Now the niece has taken over the place, made comfortable bed-and-breakfast accommodations out of the old ranch hands' quarters, and painted the outside sunny yellow trimmed with white.

The best rooms are the three upstairs. Each is a suite with a sitting room, antique furniture, good books, a private bathroom, and two entrances (or exits, depending on your point of view) leading from (or to) the porch that wraps around the building. Nicest of all is the suite with a wood-burning stove and king-size bed. The upstairs porch has a bench swing from which you can see the bucolic Sonoma Valley and surrounding mountains.

Downstairs is a small, one-room-plus-bathroom unit. It's very attractively decorated, but a bit small to consider spending much time in.

The bunkhouse is situated on a 1,600-acre parcel of land stretching to the Napa County line. Some of the ranch property is planted with grapevines, other parts have been left wild and are perfect for long walks. Guests are also welcome to use the tennis court next to the bunkhouse.

The niece-innkeeper, Rosemary Wood, is our kind of proprietor. She's a very congenial hostess who expects guests to create their own amusements. Breakfast is a complete American-style meal that can be served on the upstairs porch overlooking the Sonoma Valley.

BELTANE RANCH, *11775 Sonoma Highway (Highway 12) (mailing address: P.O. Box 395, Glen Ellen, CA 95442); (707) 996-6501. Four-bedroom bed-and-breakfast inn. All rooms with private bath. Full breakfast. No phone or TV in rooms; down pillows optional. Tennis court and Ping-Pong on premises. No pets. Children "negotiable." Smoking in rooms discouraged. Rate range: $75 to $90, plus 8% tax. No credit cards. No minimum stay.*

✔ **Gaige House.** The Gaige House itself is a remarkably ornate and huge Italianate Queen Anne–style home, originally constructed in about 1890 for the town butcher, A. E. Gaige. Over the years the large Victorian was used as a boarding house, a school, and, finally, remodeled in 1980 as a bed-and-breakfast inn.

Although most of the rooms are pleasant enough, though small, we recommend staying in the Gaige Suite. Inevitably, it is also the most expensive in the place, but it is large and airy, and decorated with beautiful antiques and linens. It has a king-size bed, a lounging area with a puffy sofa, plus a private deck overlooking Calabasas Creek. Last but not least it has the bathroom of one's dreams, very spacious and modern. Breakfast can be served in the room—all adding up to an ideal setting for a romantic getaway, though the Jacuzzi in the wondrous bathroom is large enough to accommodate all your friends and relatives, if you want the company.

A full breakfast is included in the room rate, all rooms have private baths, and guests are invited to use the swimming pool out back.

GAIGE HOUSE, *13540 Arnold Drive, Glen Ellen, CA 95442; (707) 935-0237. Seven-bedroom bed-and-breakfast inn. All rooms with private bath. Full breakfast. No phone or TV in rooms. Pool on premises. No pets. No children under sixteen. No smoking in rooms. Rate range: $75 to $145, plus 8% tax. MC, Visa. Two-night minimum stay on weekends.*

✔ **Stone Tree Ranch.** By telling you about this place we are probably never going to get to stay here again. This is a unique bed and breakfast in the Sonoma hills that has just one guest cottage to rent, upstairs above what was once a stable. It comes complete with a small kitchen, and the place can be used as a romantic spot for two, or converted to sleep six.

The Gavigans, who live in the ranch house on the property, will stock the cottage with everything you will need for breakfast, including fresh coffee beans and a grinder, then leave you to your own devices. You can use the hot tub on their deck if you like, and you can roam around the ranch, which affords a sweeping view of the valley. It's a good idea to make your reservation for this place well in advance.

STONE TREE RANCH, *7910 Sonoma Mountain Road, P.O. Box 173, Glen Ellen, CA 95442; (707) 996-1114. One-bedroom suite with private bath. Fixings for full breakfast provided. No phone or TV; radio and down pillows available. Hot tub on premises. Pets allowed. Children welcome. No smoking. Price: $125 for two, $25 per additional person, plus 8% tax. No credit cards. Flexible minimum-stay requirement.*

GUERNEVILLE

✔ **The Estate.** As you drive a few minutes out of Guerneville on Route 116, you'll come to one of the best places to stay in the Russian River resort area, and, we should add, one of the most expensive in the county. The Estate is the former country home of a wealthy banker that has been taken over by two gentlemen from San Francisco and converted into an elegant bed-and-breakfast inn.

The ten guestrooms offer the best of bed-and-breakfast charm with the convenience of a first-class hotel. Like the former, the rooms are luxuriously appointed with tasteful antiques, down comforters, and lovely paintings; like the latter, each room has a private bath with tub and shower, business-caliber telephone, and remote-control TV. If you choose to leave your room, guests can socialize in one of two common rooms, read a book by the fireplace, or hang out around the swimming pool.

A full breakfast is served each morning in the dining room, and, with prior arrangement, registered guests may have dinner there as well.

The big crowds arrive on the weekends, so if you can visit during the week you'll have lots of privacy. During the slow times, midweek in winter in partic-

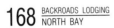

ular, special rates are often available; the room may be discounted as much as 40 percent from the weekend rate.

THE ESTATE, *13555 Highway 116, Guerneville, CA 95446; (707) 869-9093. Ten-bedroom bed-and-breakfast inn. All rooms with private bath, phone, TV, and down comforters and pillows. Pool and hot tub on premises. No pets. No children. No smoking. Rate range: Midweek and off-season $75 to 125; weekends $100 to $150, plus 8% tax. MC, Visa, Am Ex. Two-night minimum stay on weekends.*

✔ **Belle de Jour Inn.** It took us several passes to find Belle de Jour, which is a good sign for anyone looking for a place to stay that's away from it all. Even though it's only a few minutes from the Healdsburg town square and not far from Highway 101, Belle de Jour is nicely isolated on a remote hilltop, set amid six wanderable acres. The farmhouse that you see when you pull up the long driveway is the home of the innkeepers, Tom and Brenda Hearn. They serve a full breakfast in their kitchen each morning, or on the deck in the garden when the weather is inviting. Guests may also have a continental breakfast—complete with china and crystal—delivered to their door.

The guest quarters are four separate cottages, each with a distinct atmosphere. The largest cottage is called The Caretaker's Suite and features such niceties as a king-size canopy bed, a whirlpool tub for two, and a trellised deck with a view. The smallest, called the Morning Hill Room, is compact but cozy, featuring a wood stove and probably the best view. All guests have access to the giant hot tub that overlooks the valley.

A special feature offered here costs extra but is a lavishly decadent way to tour the local wine country. For $80 per couple, you can be driven in a beautifully restored 1923 Star roadster. It's a three-hour tour, followed by lunch. And since someone else is driving, you can taste wine to your heart's content.

BELLE DE JOUR INN, *16276 Healdsburg Avenue, Healdsburg, CA 95448; (707) 433-7892. Four guest cottages, all with private baths and Jacuzzis. Full breakfast. No phone or TV in rooms; down pillow optional. No pets. Children "not encouraged." No smoking inside cottages. Rate range: $85 to $125, plus 8% tax. MC, Visa. Two-night minimum stay on weekends.*

✔ **Camellia Inn.** Some Victorian homes and inns are so spectacular it's hard to imagine anyone ever really living there. This finely preserved example of an Italianate Victorian townhouse is more like a geniune home, situated on a neighborhood block. Not that it isn't of great interest to Victoriana buffs, with its double parlor, many of the original fixtures, and period decorations: antiques, inlaid hardwood floors, and oriental rugs. The house was built in 1869 and was for a time used as the town's hospital.

Most of the rooms are named for types of camellias. There's the Firelight Room, which features a carved oak mantle, antique armoire, a queen-size canopy bed, a Queen Anne bay window, and the innkeeper's grandfather's shaving mirror. The Royalty Room is the house's original dining room and has a massive maple-canopied bedstand and three tall arched windows that look out on the veranda. The Caprice has a four-poster canopy bed accompanied by a footstool to assist getting into the tall bed. The Firelight, Royalty, and Caprice rooms have private entrances; the Momento and Tiffany rooms have clawfoot bathtubs.

Several years ago a tower addition with two rooms was added. These are the most expensive rooms in the house—large, suitelike rooms with Jacuzzi baths built for two.

Breakfast is expanded continental fare including hard-boiled eggs, fresh fruit, and housemade nut breads and jam (when we were there, the smell of apple butter being cooked permeated the house). Out back is a swimming pool with terrace for relaxing poolside in the afternoon. The house is nicely situated in a residential neighborhood, just two blocks off the town plaza.

CAMELLIA INN, *211 North Street, Healdsburg, CA 95448; (707) 433-8182. Nine-guestroom bed-and-breakfast inn. Two rooms share a bath; two rooms have whirlpool spas. Full breakfast. No phone or TV; down pillow optional. Pool on premises. No pets. Children welcome. No smoking in rooms. Rate range: $55 to $95, plus 8% tax. MC, Visa. Two-night minimum stay on weekends.*

✓ **Healdsburg Inn.** On the south side of the plaza in the center of town, the Healdsburg Inn is in a lovely old three-story building. On the ground floor is a gift shop, art gallery, and bakery; on the next two floors are a bed-and-breakfast inn complete with a rooftop garden and solarium. It's also within walking distance of three good restaurants and a great bakery (see Healdsburg dining section, which begins on page 28) and a short ride from the wineries on beautiful West Side Road.

It was originally built in 1900 as the town's Wells Fargo Bank building. In the communal sitting area where you can read, assemble puzzles, or play cards, you will find reprints of the March 7, 1901, *Healdsburg Tribune* with a front-page story about the building—it created quite a to-do in this little town at the turn of the century.

Guest rooms come in a variety of sizes. Some are large enough to hang out in all day; others are small enough to encourage outings. All rooms have queen-size beds and private baths, some with old-fashioned tubs, all with showers. Three rooms have fireplaces, bay windows, and a view of the town plaza; three others rooms have extra beds in the room. The decorative style is quaint, antique country charm. A television set is available by request; a pay phone is in the hallway. All rooms are air conditioned, a very important consideration during summer and Indian summer months.

Breakfast is served at 9 A.M. in the solarium. This is quite a spread, with a hot entree of eggs, cheese and vegetables, and a platter of fresh fruits accompanying coffee, juice, toast, and cereal. All afternoon, housemade cookies, cakes, popcorn, coffee, and solar tea are available in the solarium. Those with a problem with stairs may wish to note that there is no elevator in this establishment. One room is on the main floor; everything else, including the solarium, is up a flight.

HEALDSBURG INN, *116 Matheson Street, Healdsburg, CA 95448; (707) 433-6991. Nine-bedroom bed-and-breakfast inn. All rooms with private bath. Full breakfast. No pets. No children. No smoking allowed in rooms. Rate range: December through June: $65 to $115; July through November midweek: $75 to $95, weekends: $105 to $125. Plus 8% tax. MC, Visa. No minimum stay.*

✔ **Huckleberry Springs.**   This is a truly unique place and a remarkable bargain. For one thing, it's one of the few places to stay around here that serves both breakfast and dinner, and, considering that the Russian River area is no one's idea of a culinary heaven, that's good news. The inn itself is situated on fifty-six forested acres; accommodations are four modern cottages spread out a friendly distance from one another. Three of the cottages are an easy walk (the fourth is a not-so-easy journey) to the main house, where meals are served. The main house also has a large living room with comfortable chairs, fireplace, books, games, and minipool table, if one cares to partake. Otherwise you can isolate yourself in your cottage, with no phone, television, or other people to distract you.

To get here, you drive a long way down a private, occasionally unpaved, road lined with Douglas fir trees and huckleberry bushes. Before the current owners bought it, the property was owned by a commune. One of the nicest cottages, called the Cherry Barrel Cabin, was the spiritual gathering place for the group. It's made from the wood of an old maraschino cherry vat; the wood still has a faintly sweet smell. The room is round, like a barrel, and features a skylight for star-watching and a wood stove.

The Orchard Cottage holds up to four, though it strikes us as the ideal place for a lone soul finishing up a long-term project or getting a start on the Great American Novel; it has both a queen-size bed and a sleeping loft with a double bed, ceramic fixtures in the bathroom, and lots of books lying around. The Gate Cottage features a sleeping platform and window seat. The Spring Trail Cabin is the most secluded. The loft with cushions and French doors leading out to a deck are its best features, but it's a bit of a hike to get there.

Cabin rates include breakfast and dinner. Innkeeper Suzanne Greene prepares the meals, incorporating vegetables and herbs grown on the property.

MONTE RIO

Dinner includes a choice of three entrees each night, and special dietary needs can be accommodated with advance notice.

HUCKLEBERRY SPRINGS, *8105 Old Beedle Road (mailing address: P.O. Box 400, Monte Rio, CA 95462); (707) 865-2683. Four-cottage country inn. All cottages with private baths, radios, and down comforters. Full breakfast and dinner served in the main house. Pool and spa tub on premises. No pets. No children. No smoking in cabins. All cabins $125 midweek, $150 weekends, plus 8% tax; includes breakfast and dinner. MC, Visa, Am Ex. Two-night minimum stay on weekends.*

OCCIDENTAL ✔ **Heart's Desire Inn.** Perched on a hillside above the town, just a block or so up from the main drag, is a very inviting inn called Heart's Desire. The original house was a two-story Victorian built in the 1860s; a heart shape was laid into the brick on the chimney outside. In 1988 the home was totally renovated as an inn with eight guestrooms, each with a private bath. Whereas traditional Victorians tend to have dark walls and small rooms, the Heart's Desire is open and airy; all the walls are painted white. In effect, the place seems brand-new.

Upstairs is a "honeymoon suite"—a perfect getaway room with a stone fireplace, four-poster bed, and large double shower; breakfast can be served here or on a private balcony overlooking rooftops and the antique church steeple in town.

A room on the first floor has been designed to accommodate the needs of handicapped travelers, complete with wide doorways and a large shower stall with bench. All rooms are tastefully decorated with lovely antiques (the innkeeper, Justina Selinger, used to be an antiques dealer) and come with huge European down pillows, the kind that are perfect when you're reading in bed.

There's no television on the premises; because a lot of businesspeople stay here, Justine has consented to keeping in touch with civilization via a pay phone in the hall. She serves a modest breakfast of housemade baked goods, fruit, and beverages; Justine says her guests want to eat in the good restaurants in the area and tend not to want a lot of breakfast.

All in all it's a lovely place, with a comfortable parlor, large porches with elegant white wicker furniture, and two charming house pets: a lovebird named Chicken and a cat named Jake the Rake, who gets fan mail from past guests.

HEART'S DESIRE INN, *3657 Church Street (mailing address: P.O. Box 857, Occidental, CA 95465); (707) 874-1311. Eight-bedroom bed-and-breakfast inn. All rooms have private bathrooms, showers only. One room equipped for handicap access. Continental breakfast. No phone or TV in rooms; down pillow optional. No pets. No children under sixteen. No smoking in rooms. Rate range: $75 to $135, plus 8% tax. MC, Visa, Am Ex. Two-night minimum stay on weekends and holidays.*

✔ **Melitta Station Inn.**   Once upon a time there was a little town called Melitta, a name derived from the Miwok Indian word *matilija*, meaning poppy. In the late 1800s the little town built a stagecoach stop; later the building was used as a freight station, then as housing for the Italian immigrants who hauled basalt stones from the nearby quarries (this stone was sent to San Francisco to be used for the cobblestone streets). Somewhere along the line the old stage stop also served as the town's general store and post office.

As time passed, Melitta was integrated into the growing metropolis of Santa Rosa, and the station was converted into a bed-and-breakfast inn. We like it because it is incredibly cute, nicely run, and is located on the Backroads in the country yet just minutes away from the main part of Santa Rosa.

At first glance the place appears funky. But that's because it's old, not because it's not kept up. It is decorated with country-style folk art—carved duck silhouettes, dried flowers, and the like—and is very comfortable, like a well-worn and favorite pair of shoes. There's an herb garden out back, the bounty of which makes its way into the morning meal (which also includes Peet's coffee, thus scoring twenty-five additional bonus points from us). You may have your breakfast in the parlor with the other guests, or in the privacy of your own room.

There is a comfortable sitting room with a wood-burning stove, though most of the rooms are large enough to spend time in if you prefer. Also, families or couples traveling together can arrange for adjacent rooms that can be transformed into a suite by simply leaving the doors open.

MELITTA STATION INN, *5850 Melitta Road, Santa Rosa, CA 95405; (707) 538-7712. Six-bedroom bed-and-breakfast inn. Four rooms have private baths. Full breakfast. No phone or TV in rooms. No pets. Children welcome. Rate range: $60 to $80 midweek; $80 to $90 weekends, plus 8% tax. MC, Visa. Two-night minimum stay weekends May through October.*

✔ **Vintner's Inn.**   This place has the charm of a country inn and all the advantages of a good hotel: room service, private bath, remote-control TV, a phone, and concierge. Built in 1985, the idea was to create Provençal-style buildings in the heart of the booming Sonoma wine country. Voila! Just off the main highway and surrounded by a forty-five-acre vineyard, the four rather tasteful buildings are arranged around a central plaza with fountain. The rooms are decorated in elegant French country style, featuring brass and porcelain fixtures in the bathrooms and antique European pine furnishings. Open the beautifully carved armoire to discover the television discreetly hidden inside.

The least expensive rooms are on the ground floor. There's no view, but they are nicely decorated and roomy. The most expensive rooms are the Junior Suites; these come complete with view, fireplaces, wet bar, refrigerator, comfy couches and armchairs, and a room rate to match. In the main-lobby building is the dining room, where a complimentary continental breakfast (including fruit, Belgian waffles, and cereals) is served, and a recreation room with games like Trivial Pursuit and backgammon, a VCR for watching movies, and a library of books. Outside is a sundeck and outdoor whirlpool bath.

Santa Rosa's trend-setting restaurant, John Ash and Company, is located on the premises. (See page 34 of Dining section.)

VINTNER'S INN, *4350 Barnes Road, Santa Rosa, CA 95401; (707) 575-7350 or toll-free in California 1-800-421-2584. Forty-four-room hotel. Continental breakfast. All rooms have phones, TVs, radios; VCRs available at extra charge. Hot tub on premises; tennis access at local club. Pets allowed; extra charge. Children welcome. Rate range: $98 to $155 midweek; $108 to $165 weekends, plus 8% tax. MC, Visa, Am Ex, Diners. Two-night minimum stay on weekends May through October.*

SEA RANCH

✔ **The Sea Ranch Lodge and Condominiums.**   In the mid 1960s, a considerable amount of controversy surrounded the building of the Sea Ranch. This colony of environmentally-sensitive vacation homes was the last major development allowed on the Northern California coast, and many thought that even this should not have been permitted. Now, more than twenty years later, the ranch has proven to be not only an interesting fixture on the shoreline but also a good getaway spot, especially for families.

There are two ways to stay at the Sea Ranch. First, there's the lodge, which is operated like a small hotel, complete with restaurant and bar. All rooms have ocean views and are good for guests who don't want to do anything but laze around in comfort or perhaps stroll to the beach or community swimming pool or tennis courts.

The other option, perfect for families, is to rent a house. They are available in a variety of sizes, some accommodating up to eight people. When you rent a home you provide your own sheets, pillow cases, and towels. Everything else, including dishes and utensils, is provided. Home renters also have use of the community swimming pool and tennis courts. If you do rent a house, be sure to stock up on groceries before you arrive. It's a long drive to the nearest store, although there is a small nook in the lodge where you can get necessities like milk and aspirin.

Both the lodge and homes are designed to blend harmoniously with the environment. All are woody and modern, with lots of glass providing views of the ocean and trees. The entire ranch is well maintained, and there are trails leading out to the bluffs over the water and down to the beaches. In addition, at the northernmost end of the ranch, is a rugged nine-hole golf course; this and horseback riding are available to Sea Ranch guests for additional fees. Just make sure you get your visitor's pass for your car when you check in; you'll need it to gain access to all the facilities.

THE SEA RANCH LODGE AND CONDOMINIUMS, *60 Sea Walk Drive (mailing address: P. O. Box 44, The Sea Ranch, CA 95497); (707)785-2371. Twenty-bedroom lodge. All rooms with private bath; two rooms with hot tubs on deck. No phone or TV in room; down pillows optional. Two pools, four tennis courts, golf course, basketball, volleyball, and saunas on premises. Nonsmoking rooms available. Rate range: summer: $97 to $135; winter: $87 to $135, plus 8% tax. MC, Visa, Am Ex. Two-night minimum stay on summer weekends.*

To rent a home: Several real estate agencies in the area rent homes for the weekend or by the week and month. Accommodations for two people for two nights can range from about $125 to $1,000; two people can usually get a nice home for the weekend for about $150. A cleaning and security deposit is required. Agencies include The Don Berard Agency, P.O. Box 153, The Sea Ranch, CA 95497; phone (707) 884-3211. You can also inquire about home rentals at the lodge.

✔ **Chalet Bed and Breakfast.**   Right from the start, let us make it clear that this inn is for people with a taste for the out of the ordinary. Outside there are guinea hens, turkeys, ducks, and geese; inside is a large quantity of things, including antique dolls, period furniture, and ceramics from the forties.

SONOMA

The farmhouse itself was built in the forties, sitting on three acres outside town. On clear nights you're far enough away from the lights of the town to get a pretty good star show. Within the house are four sleeping rooms, two downstairs and two upstairs, with one bathroom on each floor. This situation can be attractive for two couples traveling together; you can have your own floor of the house (complete with a sitting area) plus the discount that comes with sharing a bath.

For more privacy, there are two guest cottages. Each has the wacky, funky-chic decor of the main house, plus private bathrooms.

About those guinea hens. This is a farm out in the country, so the dog and geese and ducks come as no surprise. The surprise is these guinea hens, which look like mutant chickens that make an undescribable sound; if you're the kind of person who does not love all animals, the morning noise might drive you nuts.

Guests have access to a refrigerator for keeping goodies on hand for snacking, plus a hot tub in a lovely, secluded setting.

As this book was heading to the press, we were informed that the property was sold to new owners and management, but that it would be run like the old Chalet.

CHALET BED AND BREAKFAST, *18935 Fifth Street West, Sonoma, CA 95476; (707) 938-3129. Six-bedroom (including two private cottages) bed-and-breakfast*

inn. Private bathrooms in cottage; private bathrooms in main house if you oc-
cupy the entire floor. Continental breakfast. Phone in one room; no TV in rooms;
down pillows optional in all accommodations. Hot tub on premises. No pets.
Children "not encouraged." Smoking permitted inside. Rate range: $75 to $110,
plus $25 for third person in cottage; plus 8% tax. MC, Visa. No minimum stay.

✔ **Thistle Dew Inn.**   This is the kind of inn that encourages social interaction between guests. So if one of the pleasures for you in staying at a bed and breakfast
is meeting interesting new people, you'll be happy at this charming and well-run
inn, located on a residential street within easy walking distance of the Sonoma
Plaza.

The inn consists of two buildings, the main house and a cottage in back. Both
were built around 1910. In the main house are the communal living and dining
rooms plus two guestrooms, both with private baths. The cottage in back has
four guestrooms and a sitting area. Two rooms share a bath; two rooms have
entrances onto a private backyard deck.

All rooms are decorated with antiques and touches of folksy country charm.
Feather and down pillows are available, and each guest is tempted by chocolate
truffles, homemade by the innkeeper and left seductively under a wine glass.

These are historic buildings, so smoking is not allowed. The houses and the
rooms are small, so you will feel you are staying in close quarters with the other
guests; on the other hand, you can't beat the price and you might make new
friends.

THISTLE DEW INN, *171 West Spain Street (mailing address: P.O. Box 1326,*
Sonoma, CA 95476); (707) 938-2909. Six-bedroom bed-and-breakfast inn. Four
rooms with private baths. Full breakfast. No phone or TV in room; down pillow
optional. Hot tub on premises. No pets. No children under twelve. No smoking
in rooms. Rate range: November 1 to April 1: $50 to $75; April 2 to October 31:
$60 to $85, plus 8% tax. MC, Visa, Am Ex. No minimum stay.

CHAPTER **18** Napa County

(See map on page 45.) The Napa wine country is world famous, and people arrive in droves to experience the sights and tastes this beautiful valley offers. If your schedule allows we
suggest visiting in the fall. The changing foliage is breathtaking and you'll practically have the place to yourself, especially on weekdays. But best of all many
inns offer enticing off-season rates and special package deals.

You will notice that many of the places we recommend in this section do not serve full breakfasts. That's often because of licensing restrictions, which forbid the inns from operating as restaurants. Usually, the "continental breakfast" is quite substantial, with fresh fruit, homemade pastries and muffins, good coffee, and the like.

Our recommendations are mostly in the northern part of Napa County, where you can take advantage of visiting the many wineries plus the baths and spas of Calistoga. Also, Calistoga and St. Helena are small towns that have styles and paces of their own and are not built exclusively around tourism.

One curious medical note for those who are allergic to cats: we were struck by the fact that though many inns on the Bay Area's Backroads have house cats, in Calistoga they seem to be allowed the run of the place, on the furniture, in the kitchen, sometimes even on the dining room tables. Though we love cats (we have two at home), we also have friends with allergies who would be subjected to a living hell if they stayed in such a place. If cats are a problem for you, be sure to ask the individual innkeepers about house policy regarding the whereabouts of their pets.

✔ **Foothill House.**   Innkeepers Michael and Susan Clow have worked hard to provide something most of us are looking for: country inn accommodations at an affordable price.

CALISTOGA

The main house is a turn-of-the-century farmhouse divided into three very spacious rooms. Each has its own bath, private entrance, and refrigerator and is decorated with country antiques. Attention to detail is evident everywhere. The rooms have fresh flowers, plenty of towels, and an AM-FM radio/cassette player (tapes are provided, but you might want to bring your favorite tunes). A handmade quilt adorns the queen-size four-poster beds; both feather and foam pillows are provided. For cold weather there's a wood-burning fireplace; for hot weather fans and air-conditioning. The largest of the rooms, the Evergreen Suite, has a bay window view of Mount St. Helena and its own garden deck. All three rooms are large enough to hang out in for a while without feeling claustrophobic.

Like most bed and breakfasts, the rooms are without phones or TV, but a portable black and white set can be provided *if both* members of a couple approve.

Breakfast is a large continental fare: fresh fruit and orange juice, homemade breads, pastries, and muffins, which can be eaten in the sunroom of the main house, outside on the terrace, or in your room.

For even more privacy there is a cottage separate from the main house where the innkeepers used to live before moving to the place next door. The cottage has a kitchenette and fireplace, and breakfast makings are on hand when you arrive so you can enjoy your morning meal anytime you like.

FOOTHILL HOUSE, *3037 Foothill Boulevard, Calistoga, CA 94515; (707) 942-*

6933. Three-bedroom bed-and-breakfast inn, plus cottage. All accommodations have private baths, cassette players, and radio. Continental breakfast. No phone in room; TV optional. No pets. "Well-behaved teens" welcome. No smoking in rooms. Rate range: $85 to $105, plus 8% tax. MC, Visa. Two-night minimum on weekends.

✔ **Meadowlark.** What a wonderful blending of old and new. The original farmhouse was built in 1886 and was recently remodeled with contemporary colors and furnishings. Even though the interior looks like a spread from one of those slick decorating magazines, this is a place where you can feel comfortable and be informal.

The downstairs is shared by all the inn's guests. You can make yourself right at home in the open, airy living room, help yourself to the beverages in the refrigerator, and stroll out onto the veranda overlooking the English garden. The four guestrooms, each with its own bath, are upstairs. The bedrooms are bright and airy, painted in pastel hues and decorated with contemporary furniture and art.

Perhaps the nicest feature of this inn is the setting, twenty strollable acres of pine, fir, mimosa, and cherry trees, plus a swimming pool and sun deck. Innkeeper Kurt Stevens, who lives in the house next door, keeps horses on the property; however, they are not available for riding.

Stevens is the kind of innkeeper who makes you feel at home, provides you with local information, restaurant recommendations and reservations, then disappears. If you want lots and lots of attention from your host, this is not the place for you. In fact, he may not even be there when you arrive. It's not unusual to find a note of welcome with directions to your room. He serves a bountiful breakfast, given the limits imposed by operating permits. Breakfast is served inside or on the terrace overlooking the garden.

MEADOWLARK, *601 Petrified Forest Road, Calistoga, CA 94515; (707) 942-5651. Four-bedroom bed and breakfast. All rooms with private bath. Expanded continental breakfast. No phone or TV in rooms; down pillow optional. Pool on premises. No pets. Children "not encouraged." No smoking in rooms. Rate range: $100 to $125, plus 10% tax. No credit cards. Two-night minimum stay on weekends.*

✔ **Mount View Hotel.** Right in the heart of town is this art deco landmark, built in 1917, famous for the fanciful names given to its guestrooms. The most popular is the Carole Lombard Suite, a Hollywood-esque fantasy done in pink tones and featuring a mirrored bedroom and lots of Carole Lombard–Clark Gable memorabilia. Another popular suite is The Lily Coit. Named after the legendary San Francisco belle, it is decorated in high-Victorian style.

The more modest rooms are small but inexpensive and decorated in an art deco fashion. The hotel also has a pool and a Jacuzzi and is located right on the main drag of town, close to the spas and mudbaths.

MOUNT VIEW HOTEL, *1457 Lincoln Boulevard, Calistoga, CA 94515; (707) 942-6877. Hotel with nine suites, twenty-five rooms. All accommodations have private bath and phones; no TV in rooms. Continental breakfast. Pool and Jacuzzi on premises. No pets. Children welcome. Price range: $60 to $120, plus 10% tax. MC, Visa, Am Ex, Diners. No minimum stay in winter; Fridays and Saturdays must be booked together during the summer.*

✔ **The Pink Mansion.** Before this stately Victorian home was painted shocking pink, it was the site of grand soirées given by the original owner, the founder of Calistoga's stagecoach line, William F. Fisher. The next occupant was an Auntie Mame–type character named Alma Simic, who, to the dismay of her neighbors, painted the place its present color.

The current innkeeper, Jeff Seyfried, is Alma's nephew, and he has lots of stories to tell about childhood visits with his aunt. Aunt Alma collected cherubs, crystal chandeliers, Victoriana, and oriental paraphernalia, all of which adorn the place; in fact, The Pink Mansion looks a lot like the home of an eccentric maiden aunt—the kind who would win a jackpot in Reno and use the loot to build an indoor swimming pool in her shockingly pink house (true story). By the way, guests have full use of the pool.

Five rooms have been converted into guest bedrooms, each with a private bath. Upstairs, the Angel Room bears the weight of Aunt Alma's angel and cherub collection and also features a window seat with a view of Mount St. Helena and the Palisades; the bathroom has the home's original claw-foot tub. Downstairs, the Rose Room has a private entrance and garden and the Oriental Room features a sundeck, private entrance, large corner shower, and Ms. Simic's Japanese and Chinese antiques. All rooms have queen-size beds and nice views.

THE PINK MANSION, *1415 Foothill Boulevard, Calistoga, CA 94515; (707) 942-0558. Five-bedroom bed and breakfast. All rooms with private bath; one room has a phone, one room has a TV and a VCR. Indoor pool. Small, well-behaved pets allowed. Children "not encouraged." No smoking in rooms. Rate range: $65 to $125 in winter, $85 to $145 in summer, less $20 midweek; 10% tax. MC, Visa. Two-night minimum stay on weekends.*

✔ **Wayside Inn.** This modest, charming place is like a Hollywood version of a Spanish bungalow. The hacienda-style home was built in the twenties, tucked away on a wooded hillside with a flagstone terrace complete with goldfish pond and miniwaterfall. Above, a second terrace is surrounded by flowering trees, a perfect spot to take your breakfast on a warm morning.

This tranquil bed-and-breakfast inn has only three guestrooms, one with a private bath. Now, as a rule of thumb we don't recommend places where the majority of guests have to share a bathroom, but since the bathroom in question is really great (huge, with lovely tile and fixtures) we are willing to make an exception. (This setup would be ideal for two couples traveling together, or, if you stay in the winter off-season you might get the bathroom to yourselves.)

The rooms that share the bath are upstairs. One room is decorated with antique furniture and features a king-size waterbed (admittedly a strange combination). The other upstairs room is decorated in French Provincial, has a queen-size bed and French windows that look out over the terrace and water fountains.

The larger bedroom with its own bath is downstairs, overlooking the lower terrace and entrance to the inn. All the rooms have down comforters and feather pillows; all guests have use of the Jacuzzi and the sitting room, which has a library of books.

WAYSIDE INN, *1523 Foothill Boulevard, Calistoga, CA 94515; (707) 942-0645. Three-bedroom bed-and-breakfast inn. One room with private bath. Full breakfast. No phone or TV in rooms; down pillow optional. Jacuzzi on premises. Pets "negotiable." Children over thirteen welcome. No smoking inside. Rate range: $85 to $95, plus 10% tax (room rates 10% lower in winter). MC, Visa. Two-night minimum stay on holidays.*

RUTHERFORD ✓ **Auberge du Soleil.** Even though we usually search for bargains, or at least good values, we have included a few places in this book for people who only fly first class.

Perched on the hillside just below the world-famous and very expensive restaurant are the elegant and very expensive rooms and suites with million-dollar views of the grapevines and olive groves of Napa Valley. Though the brochure says the inn's intention is "to portray the informal but elegant tradition of the finest European country inns," the interior design of the rooms reminded us of the American Southwest, with terra cotta tile floors, peach-hued walls, and colorful woven throw rugs.

The inn is set up with clusters of "châteaux," each named for a wine region in France. All rooms are large and deluxe and have a private balcony, fireplace, minirefrigerator, wet bar, and coffeemaker. The more expensive accommodations come with a whirlpool tub. In the morning a continental breakfast of juice, pastries, and coffee is delivered to your door, along with a newspaper. For those really interested in staying in touch with the rest of the world, all rooms come equipped with a television and phone.

The lowest price accommodations (at $220 and $260 per night) are one-bedroom affairs designed for up to two persons. The one-bedroom suites ($325 and $385 per night) can accommodate up to four persons (if you're traveling with another couple you can flip for who gets the couch), and the two-bedroom suites ($510) can sleep six (the kids can have the couch).

For recreational pleasure after a tour of the valley, or to burn some of the calories consumed in the restaurant, châteaux guests have use of the Auberge du Soleil tennis courts (lessons are available) and swimming pool. (If you plan to take advantage of the latter, be forewarned: the pool is visible from the terrace of the restaurant, so you will probably want to pack your most flattering bathing suit.)

AUBERGE DU SOLEIL, *180 Rutherford Hill Road, Rutherford, CA 94573; (707) 963-1211. Forty-eight-bedroom hotel. All rooms with private bath, phone, TV, radio; down pillow optional. Continental breakfast. Pool, hot tub, and tennis courts on premises. Pets allowed. Children welcome. Smoking allowed in rooms. Rate range: $220 to $510, plus 8% tax. MC, Visa. Two-night minimum on weekends.*

✔ **Rancho Caymus Inn.** Whereas Auberge du Soleil is a starkly elegant imitation of European country charm, Rancho Caymus Inn is a folksy homage to California's Spanish heritage and to the artists and craftspersons of California's past and present. The Rancho is a few minutes from the main route of the wine country, Route 29, in the tiny village of Rutherford.

Built in 1985, this twenty-six-unit inn is the project of sculptor–local character Mary Tilden Morton. Right away you know you are somewhere unique when you arrive and try to open the lobby door—a massive, hand-carved wooden affair, several hundred years old and weighing several hundred pounds. Elsewhere in the inn you'll see rough-hewn wooden beams and doors (the remnants of an antique barn in Ohio); giant wrought-iron light fixtures and bed tapestries from South America; handmade sinks and stained glass made by local artisans.

Each room is named for a famous Californian, including Black Bart, Lily Coit, and the town's first grocer (Joshua Frye). A typed biography of the person has been hung on the wall of the appropriate room. The rooms are called suites, each one a large open room with a separate sitting area. You have a choice of a variety of accommodations, and the price is determined accordingly. The top-of-the-line Master Suites feature Jacuzzi bathtubs next to a stained-glass window, kitchenette, and private balcony. Most of the rooms have fireplaces—not ordinary fireplaces, mind you, but beehivelike structures made by Mrs. Morton herself (her contractor couldn't understand what she wanted, so she just rolled up her shirt sleeves and made them herself). All rooms have television, phone, and air-conditioning, and two suites are designed to accommodate handicapped persons.

Breakfast is a deluxe continental affair complete with espresso coffee, and you can enjoy it in the dining room or in the privacy of your own suite.

The Inn is right on the road, which is not heavily traveled, so noise shouldn't be a problem. There is a lovely courtyard in the center of things.

RANCHO CAYMUS INN, *Rutherford Road (mailing address: P.O. Box 78, Rutherford, CA 94573); (707) 963-1777. Twenty-six-bedroom inn. All rooms with private bath, phone, TV, radio; down pillow optional. Five in-room Jacuzzis. Continental breakfast. No pets. Children welcome. Price range: $90 to $275 midweek; $95 to $295 weekends, plus 8% tax. MC, Visa. Two-night minimum stay on weekends.*

ST. HELENA ✔ **Bartels Ranch and Country Inn.** Talk about the Backroads! If nothing else, the drive on the twisting country lanes to this charming bed-and-breakfast place is almost worth the price of a night's lodging. But have no fear, you'll get your money's worth during the length of your stay. Innkeeper Jami Bartels expends more energy per minute than most of us can muster in a day. When she gives you a tour of the place you'll hear all about the plans to knock out this wall and that, add a fireplace here, plant grapevines down there.

Years ago that energy was expended to create a home for her daughters. Now that said daughters are grown, Jami has converted the home into a four guest-room bed-and-breakfast inn, complete with swimming pool and surrounded by acres and acres of vineyards, ranchland, and not a neighbor in sight.

As for the main house, the living room and library area offers a pool table, Ping-Pong, antique jukebox, stereo, exercise bike, and television with satellite reception. Guests are welcome to use the household clothes washer and dryer, and there's always an ironing board and iron set up in the laundry room if you need to spruce up the collar of a poorly packed shirt. If you're tired of being indoors you can stroll on Jami's sixty acres or borrow a ten-speed bicycle and peddle to nearby Lake Hennessey. Each room comes equipped with a picnic basket packed with utensils and ground cover; guests share a refrigerator where they can store picnic supplies. The Blue Valley Room and the Brass Room are furnished with antiques, the latter with a 150-year-old bedframe. The Sunset Room has a mural of a remarkable tropical scene occupying an entire wall and an orthopedic king-size waterbed.

The newest addition is called the Honeymoon Suite, though just about anybody trying to get away from it all could find a use for the Jacuzzi-for-two, sauna, fireplace, and private deck.

If you're planning a romantic weekend and would prefer to be left alone, just tell Jami and she will gracefully make herself scarce; but if you want company or lots of information, she can accommodate those needs.

BARTELS RANCH AND COUNTRY INN, *1200 Conn Valley Road, St. Helena, CA 94574; (707) 963-4001. Four-bedroom bed-and-breakfast inn. All rooms with pri-*

vate bath, cassette players, and radio. Continental breakfast. No TV in room; phone and down pillow optional. Pool on premises. No pets. Children allowed by prior arrangement. Smoking allowed in rooms. Price range: $130 to $165 for the regular rooms; $300 for Honeymoon Suite, plus 9% tax. MC, Visa, Am Ex. Two-night minimum stay.

✔ **El Bonita Motel.** If you are nostalgic about traveling in the forties and fifties you will enjoy a stay at the El Bonita Motel, right on the main drag through the Napa Valley. It is unusual for us to recommend a place right on the highway, but this place originally built in the thirties is cute, well-run, and inexpensive. The current owners have jazzed up the decor to look art deco, eighties-style. At night from the highway, you can't miss the neon lily in the office window.

There are two types of accommodations offered at El Bonita. Closest to the road is a group of sixteen poolside units—small rooms with TV, phone, deco-style furnishings. Set back off the highway, behind the other units, there are six "garden units"—larger and quieter than the ones up front—and all have kitchenettes. All guests have use of the kidney-shaped swimming pool, and all units have air-conditioning (a must during the Napa Valley summers).

Do keep in mind that the motel is right on a busy highway, although traffic is reasonably light at night. It just starts up pretty early in the mornings. Cribs and roll-a-way beds are available for a slight additional charge.

EL BONITA MOTEL, 195 Main Street (Highway 29), St. Helena, CA 94574; (707) 963-3216, or national toll-free number 1-800-541-3284. Twenty-two-room motel. Phone, TV, radio, and down pillows in all rooms. Pool on premises. No pets. Children welcome. Some nonsmoking rooms available. Rate range: $53 to $78, plus 10% tax. MC, Visa, Am Ex. Two-night minimum stay on summer weekends.

✔ **Meadowood.** There are many luxury resorts in the wine country. If you're in the mood to splurge and get some exercise you can do both elegantly at Meadowood. Not only will you get the usual resort facilities—a pool, an exercise par course, tennis courts, a pro to give you lessons, and a nine-hole golf course—you will get the unusual, including a professional croquet course, 250 wooded acres for hiking, and a wine school, where you can participate in all-day Saturday courses, two-day courses, festive dinners (with many courses), and tours of the famous Napa Valley wineries. This is a very large and complete compound.

Last but not least, most of the overnight accommodations are extremely comfortable. Although a few of the rooms are surprisingly small, the majority of the rooms and suites are beautifully decorated and spacious; several are equipped to accommodate handicapped persons. It's all tucked away in a woody, secluded section of Napa Valley yet right in the heart of the wine country and with lots of good restaurants in the area.

Please note that rates vary at different times of the week and the year, Sunday through Thursday being the least expensive nights, with rates for Friday and Saturday nights being slightly higher; rates are lowest in late November through March.

MEADOWOOD, *900 Meadowood Lane, St. Helena, CA 94574; (707) 963-3646, or toll-free in California 1-800-458-8080. Country club resort with seventy guest units, including studios, one-bedroom suites, and chalets. All accommodations with phone, TV, minifridge, and down pillows. Pool, tennis courts, and croquet and golf courses on premises. No pets. Children welcome. Smoking allowed in rooms. Rate range: $195 to $445 ($545 for two couples), plus 8% tax. MC, Visa, Am Ex, Diners. Two-night minimum stay on weekends.*

✔ **Villa St. Helena.**   To give you an idea of how showy this place is, the living room has been used as a set on the TV series "Falcon Crest." Villa St. Helena was the last major project of the architect Robert M. Carrere, noted for his villas and châteaux in Europe and mansions in the eastern United States. This is one of two homes he designed in California. Carrere was commissioned to create a one-of-a-kind grand vacation home suitable for elaborate entertaining, and he created a unique blend of Mediterranean villa, Mexican hacienda, and California ranch.

Now the rambling mansion has been converted into a bed-and-breakfast inn. Somehow, calling Villa St. Helena a bed-and-breakfast inn is a bit like describing Marilyn Monroe as "a nice-looking female"—it's true, but misses the point. The Villa is secluded from the rest of the world, surrounded by twenty acres atop a hill at the end of a long, winding driveway.

The terra cotta tile floors, high exposed-beam ceilings, antique tapestries, sculptures, oil paintings, and crystal objects that adorn the interior create an elegant setting; you expect to see Lauren Bacall in silk pajamas lounging around the Romanesque swimming pool, or the characters of "Falcon Crest" scratching one another's eyes out in front of the living room's massive stone hearth.

There are only two guestrooms and a two-bedroom suite. One of the rooms and the suite have marble fireplaces, and the suite has the added convenience of a kitchenette. All have their own private entrances. Remarkably, the price is not as astronomical as one might imagine. The secluded two-bedroom suite is about the price of the most modest room at Auberge du Soleil. And there are reduced midweek rates.

Breakfast is continental; perhaps it might include pecan tea cakes or cheesy apple crisp and coffee or tea, served buffet style. Weather permitting, you may have your breakfast poolside.

VILLA ST. HELENA, 2727 *Sulphur Springs Avenue, St. Helena, CA 94574. (707) 963-2514. Three-bedroom bed-and-breakfast inn. All rooms with private bath. Continental breakfast. Phones and down pillows optional. Pool on premises. No pets. No children under sixteen. Rate range: $145 to $225 (midweek in January and February, $145 to $195), plus 8% tax. MC, Visa, Am Ex. Two-night minimum stay on weekends.*

South Bay

CHAPTER **19** San Mateo County

San Mateo County begins where the city of San Francisco ends. Here you'll find the flower capital of the Bay Area, especially around the city of South San Francisco and along the coast by Half Moon Bay. Farther down the coast are farms that grow foods like kiwis, artichokes, and brussels sprouts.

The San Mateo coast also offers nine state beaches, some very rocky and rugged, others good for sunbathing and surfing, and most of them good for tidepooling and beachcombing.

All of the places that we recommend in San Mateo County are along the coast. Generally, that is the most scenic part of the county. There are also several hotels and motels along Highway 101, serving the airport and the many corporations in the area.

(*See map on page* 55.)

✔ Mill Rose Inn.   Just the fact that all the rooms are named for roses would be enough to make Catherine want to stay here. However, the Mill Rose Inn has much, much more going for it. This is a place to stay when you're willing to splurge and want the option of spending a lot of time around the inn: in your room cuddled up in bed or on the window seat, strolling in the gardens, or nestled in the secluded whirlpool tub out back inside a Victorian gazebo.

Located just a block or so off Main Street in a quiet residential neighborhood, the Mill Rose Inn is tended by two horticulturists who treat the place as if it were an elegant English manor house. The original house was built around the turn

HALF MOON BAY

187

of the century, with various rooms and wings and additions being added on over the years by various owners. The bathrooms have hand-painted ceramic sinks; the walls are adorned by ornate Victorian-style wallpaper. All rooms come equipped with televisions, telephones, hair dryers, and fluffy robes. The minirefrigerators are stocked with a variety of beverages, alcoholic and nonalcoholic—all included in the price of the room. A VCR can be carted up to the room should you desire to rent movies.

The rooms are spacious, with several areas of lounging about: Within each room or suite there are private lounging areas, i.e., windowseats in some rooms, armchairs with lots of leg room in others. In addition, the inn provides communal lounging areas. One of the loveliest rooms is the Renaissance Rose Suite, which features a fireplace with painted tiles, a bathtub for two, a king-size brass bed, and a comfortable sitting area with a sleeper sofa.

Breakfast is served communally in the dining room or privately in your room. You and your companion may also sign up for private time in the gazebo spa.

MILL ROSE INN, *615 Mill Street, Half Moon Bay, CA 94019; (415) 726-9794. Twelve-bedroom bed-and-breakfast inn. All rooms with private baths, phone, TV, cassette player, radio, minirefrigerator; VCR and down pillows optional. Full breakfast. Jacuzzi on premises. No pets. No children under twelve. No smoking inside. Rate range: $125 to $225 weekdays, $135 to $235 weekends, plus 8% tax. MC, Visa, Am Ex. Two-night minimum stay on weekends.*

✓ **Old Thyme Inn.** If the Mill Rose Inn is like an elegant, showy country house, the Old Thyme Inn is like a cozy country cottage. The Old Thyme Inn is located on Main Street, which is well removed from the highway but within strolling distance of the shops and restaurants, and it can be a relative bargain, especially midweek. Though the decor is lovely and full of British charm, the rooms are small enough to encourage you to spend the day out on the coast or around town, returning in the late afternoon for sherry and tea before venturing out to dinner.

The house itself was built in 1899 for the town's superintendent of schools; thus, it has a respectable past and is nothing fancy. The old house was restored and decorated by the current innkeepers, Anne and Simon Lowing. The centerpiece of this inn is the impressive herb garden in the patio around back. Not only are the herbs lovely to look at, but they have been labeled with their names and ways to use them in cooking. Best of all, their scents and flavors make their way into the potpourris in the guestrooms and into the morning meal, which includes egg dishes like frittata and Simon's own buttermilk scones.

Not surprisingly, each of the guestrooms at the Old Thyme Inn is named for an herb. Those on a budget may wish to make note that the Lavender and Chamomile rooms go for $60 and $65 midweek ($70 and $75 on weekends). The catch is that the two rooms share a bath, which isn't such a big deal for some folks (and if no one occupies the other room, you will get a private bath anyway).

The more deluxe rooms are the Thyme and Mint rooms. The Thyme Room is downstairs on the first floor and has a whirpool tub-for-two, a fireplace, and a queen-size canopy bed. The Mint Room is upstairs, has a fireplace, and an old-fashioned showerhead in an antique claw-foot tub. However, we should point out that this room is very, very green, so if you have an aversion to this color be sure to book another room.

The most romantic accommodations are in the Garden Suite, which has a private entrance and goes for $110 during the week, $150 on weekends. The suite is located out back, through the herb garden, and up a flight of stairs. Inside is a large room with a fireplace and carved mantle, a four-poster bed, a whirlpool tub-for-two in the room, and a TV set and VCR tastefully hidden inside an antique armoire. To enhance the sense of seclusion, breakfast is delivered to the door.

The other guests have the option of meeting in the dining room for breakfast, which is served at 9 A.M., or they can make arrangements to eat privately in the room.

OLD THYME INN, *779 Main Street, Half Moon Bay, CA 94019; (415) 726-1616. Seven-bedroom bed-and-breakfast inn. Five rooms with private bath, some with Jacuzzi tubs. Full breakfast. No phones in rooms; Garden Suite has a TV with VCR; down pillows optional. Pets OK. Children welcome. No smoking inside. Rate range: $70 to $150 weekends, $60 to $110 weekdays, plus 8% tax. MC, Visa, Am Ex. No minimum stay.*

✔ **San Benito House.**   Not only is the old hotel a fine place for food (see Dining section, page 56), it is a bargain hunter's haven for lodging. This is the kind of place owner Carol Mickelsen likes to stay in when she's traveling: clean, nothing fancy, and really cheap. Keep that in mind if you're simply looking for a place to flop that also happens to have freshly cut flowers in the room, a sauna down the hall, a nice garden outside, and a deli and restaurant below.

The original hotel was built in 1904. In 1979 it was purchased by Carol and a group of investors who wanted to use the first floor as a restaurant. This was such a successful venture that Carol decided to fix up the rooms upstairs. Rooms on the street side go for $55 to $75, tax included; three of these share a bath. Rooms along the garden side are more elaborately decorated, are quieter, have their own bathrooms (featuring tubs accompanied by lovely stained-glass panels), and rent for $90. One suite is painted a remarkable shade of red (Whorehouse Red perhaps describes it best), with a sitting room and a view of the world going by at the corner of Main and Mill streets.

The room rate also includes a hearty continental breakfast, which can be served to you in bed if you wish, plus a 10 percent discount at dinner in the restaurant.

Hotel guests also have access to an upstairs sundeck and a lovely English-style garden; Carol's husband happens to operate one of the largest commercial nurseries in this area, which is famous for its flower nurseries, so needless to say the grounds are terrific, especially in spring and summer (things can get pretty bleak on this part of the coast in the dead of winter). The garden includes a large grassy area, a gazebo with a swing, and a huge firepit lit at night so guests of the inn and restaurant can sit outside to enjoy the stars and night air.

SAN BENITO HOUSE, *356 Main Street, Half Moon Bay, CA 94019; (415) 726-3425. Twelve-bedroom hotel. Nine rooms with private baths. Continental breakfast. No TV in room; phone and down pillow optional. Sauna on premises. No pets. No children. Smoking permitted in rooms. Rate range: $55 to $112, tax and 10% discount in restaurant included. MC, Visa, Am Ex. No minimum stay.*

MONTARA

✔ **Goose and Turrets Bed and Breakfast.** If the name isn't enough to arouse one's curiosity, perhaps the history of the place will. What is now a cozy bed-and-breakfast inn was built as the Spanish-American War Veterans' Club. Cannons flank the front door, thus explaining the "turrets" in the name. Out back is a pond with a small population of geese, thus explaining the other half of the name. There's an air of eclecticism and whimsy about this place, accentuated by such surprise touches as electric towel warmers in the bathrooms, and *Federbett* mattresses.

The setting is a residential neighborhood in a rugged little beach town, not where you would expect to find such lodging. At the turn of the century, Montara was an artists' colony, much as Sausalito or Carmel used to be. It was also a popular spot during Prohibition; rum runners could anchor offshore and row the alcoholic contraband onto the sparsely patrolled shoreline. Today, the main things going around here are horse ranches, strawflower farms, the state beach a few miles away, and a lovely eight-mile drive down the coast to the action in Half Moon Bay.

The inn is set up with the veterans' old sitting room arranged for guests to lounge around in, read, play the piano, and shoot the breeze. English-style tea is served here in the afternoon. The handy nearby half bath is, for some reason, wall-papered with *New Yorker* covers.

The five modestly decorated guestrooms are in the back section of the building, and they are all on the small side. One of the most unusual is called Lascaux, named for the prehistoric French caves. It contains two single beds, one with a canopy, the other tucked away and hidden around a corner, a rather cozy and very pink hideaway for people who don't mind sleeping in twin beds. Other rooms have names like the Hummingbird Room and the Whale Room (so named because it has blue whale wallpaper), with a private entrance leading out to the rose garden, pond, and geese.

Breakfast is a hearty and communal affair, which may include such items as Tennessee spoon bread with country sausage (Emily, one of the innkeepers, is originally from Nashville), broiled tomatoes with pesto and Parmesan cheese, warm compote of cranberries and orange slices, corn and green pepper pancakes.

GOOSE AND TURRETS BED AND BREAKFAST, *835 George Street (mailing address: Box 937, Montara, CA 94037); (415) 728-5451. Five-bedroom bed-and-breakfast inn. Two with private bath. All rooms with German Federbett and down pillows. Full breakfast. No phones or TVs in rooms. No pets. Children welcome. Rate range: $70 to $80, tax included. MC, Visa, Am Ex. No minimum stay.*

✔ **Montara Lighthouse Hostel.**   Within an hour of San Francisco you can have ocean-front accommodations in an historic setting for just $6.50 a night. All you have to do is pitch in a bit and suspend the desire for room service and privacy. We're talking about staying in a place run by the American Youth Hostel Service, an organization for anyone who feels young. The goal of AYH is to make hosteling as popular in this country as it is in Europe.

Along this stretch of the San Mateo Coast are two lighthouse accommodations run by the AYH: this one, which is located about twenty-five miles south of San Francisco, and the Pigeon Point Lighthouse Hostel, about fifty miles south of the city (see page 192). Both establishments are clean, friendly places. If you're not familiar with the hostel kind of setup, the hostel provides shelter, a bed, and kitchen facilities; the visitors provide their own food, bedding, towels, etc., and pitch in with at least one chore, like helping clean up the kitchen.

The Montara Hostel is set in a restored 1875 lighthouse and fog signal station. The seven-bedroom duplex can accommodate forty-five guests, with two fully equipped dining rooms, a common living room, and a laundry. Most of the sleeping is done in dormitory rooms, but there are separate units available. The inside of the hostel is closed during the day, so you must come up with some interesting activities to keep you busy.

Like most hostels, the accommodations at the Montara Lighthouse are available on a first-come, first-served basis. Reservations can be made by sending the first night's fees in advance.

MONTARA LIGHTHOUSE HOSTEL, *16th Street and Cabrillo Highway (Highway 1) (mailing address: P.O. Box 737, Montara, CA 94037); (415) 728-7177. Forty-five-bed hostel, with rooms for couples and families available. No private bathrooms, phones, or TVs. Hot tub, volleyball, and croquet on premises. No pets. Children welcome. No smoking inside. Rate range: $6.50 for AYH members,*

$9.50 for nonmembers. Kids half price; private rooms $4 additional. No credit cards. Maximum stay: three days.

PRINCETON-BY-THE-SEA

✔ **Pillar Point Inn.** This unincorporated town (population 200 if everybody's home), located about a mile and a half north of Half Moon Bay, is somebody's fantasy of Cape Cod; in fact, "Cape Cod on the California coast" is the local slogan. There's a harbor with lots of fishing and pleasure boats, good fish restaurants (see Dining section, page 60), and buildings painted light blue and built to resemble East Coast turn-of-the-century architecture. In the midst of this is a very nice place to stay that combines the charm of a bed-and-breakfast inn with the amenities of a businessperson's hotel.

The rooms at the Pillar Point Inn have feather mattresses, four-poster beds, and antique furniture plus TV sets, VCRs, telephones, and minirefrigerators. The rooms on the second floor have the best view of the harbor. The views from the rooms on the first floor aren't bad, but occupants are compensated by the luxury of private steam baths in each bathroom (each bathtub has jets that spew steam; by shutting the glass doors that surround the tub you effectively create a mini–steam bath). One of these rooms is equipped for handicapped access and has the best of the steam baths.

Breakfast is expanded continental fare and can be served in the room.

PILLAR POINT INN, *380 Capistrano Road, Princeton-by-the-Sea, CA 94018; (415) 728-7377. Eleven-bedroom hotel. Continental breakfast included in room rate. All rooms with phone, TV, VCR, radio, and down pillows. No pets. Children welcome. No smoking inside. Rate range: $129.30 to $145.50 Sunday through Thursday; $150.90 to $167.10 weekends, tax included. MC, Visa, Am Ex. No minimum stay.*

PESCADERO

✔ **Pigeon Point Lighthouse Youth Hostel.** The American Youth Hostel at Pigeon Point is located seven miles south of the turnoff for Pescadero, and just a few miles north from Año Nuevo Beach. So if you're planning to visit the elephant seals and don't mind rustic accommodations, here's a chance to stay in a historic lighthouse for cheap (see entry on page 191 for Montara Lighthouse Hostel).

The setting here is a former coast guard residence that includes three bungalows, each with its own kitchen, accommodating a total of fifty persons. The former fog signal building has been converted into a communal recreational lounge. The lighthouse itself is a beauty, one of the tallest in the United States. It's open for tours on Sundays to those willing to make the 150-step climb to the top. Hostel sleeping space goes for $6.50 to $9.50 per adult and is available on a first-come, first-served basis. Reservations can be made by sending the first night's fees in advance. Remember, these are minimal accommodations, an experience that is not enjoyed by everyone.

PIGEON POINT LIGHTHOUSE YOUTH HOSTEL, *Pigeon Point Road and Highway 1, Pescadero, CA 94060; (415) 879-0633 between 7:30 A.M. and 9:30 A.M., or between 4:30 P.M. and 9:30 P.M. Fifty-two-bed youth hostel; four rooms available for couples, one for groups or a family. No private baths, phone, or TV. Hot tub on premises. No pets. Children welcome. No smoking inside. Rate range: $6.50 for AYH members, $9.50 for nonmembers. Kids half price; private rooms $4 additional. No credit cards. Maximum stay: three days.*

CHAPTER **20** Santa Clara County

In Santa Clara County you'll find Silicon Valley, Stanford University, and what's left of this once-rich agricultural region. Though there are many destinations to visit and wonderful places to eat, we haven't come across a lot of lodging we can whole-heartedly recommend. People who come here on business will find lots of chain-operation motels and hotels, but Backroads travelers have fewer options. These we whole-heartedly recommend.

(*See map on page 67.*)

✓ **La Hacienda Inn.** At the turn of the century, when there was little more than trees around Los Gatos, La Hacienda opened as a one-building inn, with an Italian restaurant downstairs and overnight accommodations above. In 1962, the owners expanded and built a very nice, lodge-style motel on the property, so now there are twenty rooms situated on eight woodsy acres.

LOS GATOS

La Hacienda combines the charm of a well-run inn with the necessities of being located near Silicon Valley. Each room is decorated with hand-crafted wooden furniture, made especially for the inn (no plastic stuff) and has a little private terrace. Continental breakfast fare is laid out in the front office each morning; guests can take their food back to the room, or eat outside, on the patio or under an umbrella at one of the tables around the pool. Each room comes equipped with such modern conveniences as a minirefrigerator, computer-compatible telephones, and, of course, television. Guests have use of the swimming pool, hot tub, and a little exercise room with a stationary bicycle. If you're in the mood to dreamily while away some time, there's a lovely lawn area behind the inn; it's trimmed with flowers and has garden benches for sitting a spell.

Three types of accommodations are available. The most modest, which seems to appeal to businesspersons, is the room with the queen-size bed and shower only (no tub). The King rooms have king-size beds, wood-burning fireplaces, additional sofa beds, and a good-size vanity area in the bathrooms (though most of these have showers only). The suites have king-size beds, additional sofa beds, and a full kitchen, complete with stoves and microwave ovens.

This is a very friendly, nicely run place that gets lots of repeat business.

LA HACIENDA INN, *18840 Saratoga–Los Gatos Road, Los Gatos, CA 95030; (408) 354-9230. Twenty-bedroom deluxe motel. Continental breakfast. All rooms with private baths, telephones, TVs, and radios. Pool and Jacuzzis on premises. No pets. Children welcome. Smoking allowed inside. Rate range: $75 to $105, plus 8% tax. MC, Visa, Am Ex, Diners. No minimum stay.*

PALO ALTO   ✓ **Cowper Inn.**   This bed-and-breakfast inn consists of two brown shingle Craftsman-style homes, joined by a porch adorned with white wicker furniture, plus a carriage house in back. The main house was built for a coal merchant in 1897; the house next door was built in 1893 and was occupied for many years by schoolteachers. In other words, these were comfortable, middle-class homes that make for a cozy place to stay within a mile of the Stanford campus, just two blocks from University Avenue, Palo Alto's main drag of shops and restaurants.

The inn opened in November 1986. It is owned and run by a former elementary schoolteacher, Peggy Woodworth, who wanted to open a low-cost bed-and-breakfast inn. When she acquired the property, the place was such a wreck that the others who had bid on the property planned to tear it down. Instead, Peggy renovated the place and decorated the rooms beautifully, complete with stitched quilts and lace curtains.

With the exception of the Carriage House, the rooms are quite small. And though they have television sets, they are not the kind of accommodations for prolonged lounging. It's an ideal place to stay if you plan to be out and about. If you are in the mood to read or be sociable, the main house has a parlor with a fireplace, upright piano, and chairs comfortable enough for an evening of reading and conversation.

The top-of-the-line room—which is the Carriage House, set back from the street, away from the other guests, and with a full kitchen—is $90 a night for two. The least expensive room is $60 for two, though it shares a bathroom with another room. All guests have access to a refrigerator and an iron and ironing board.

Breakfast is served in the parlor and dining room in the main house, though guests may take a tray to their rooms. The continental breakfast usually features Peggy's housemade granola and freshly baked breads or muffins.

COWPER INN, *705 Cowper Street, Palo Alto, CA 94301; (415) 327-4475. Fourteen-bedroom bed-and-breakfast inn. Twelve rooms with private bath. Continental breakfast. All rooms with phone, TV, radio; down pillow optional. No pets. Children welcome. No smoking inside. Rate range: $60 to $90, plus 10% tax. MC, Visa, Am Ex. No minimum stay.*

✔ The Victorian on Lytton. If you're in Palo Alto and plan to spend a significant amount of time in your room, The Victorian on Lytton is a wonderful place to stay. The owner, Susan Hall, is an artist, and she has applied her eye for soothing colors and decor to each room. The main house is a registered historic landmark, a Queen Anne–style Victorian built in 1895 for a colorful character named Hanna Clapp. The legendary Ms. Clapp, a suffragette who is said to have ridden to the West on horseback, purchased the entire block in 1890. Over the decades her home went through several incarnations: as an apartment building in the twenties, a hippie crash pad in the sixties. Susan bought the place in the eighties, gutted the house, built a new annex in back, and named each of the rooms for Queen Victoria and her nine children.

Both the old and the new structures are very appealing, with attention paid to air and light; the upscale magazine *Architectural Digest* described the atmosphere as "understated elegance." All the rooms are done in pastels and each has its own bath; the annex rooms are graced with the old claw-foot bathtubs. Several rooms have canopy beds, and all are accented by antique botanical prints; there's also a small but lovely English-style garden in back, between the main house and the annex. One of the rooms off the garden is equipped for handicap access.

Breakfast is served on a tray at your door, delivered between 7 A.M. and 9 A.M., according to your preference; arrangements can be made to accommodate an earlier departure. The Victorian on Lytton is located near the Stanford campus, within walking distance of Palo Alto's main shopping and restaurant district.

THE VICTORIAN ON LYTTON, *555 Lytton Avenue, Palo Alto, CA 94301; (415) 322-8555. Ten-bedroom bed-and-breakfast inn. All rooms with private bath, phone, and radios; TVs and down pillows optional. Continental breakfast. No pets. Children "not encouraged." No smoking inside. Rate range: $90 to $135. MC, Visa, Am Ex. No minimum stay.*

SARATOGA

✔ Sanborn Park Hostel. On the Backroads program we have visited many wonderful hostels, those overnight accommodations where guests can "rough it" and spend the night for next to nothing. In the San Mateo County section we recommended two such places, both of them lighthouse hostels dramatically situated on the coast.

One of the most beautiful of these hostel setups is located in Sanborn Park, about ten minutes from the town of Saratoga. In fact, it's worth visiting even if you're not planning to stay there. This is one of the few hostels in the official American Youth Hostel (AYH) system that welcomes day visitors.

Nestled in the woods near a pond, this looks more like a country estate than a youth hostel—probably because it *was* a country estate. It was built as a summer "cabin" for the county's first Superior Court judge, James Welch. Most of us would not call this place a "cabin." The rooms are large and airy, the use of wood lavish; most impressive is the curving redwood staircase leading to the second floor. There's an inviting and large kitchen, a hexagonal dining room, and beautiful grounds with acres of oaks and redwoods and a large, cool gazebo.

As with all hostels, the accommodations are Spartan and you are expected to pitch in with the chores. For a further explanation of hostels, see Montara Lighthouse Hostel, page 191, and Pigeon Point Lighthouse Youth Hostel, page 192.

SANBORN PARK YOUTH HOSTEL, *15808 Sanborn Road, Saratoga, CA 95070; (408) 741-9555. Thirty-nine-bed youth hostel. No private bathrooms. Pets must stay in the car overnight. Children welcome. No smoking inside. Rate range: $6 AYH members, $8 AYH nonmembers; children half price. Maximum stay: three nights.*

CHAPTER **21** Santa Cruz County

(*See map on page 81.*) The beach resort towns of Santa Cruz and Capitola developed as turn-of-the-century day resorts; visitors would take the train from San Francisco or San Jose in the morning, then depart on the evening train. Perhaps this history explains the curious lack of quality places to stay in this area. This is not to say that there is a lack of places to stay; on the contrary, there are many hotel, motel, and bed-and-breakfast establishments near the coast and in the mountains. However, most are not of the quality one finds in such regions as the wine country to the north.

Here are the places we've found that are as comfortable and professionally run as the lodging found elsewhere in the Bay Area. If you're partial to the mountains, you will probably enjoy the accommodations around Ben Lomond and Boulder Creek; if you'd rather be near the ocean, check out the rugged coastline around Davenport or the swimming-and-sunning beaches in Aptos and Santa Cruz.

APTOS ✔ **Apple Lane Inn.**   To give you an idea of the unpretentious manner with which this inn is run, a little plaque on the outside of the old farmhouse inn announces "On this site in 1897 nothing happened." Fortunately, on this site in the 1990s what's happening is a very nice place to stay, situated well off the highway on three acres of ranch land. The entrance to the inn is a long driveway, which has officially made its way onto the city map as Apple Lane. As you approach the inn, on both sides you'll see the workings of an active ranch: horses, corrals, a

barn, and farm machinery. In the distance behind the inn is the untended part of the ranch, where the deer and quail play, with the appearance of an occasional fox or bobcat.

The inn itself was built as a modest farmhouse in the 1870s; today it is as cozy and comfortable as a country inn should be. The parlor is graced by elegant Victorian wallpaper and a player piano. Down below in the basement is a wine cellar and modern "rec room," complete with games, comfortable seating, and an entrance to the English-style garden graced by a gazebo and wisteria arbor.

The bedroom accommodations are on the second and third floors of the house. The three rooms on the second floor all have private baths. The most romantic is the Blossom Room, which features a lace canopy over the queen-size bed, and a terrific bathroom: large enough to accommodate a claw-foot tub and a chaise longue. Granny Smith's Room has the home's original tin ceiling, and though the bathroom is small it still does have the original, old-fashioned pull chain toilet.

On the third floor are two rooms that share a bath. These rooms were formerly the attic and have dormer ceilings—a word to the wise if you happen to be a tall person.

All guests have access to an additional sitting room on the second floor, where you'll find a pot of coffee brewing first thing in the morning; also, a minirefrigerator for guests' use is tastefully hidden inside an antique table in the hallway. Breakfast is served at 9 A.M. in the parlor. If that time is not convenient, a breakfast basket will be delivered to your door; you will miss out on the hot egg dishes, but the basket will have freshly baked muffins and a hard-boiled egg, and you can get a glass of fresh orange juice waiting for you in the communal refrigerator.

A tip: This is a romantic place and is one of the few in the area with no minimum-stay requirements on weekends.

APPLE LANE INN, *6265 Soquel Drive, Aptos, CA 95003; (408) 475-6868. Five-bedroom bed-and-breakfast inn. Three rooms with private bathrooms. Full breakfast. No phone or TV in rooms; down pillow optional. No pets. Children "negotiable." No smoking inside. Rate range: $75 to $105 weekends, $65 to $95 weekdays May through September, ten dollars less October through April; plus 9½% tax. No minimum stay.*

✔ **Mangels House.**   The setting for this place is hard to believe: an antebellum-style summer home smack dab in the middle of a 10,000-acre state park. Mangels House was built in 1880 as the summer "cottage" (the rest of us might consider it a mansion) for one Claus Mangels, brother-in-law of Adolph Spreckels, who together founded the sugar beet industry in California. The Spreckels family built an identical home a few miles away. The Mangels family occupied their digs until 1979 when it was purchased by the current owners, Jackie and Ron Fisher. After their children grew up and vacated the premises, the Fishers converted the home into a bed-and-breakfast inn.

As you might imagine, the entrance to the inn is quite remarkable. You enter the state park and drive down a woodsy and winding road until you see a clearing and a large, white monument to civilization. The style is rich person's rustic: not as finely finished as a stone and brick home in the city might be, but impressive enough. Downstairs in the parlor is a huge stone fireplace, reminiscent of the Hearst palaces, and a large formal dining room with portraits of Mr. Mangels and his first and second wives.

The bedrooms are upstairs, and not a lot of conversion was necessary to transform the home into a bed-and-breakfast inn; you really feel like you are staying in someone's home. One room has a private terrace, another a marble fireplace. Most unique is the room painted brown and decorated with the masks, icons, and various artifacts collected when the Fishers lived in central Africa. Two of the bedrooms share a bath; another, called Martha's Room, has its own bath, but it is located down the hall. Each room has a thermostat, so you can control your own heat.

The house is situated on four private acres, some of which has been landscaped with gardens of herbs, vegetables, and cutting flowers. Breakfast is served at 9:15 on weekends, and just about any time you wish during the week. From Mangels House it is an easy drive to the beach and restaurants in Aptos, Capitola, and Santa Cruz. We would classify it as rustic-historic, rather than particularly romantic, better suited for an outdoorsy weekend than an anniversary celebration.

MANGELS HOUSE, *570 Aptos Creek Road (mailing address: P.O. Box 302, Aptos, CA 95001); (408) 688-7982. Five-bedroom bed-and-breakfast inn. Three guestrooms with private bathrooms. Full breakfast. No phones in room; no TV on premises. Some rooms with down pillows. No pets inside; some allowed in car. No children under twelve. No smoking inside. Rate range: $90 to $105, plus 9½% tax. Discount for multi-night. MC, Visa. Two-night minimum stay on weekends.*

BEN LOMOND ✔ **Fairview Manor.**   This was once the site of the Ben Lomond Hotel, destroyed by fire in 1906. It was replaced in 1924 by a summer home for a wealthy patent attorney, and it stayed in the family until 1981 when it was purchased by the current owner-innkeeper, Frank Feely, a retired firefighter.

The converted summer home is built entirely of redwood; the walls in all the rooms have redwood walls. The five bedrooms are all located on the first floor. All have private bathrooms; two have claw-foot tubs, others have a shower only. In the dining room is a little refrigerator stocked with beverages for the guests.

This is a modest place, but very comfortable, like visiting a friend's cabin—one that happens to have silver utensils and linen napkins at breakfast. The setting is ideal for those who want to stay in a quiet neighborhood in a small mountain town just a short drive from Big Basin State Park, Roaring Camp Railroad, golf in Boulder Creek, and twenty minutes by car from the beach and Boardwalk in Santa Cruz.

The house is situated on two and a half acres of wooded land; the San Lorenzo River runs through the property, so guests have access to a little private beach. Beach towels and an ice chest can be provided upon request.

By the way, instead of a house cat, the innkeeper keeps a trained rabbit named Bert on the premises.

FAIRVIEW MANOR, *245 Fairview Avenue (mailing address: P.O. Box 74, Ben Lomond, CA 95005); (408) 336-3355. Five-bedroom bed-and-breakfast inn. All rooms with private bathrooms. Full breakfast. No phone or TV in rooms. Volleyball court and river beach on premises. No pets. No children. No smoking inside. Rate range: $89 to $99, plus 9½% tax; midweek off-season rates "negotiable." MC, Visa. No minimum stay.*

✔ **Boulder Creek Country Club Condominiums.** Nestled in the Santa Cruz mountains is a country club based around an eighteen-hole golf course. Built in the early sixties, the Boulder Creek Country Club has a neighborhood of 150 condominium units, 40 of which are for rent through the club's main office. The units are well-maintained and come in a range of sizes and prices. One-bedroom units start at $75; three-bedroom units start at $136. These come with fully equipped kitchens, phones, televisions, fireplaces, wall-to-wall carpeting, and the usual comforts of home plus daily maid service. There is no minimum-stay requirement (except on major holidays), so you can spend a night or a week or two.

BOULDER CREEK

If you golf, the setting is unique: How many golf courses in the world have redwood tree hazards? Country club guests also have access to tennis courts and small swimming pools (more for cooling off than swimming laps); you can also buy a package deal that includes reduced rates on the condo, unlimited tennis court time and lessons, use of the golf course, and cocktails.

One warning: These are privately owned condos, and in terms of interior decor you are left at the mercy of the owner's taste. If the owner is into brightly colored polyester shag furniture, that's what you'll get.

BOULDER CREEK COUNTRY CLUB CONDOMINIUMS, *16901 Big Basin Highway, Boulder Creek, CA 95006; (408) 338-2111. Forty condominium units. Six pools and six tennis courts on premises. No pets. Children welcome. Non-smoking units available. Rate range: $75 to $173 per night, less 20% for multi-night stays, plus 9½% tax. MC, Visa, Am Ex. Two-night minimum stay on holidays.*

DAVENPORT ✓ **The New Davenport Bed and Breakfast Inn.** The seaside town of Davenport was named for Captain John Davenport, who came to this part of the coast to harvest gray whales. In what seems like an act of divine justice, Davenport is now a prime whale-watching spot. The oldest remaining home in town has had a long history; for a while it was a public bath, then later a dance hall, and later still, a pottery gallery. Today it is the New Davenport Cash Store, a very nice gallery and excellent cafe (see Dining section, page 84), with eight rooms and a cottage available for overnight accommodations.

Atop the Cash Store, in what used to be potters' studios, are eight rooms, each with a private entrance from the veranda, which sweeps around the second floor. The inn is located directly across the street from the Pacific Ocean, and many of the rooms have an ocean view. The bad news is that some of those rooms also face Highway 1, so if you are sensitive to noise ask for a back room, or one of the less expensive and smaller rooms in the cottage next to the inn. Mike's Room, in the cottage, is a great pick; it's small but secluded and charming. It's also the lowest priced accommodation. On the other end of the scale, Captain Davenport's retreat, in the main building, is huge with a great view of the ocean without being directly on Highway 1. It has two large beds, many areas for sitting, and is more like a suite.

The cottage has four bedrooms, with a public room where breakfast is served on weekends; other days, guests eat in the cafe. On weekends, the breakfast is continental fare with housebaked pastry, freshly squeezed juice, and tea or freshly ground coffee. During the week, guests can have a full breakfast in the cafe.

THE NEW DAVENPORT BED AND BREAKFAST INN, *31 Davenport Avenue, Davenport, CA 95017; (408) 425-1818. Twelve-bedroom bed-and-breakfast inn. All rooms with private bath, some rather small. All rooms have phones, but no TV. No pets. Children welcome. No smoking inside. Rate range: $55 to $105, plus 6½% tax. MC, Visa, Am Ex. Two-night minimum some weekends and holidays.*

SANTA CRUZ ✓ **The Babbling Brook Inn.** Now here is a place with some history. Centuries ago, Ohlone Indians lived on the cliffs and fished in Laurel Creek. During the Spanish era, the Mission fathers built a grist mill on the property, later replaced by a tannery. In 1909 a log cabin was built on the site and was occupied by a series of colorful characters—actors from a touring stock company, a gourmet-gourmand who served such legendary dinners as "a suckling pig stuffed with a quail inside a pheasant," and at least one countess. In 1942, a restaurant named The Babbling Brook was established here, and, last but not least, in 1981 it was converted into a bed-and-breakfast inn.

The Babbling Brook Inn offers accommodations within the main house and a collection of two-story "chalets." Though decorated like an elegant country inn, the rooms have the amenities of a hotel: private baths, phones, TVs; most rooms have fireplaces, and those that don't, have Jacuzzi tubs. It's all on an acre of gardens and redwoods, and, yes, a babbling brook. Amazingly, the location is just two blocks off Route 1, within walking distance of downtown, on a street that is a main thoroughfare of town. But the rooms are set back so that street noise isn't a problem. It's the ideal place to stay when visiting the University of California, Santa Cruz campus, or heading to the beach and Boardwalk. One room has been equipped for handicap access.

THE BABBLING BROOK INN, *1025 Laurel Street, Santa Cruz, CA 95060; (408) 427-2437. Twelve-bedroom bed-and-breakfast inn. All rooms with private baths, phone, TV; down pillow optional. Full breakfast. No pets. No children under twelve. No smoking inside. Rate range: $85 to $125, plus 9½% tax. MC, Visa, Am Ex, Discover. Two-night minimum stay on weekends.*

✔ **Chaminade.** On the outskirts of town is a conference center intended to accommodate large groups of people, specifically corporate groups on retreat. For this reason, the meeting rooms are well equipped and the sleeping accommodations are decorated with the bare essentials (it also explains why each room has two telephones). But for the Backroads traveler who isn't planning to spend a great deal of time in the room and would like access to health club facilities, a pool, and acres of woodsy trails, this place is terrific.

Keep in mind that you will probably be sharing the campuslike center with members of several different corporations. Fortunately, they spend most of their days in meetings, so the facilities are seldom crowded. The layout is reminiscent of a college campus, like UCSC across town. The long driveway entrance is lined with redwood trees. You walk from your room to the main building, where food is served, or to the fitness center—except you don't have to worry about being late for class.

Room rates do not include breakfast or other meals. The dining facilities are geared to serve large groups, so breakfast is served buffet style. If you prefer to eat out, there are several good cafes nearby.

CHAMINADE, *One Chaminade Lane, Santa Cruz, CA 95065; (408) 475-5600, or toll-free in California 1-800-283-6569. 152-bedroom hotel and executive conference center. All rooms with private baths, two phones, and TV. Pool, tennis courts, basketball court, Jacuzzis, and fitness center on premises. No pets. Children welcome. Smoking allowed in rooms. Rate range: $105 to $130, plus 9½% tax. MC, Visa, Am Ex, Diners, Discover. No minimum stay.*

CHAPTER **22** Alameda County

The East Bay county of Alameda includes the cities of Berkeley and Oakland to the north, Fremont and Hayward to the south, and Pleasanton and Livermore to the east. When it comes to genuine Backroads lodging, the pickin's are slim. The cities have their share of chain operations and business hotels, while the country sections of the county are not set up for tourist operations. There are some places worth noting, however, and some special situations.

For example, the Claremont Hotel in Oakland and the various hotels of Pleasanton listed below cater primarily to corporate business during the week. So, to try to fill vacant rooms on weekends, they offer special deals. These packages include reduced rates and use of fitness and recreational facilities; some places even throw breakfast into the deal. Even if you live nearby, you might want to consider a quick overnight getaway to one of these hotels.

(See map on page 93.)

✔ **Gramma's Inn.** Yes, there really was a Gramma, and this was her home. The grandchildren converted the place into a bed-and-breakfast establishment; several years later they acquired the house next door and its carriage house. Still later came a modern addition called the Garden House, so now Gramma's Inn consists of four separate buildings joined by walkways and garden landscaping and offering a variety of accommodations.

The most modest rooms are in the Main House, where the check-in desk is located and breakfast is served. The bedrooms in this turn-of-the-century house

BERKELEY

203

go for $85 each, and some are nicer (i.e., larger, with better views) than others.

Next door in The Fay House, the quarters are more elaborate and pricey. Inside is the makings of what we would call "a classic Berkeley house," with finely crafted woodwork and beautiful stained-glass ornamentation. Most spectacular is the third floor suite (Room 27), with several cushiony areas for lounging around the antique fixtures. Another nice room is Room 23. Even though it is small, the decor is cozy and the view remarkable; from one window you can see the Golden Gate Bridge and Alcatraz Island, from another the UC Berkeley campanile.

The Carriage House has been renovated to seem brand-new. Each of these rooms has a little private deck or terrace, and some have fireplaces. Midprice accommodations are in the modern Garden House; each of these rooms has a fireplace.

Since Gramma's is located close to UC Berkeley, it is convenient for visiting parents and those conducting business on campus; we have several friends who always put up their out-of-town relatives here. However, one drawback we feel obliged to mention is the neighborhood. The stretch of Telegraph Avenue between the inn and the campus attracts a crowd most visitors and many locals would not want to deal with. While on the ample grounds of the inn, one feels removed from the street; but if you plan to walk around the neighborhood be prepared to be panhandled, or, at the least, to witness the fallout of the psychedelic sixties.

GRAMMA'S INN, *2740 Telegraph Avenue, Berkeley, CA 94705; (415) 549-2145. Thirty-bedroom bed-and-breakfast inn. All rooms with private bath, phone, and TV. Continental breakfast. No pets. Children welcome. Rate range: $85 to $175, tax included. MC, Visa, Am Ex, Diners. No minimum stay.*

FREMONT ✓ **Lord Bradley's Inn.** Fremont is not a place where you would expect to find such a charming old country inn, but here it is. Lord Bradley's Inn was originally built in the 1870s as the Solon Washington Hotel. Today it's a comfortable, inexpensive spot for a getaway. Four rooms are in the main house, and four more are in an adjoining building. Two rooms are on the ground floor and are equipped for handicap access.

Lord Bradley's is located in the historic section of Fremont; in fact, the inn shares a fence line with Mission San Jose, the most recently restored of all the California missions and definitely worth a visit. Within walking distance are a number of historic buildings and nice shops. The Weibel Winery is less than a mile away, and Ardenwood Historic Park, a lovely Victorian farm, is about a twenty-minute drive.

Best of all, this place is a bargain; seven of the eight rooms go for $55 a night, including breakfast.

LORD BRADLEY'S INN, *43344 Mission Boulevard, Fremont, CA 94539; (415) 490-0520. Eight-bedroom bed-and-breakfast inn. All rooms with private bath. Continental breakfast. No TV or phones in rooms. No pets, other than Scotty dogs (the owner has several). Children welcome. No smoking in bedrooms. Rate range: $55 to $65, plus 7% tax. MC, Visa. No minimum stay. Handicap-access rooms available.*

✔ **The Claremont Hotel and Resort.**   The funny thing about this hotel, resort, and spa is that though it is surrounded on all four sides by Berkeley, it has an Oakland address. Berkeley law used to prohibit the sale of alcohol within a certain radius of the UC Berkeley campus, so the story goes that in order to get a liquor license for the restaurant and bar, the hotel changed its address.

Regardless, the Claremont Hotel is a grand place, built at the foot of the Berkeley-Oakland Hills. This location is one of the reasons we recommend this hotel. Anyone with business in Contra Costa is just a hop, skip, and jump away, over the hill and through the Caldecott Tunnel. San Francisco is less than a half hour away, and all the great restaurants of Berkeley and Oakland are nearby.

The hotel building is fabulous, a white giant of stucco and stone visible for miles. On the grounds is a pool and tennis club and a spa facility. The owners are modern-art collectors, so the grounds and public rooms of this romantic-classic hotel are enhanced by a collection of dramatic sculptures and canvases. Built in 1915, The Claremont comes equipped with several legends. One involves the original group of financiers, led by one John Spring, who liked to refer to himself as a "plaything of the winds of fortune." He proposed to his other partners that they put up their shares in the hotel as the stake in a game of dominoes. Spring lost; so much for the winds of fortune. Another legend claims that the grand hotel was designed to have a train running right into the lobby; guests could board and depart without ever having to go outside.

But even without the convenience of a train depot on the premises, The Claremont does offer all the advantages of a luxury hotel: room service, spa, pools, and tennis courts, baby-sitters on the premises, shuttle services to both the Oakland and San Francisco airports, and so on. No two rooms are alike; some rooms are done in soothing pastels and antiques, others are decorated with modern prints and lively colors. Many rooms have views of San Francisco Bay.

The Claremont is definitely in the expensive category, and on weekdays much of the hotel's business is corporate; however, there are weekend bargains to be had. For example, the weekend package for two nights for two includes room, Sunday brunch, and use of the pool and tennis club for $208 for a hillside view; $278 for a bay view room. Other getaway packages are offered from time to time; call for information about current deals.

THE CLAREMONT HOTEL AND RESORT, *Ashby and Domingo Avenues, Oakland,*

CA 94623; (415) 843-3000. 239-room hotel and resort spa. Pools, tennis courts, outdoor whirlpool tub on premises. Down pillows optional. No pets. Children welcome; baby-sitting service available. Nonsmoking rooms available. Rate range: $109 to $230 for rooms, $275 to $700 for suites, plus 10% tax. Special weekend packages available on a periodic basis. MC, Visa, Am Ex. No minimum stay. Several hotel rooms are specially equipped for the needs of handicapped persons.

PLEASANTON

✓ **The Hotels of Pleasanton.** The city of Pleasanton looks like a hundred other pleasant American towns. There's a tree-shaded Main Street and a welcoming sign on an archway crossing the heart of the downtown district. But there is another Pleasanton that has sprouted up in recent years in the form of giant industrial parks that house major corporations. With all these corporations and the huge Lawrence Livermore National Laboratory not far away, lots of business travelers come to the area. And with all those expense accounts, could Sheraton, Holiday Inn, and Hilton be far behind?

The fact is that the city of Pleasanton has plenty of huge hotels that are filled with businesspeople during the week. But the travelers go home on weekends, and that's good news for us. You see, Pleasanton is a place that enjoys good weather; when it's cool and foggy in San Francisco, chances are it's warm and sunny in Pleasanton. And since these hotels are equipped with such amenities as exercise rooms, swimming pools, saunas, and the like, they make for a nice getaway less than an hour from San Francisco and close to the Livermore Valley wine country.

But even better, the hotels want to entice you to take advantage of them, so most of them offer weekend deals. The specials will vary from month to month, hotel to hotel, but there's almost always a deal out there. Here's a list of the sort of packages that are available at the various hotels of Pleasanton. These prices do not include tax and are usually for Friday and Saturday nights.

COMPRI, *5990 Stoneridge Mall Road; (415) 463-3330. Offers a choice of three weekend packages. The regular package includes use of facilities and a cooked-to-order breakfast, $49 per night for up to four persons. The other package deals include a rent-a-car with unlimited mileage, $79 for one night, $149 for two nights.*

HILTON, *7050 Johnson Drive; (415) 463-8000. This hotel is located next door to a huge athletic club, with pools, aerobics classes, weight room, and tennis and racquetball courts. The Hilton's "Spa Package" includes Saturday afternoon check-in, one-hour massage, a bottle of champagne, brunch, and use of the athletic facilities until 5 P.M. Sunday, $140 per couple.*

SHERATON, *5155 Hopyard Road; (415) 460-8800. Two weekend packages. The*

regular package includes use of on-site facilities plus access to a nearby athletic club (additional $2 fee), $55 for two, children under seventeen free; deluxe package includes drink coupons and champagne brunch, $68 per night.

CHAPTER **23** Contra Costa County

We have recommended only three places in this large and sprawling county because this is just about all there is that fits into the category of Backroads lodging. According to at least one innkeeper, zoning regulations and other bureaucratic realities have made Contra Costa County an intimidating—if not impossible—place to establish overnight lodging. This trio offers a wide selection of experiences, ranging from a very pleasant modern hotel to a secluded country inn to luxurious accommodations on an island with a lighthouse.

(See map on page 103.)

✔ **Lafayette Park Hotel.** Situated right off the freeway on this suburban town's main street, the Lafayette Park Hotel is part of the chain of well-run hotels that includes the Bodega Bay Lodge (see Sonoma County section, page 161). This modern building was designed to resemble a French château and the rooms have nice touches like marble countertops, phones in the bathroom, wet bars, and minirefrigerators. And even though the hotel is near the freeway, the windows have been effectively sound-proofed.

Like most hotels in the East Bay, this one is geared to accommodate corporate business during the week. To help fill the place on weekends, special getaway packages are offered. Here the deal includes a $20 credit for breakfast or Sunday brunch in the hotel's Duck Club restaurant. The price is $99 for one night's lodging in a deluxe room with wet bar and minirefrigerator, or $119 in even more deluxe rooms with fireplaces or vaulted ceilings. All packages also include a complimentary bottle of wine.

LAFAYETTE PARK HOTEL, *3287 Mt. Diablo Boulevard, Lafayette, CA 94549; (415) 283-3700. 140-room hotel. All rooms with private baths, phones, and TVs; free HBO. Swimming pool. No pets. Children welcome. Nonsmoking rooms available. Rate range: $89 to $250, plus 8% tax. MC, Visa, Am Ex, Discover, Diners. No minimum stay.*

LAFAYETTE

✔ **East Brother Lighthouse.** Even natives are often surprised to learn how many islands there are in the Bay Area. Most know about Alcatraz and Treasure Island, but fewer know about East Brother Island, the site for a one-of-a-kind bed-

RICHMOND

and-breakfast inn. At one time the lighthouse on the tiny island was considered the architectural gem of the many lighthouses that dotted the bay. In 1873 a beautiful Victorian home was constructed to accommodate lighthouse keepers and their families. But with the coming of automation, lighthouse keepers became a thing of the past. The coast guard was left with a beautiful but deserted Victorian island home.

In 1976 along came a group of concerned citizens from the nearby mainland town of Richmond. The citizens offered the coast guard a deal: They'd restore and maintain the historic home by running it as a bed-and-breakfast inn at no cost to the government. The coast guard agreed, with the stipulation that the inn be run as a nonprofit operation. So today we can all enjoy an island excursion that is less than an hour from San Francisco but feels like hundreds of miles from the cares of civilization. On a fog-free day the temperature on the island is usually about fifteen degrees warmer than in San Francisco.

Overnight visitors are picked up at a Richmond marina and taken by boat to the island, where they are greeted with wine and champagne. Guests arrive at four in the afternoon and leave around eleven the next morning. Dinner is a five-course gourmet affair, cooked by innkeepers Leigh and Lindamarie Hurley, and includes several courses and wines with each course, served on china and crystal.

The inn has four rooms; the two rooms upstairs have private baths, the two downstairs share. There's no TV or radio, but the rooms are comfortable but as modest as one would expect a lighthouse keeper's digs to be. But after that meal, you'll probably be ready for bed and so tired that you won't even notice the foghorn that goes off every half hour or so. In the morning, a full breakfast is also served.

This is not an inexpensive visit. The price for overnight is $285 for two, which does include the meal, all you care to drink (there's no place to drive afterward), and your breakfast. Since this is run by a nonprofit organization, 35 percent of the fee is tax deductible. It's a good idea to plan ahead for this trip; people make reservations months in advance. The inn is closed the first two weeks of July and in late December.

By the way, if you are curious as to the whereabouts of East Brother Island, next time you're crossing the Richmond–San Rafael Bridge, look to the north when you are just a mile or so off Richmond. You can see the lighthouse from there. Visitors may take a tour of the island Thursday through Sunday; make arrangements in advance by calling the reservations number below.

EAST BROTHER LIGHTHOUSE, *on East Brother Island, north of Point Richmond (mailing address: 766 Mooney Avenue, San Lorenzo, CA 94580); (415) 278-6429. Four-bedroom Victorian home. Two rooms with private bath. No phone, TV.*

Rate includes full breakfast and dinner. No pets. No children. No smoking inside. Rate: $285 for two persons. No credit cards. No minimum stay.

✔ The Mansion at Lakewood. This very special place is so nicely tucked away that people who live in the same town stay here to "get away from it all." The Mansion at Lakewood is a former summer estate nestled behind white iron gates on three acres of gardens—some parts manicured, other parts wild. The mansion started out as a modest farmhouse, built in 1861. It and the surrounding farmland were purchased in 1906 by a wealthy San Francisco shipbuilder who wanted a weekend and summer home for entertaining guests. So he started adding rooms to the original house, including a library and parlor, now used as the inn's sitting and socializing rooms. The current owners bought the place in 1988, after the home had fallen into neglected disrepair.

Now the remodeling is finished, making for a total of seven bedrooms, each one spacious and unique. The Summerhouse Room was once part of the shipbuilder's home office; the old safe has been converted into a closet. This room has a canopy bed and its own closed-in sunporch, graced by a claw-foot tub and a day bed just right for reading and relaxing while your mate takes a luxurious bath. The Country Manor Room has a huge white porcelain shower intended for two, with room to spare. The most spectacular is the Estate Suite, the kind of place that would turn a dyed-in-the-wool grouch into a love-smitten romantic. The furnishings include an ornate antique brass canopy bed, fireplace, a private sitting area and private terrace, black marble bath with whirlpool tub-for-two.

All rooms come equipped with fluffy bathrobes, and all but one have down comforters (the exception is the room with the handmade patchwork quilt). The garden, just right for a predinner stroll, includes a formal lawn area with gazebo and an overgrown hillside of cactus and eucalyptus trees. Breakfast is served in the formal dining room (those who stay in the secluded Estate Suite have the option of a breakfast tray), at a time determined by the guest.

Keep this place in mind for the next special occasion.

THE MANSION AT LAKEWOOD, *1056 Hacienda Drive, Walnut Creek, CA 94598; (415) 946-9075. Seven-bedroom bed-and-breakfast inn. Elaborate continental breakfast. All rooms with private bath; robes provided. No TV in rooms; phone optional. No pets. Children over twelve OK. No smoking inside. Rate range: $125 to $200, plus 8% tax. MC, Visa, Am Ex. No minimum stay.*

CHAPTER **24** "Yolano" County

(*See map on page 111.*) There is no such place as Yolano County. The name comes from an association of farmers who banded together to entice visitors to visit their farms in Yolo and Solano counties. These adjoining counties cover a lot of space and border the Central Valley, which produces much of the food for the United States. Yolo is sparsely populated farm country. Solano includes the cities of Vallejo, Fairfield, and Benicia.

Although this is a bucolic and historically significant part of the Bay Area to visit, there aren't a lot of interesting places to stay. The two listed below are in the very charming waterfront town of Benicia.

BENICIA ✔ **Captain Dillingham's Inn.** Captain William Wallace Dillingham built his home in 1850. The old salt left Massachusetts in the 1840s, sailed around the horn to Hawaii, then finally settled in Benicia where he married a beguiling widow. Together they lived happily ever after in this clapboard Cape Cod–style home fronted by a white picket fence.

The house remained in Dillingham's family until the 1980s, when it was sold and converted into a bright yellow bed-and-breakfast inn; a few years ago an annex was constructed in back, adding four more rooms to the house. Today it stands in Benicia's Old Town section, on a quiet residential street that could have been used as the set for "Leave It to Beaver." You have to be careful when parking your car, though. A family of ducks lives across the street, and the folks next door to the inn like to feed them. Your attempt to park may be temporarily thwarted by the parade of ducks and ducklings waddling their way to or from a snack.

The accommodations here are extremely attractive, and the inn is very professionally run. All rooms are large and airy with TV, phones, and little refrigerators; many rooms have private decks and all but one have whirlpool bathtubs. One suite is available in the main house. The grounds surrounding the inn are beautifully landscaped with formal plantings, a redwood gazebo, and bricked walkways. It's the kind of place people reserve for weddings and receptions. If this inn were located in the Napa Valley, it would probably cost twice as much.

Two rooms are specially equipped for handicap access.

CAPTAIN DILLINGHAM'S INN, *145 East D Street, Benicia, CA 94510; (707) 746-7164, or toll-free in California 1-800-544-2278. Twelve-bedroom bed-and-breakfast inn. All rooms with private bath. Full breakfast. All rooms with phone, TV, and radio. Pets "negotiable." Children "negotiable." Rate range: midweek $70* to $160, weekends $75 to $170, plus 6% tax. MC, Visa, Am Ex, Diners, Carte Blanche. No minimum stay.

✔ **Union Hotel.** The Union Hotel was built in 1882, when Benicia was a rough-and-tumble waterfront town. Legend has it that the place once served as a twenty-room bordello ("All rooms came occupied," quips the current management). It's now a respectable three-story hotel with a street-level bar and restaurant (See Dining section, page 112).

The Union Hotel offers good, serviceable accommodations. In other words, the rooms are nice but you wouldn't want to spend a lot of time hanging out in them. It's a good place to stay if you're planning to do a lot of sightseeing or business and just need a place to change your clothes, shave, shower, and sleep. Each room is decorated with antique furniture, and each is decorated with a different theme. Two of the nicest are the Mei Ling, which has a Chinese theme, and the one with the Humphrey Bogart poster and art deco furnishings. Most of the rooms are done in Victoriana style, in keeping with the era when the hotel was built. All rooms have whirlpool tubs.

The hotel is located right on the main drag of Benicia's Old Town and is thus near to shopping and sightseeing.

UNION HOTEL, 401 First Street, Benicia, CA 94510; (707) 746-0100. Twelve-bedroom hotel. All rooms with private bath, phone, and TV; down pillows only. Continental breakfast served in dining room. No pets. Children welcome. Smoking permitted in rooms. Rate range: $74.20 to $95.40 Sunday through Thursday, $90.10 to $127.20 Friday, Saturday, and holidays; tax included. MC, Visa, Am Ex. No minimum stay.

CHAPTER **25** Central Valley

Although the Central Valley cuts a wide swath through California, the area we will concern ourselves with in this section revolves around Sacramento, the state capital.

Sacramento has been gaining new respect in recent years as an affordable and liveable city. For the visitor, it offers major attractions such as the great rail museum, the splendid Capitol building, and several mansions that are open to visitors. Not far from the city, in places like the Delta, Folsom, and Stockton, there are several quirky places to visit that offer special touches of Americana.

The area had been ignored for years by the folks who live around San Francisco. Now that there is new interest in visiting the valley, there are some surprising finds in accommodations.

✔ **Grand Island Inn.** This could be called "the best hotel in the Delta" simply because it is the only hotel in the Delta. Built in the early part of the century, it was a rather elegant place called The Ryde Hotel, and for a time was owned by Lon Chaney, Jr. In the sixties, seventies, and well into the eighties, The Ryde Hotel was a crumbling dive with a very active bar downstairs and Lord-Knows-What going on upstairs.

Then in 1989, the old hotel was purchased, renovated, and renamed by the same entrepreneur who operates the Grand Island Mansion (see Dining section, page 118). The place has been art deco-ed and painted an elegant pink. On the

DELTA: GRAND ISLAND

213

lobby level is a marble bar and a linen tablecloth–type restaurant that serves Friday and Saturday dinners and Sunday brunch.

As for the rooms, which are all upstairs, they are small, clean, and cheap. Some offer only a sofa bed and a few pieces of furniture. Suites have two rooms, with a bed and a sofa bed, plus private bathrooms. The standard singles share a common bath down the hall. All of this must be kept in the perspective of location. This is the Delta, not the Napa Valley, and there aren't many choices other than sleeping on a boat or in a modest motel.

In other words, you probably won't want to spend a lot of time in the room. But the lounge area downstairs is quite comfortable and elegant, and on the grounds are such recreational facilities as a billiard table, a pool, and tennis, volleyball, and basketball courts. A complimentary continental breakfast is served to hotel guests during the week; on weekends the more elaborate cooked breakfasts go for about $5 to $7.

GRAND ISLAND INN, *Highway 160 and Junction 220 (mailing address: P.O. Box 43, Ryde, CA 95680); (916) 776-1318. Fifty-bedroom hotel. Thirteen suites with private bathrooms; individual rooms share facilities. No phone or TV in rooms. Pool, tennis court, and other recreational facilities on the premises. No pets. Children welcome. Rate range: midweek $45 to $95, plus 10% tax, about $10 more on weekends. MC, Visa. No minimum stay.*

SACRAMENTO   ✔ **Amber House.**   All of Sacramento's bed-and-breakfast inns are fashioned out of historic homes located in tree-lined neighborhoods away from downtown and near the stylish restaurants and hip cafes that are springing up these days. In addition to being a surprisingly good getaway destination, Sacramento is a good jumping-off point for day trips to Folsom, the Delta, and some parts of the Gold Country.

One of the nicest inns is the Amber House. Built in 1905, it has the ambiance of an elegant British country house. There's lots of dark wood framing the windows, lining the bookshelves that flank the living room's large brick fireplace, and hanging overhead in the exposed ceiling beams. Downstairs are the common rooms: the dining room and the comfortable living room, with armchairs, a comfy couch, and the aforementioned fireplace, are both decorated with antiques. Each of the five guestrooms is named for a poet, and the namesake room is furnished with works by the famous writer.

The Lord Byron Room, the most deluxe of the guestrooms, is downstairs. The main attraction is the bathroom, which features Italian marble and a Jacuzzi tub for two. Upstairs, the former bedrooms of the home's original residents have been converted to individually styled guestrooms, each with a private bathroom. The prettiest is the Longfellow Room, which features an antique tub and skylight in the bathroom. The bargain is the sunny and cheerful Emily Dickenson

Room—$65 during the week, $75 on weekends. The catch is that the bathroom is detached and you must travel down the hall to use the facilities.

In the morning, an hour before breakfast, coffee service is waiting in the hall. Then a full, cooked breakfast is served, and you have the option of sitting in the dining room with the other guests or having a tray in the privacy of your room. The inn also provides bicycles for pedaling around town.

AMBER HOUSE, *1315 Twenty-second Street, Sacramento, CA 95816; (916) 444-8085. Five-bedroom bed-and-breakfast inn. All rooms with private bath, one with whirlpool tub. Full breakfast. Phone, cassette player, and radio in all rooms; TV available. No pets. Children "negotiable." Rate range: $65 to $110 weekdays, $75 to $125 weekends, plus 10% tax. MC, Visa, Am Ex. No minimum stay.*

✔ Aunt Abigail's.

The innkeeper at Aunt Abigail's, Susanne Ventura, has won several ribbons for her baking. That's enough to convince us to stay at this inn, fashioned from a Colonial Revival mansion built in 1912. The deep, long, claw-foot tub in the room named Margaret is another reason.

Of course, Margaret is the most expensive room in the place ($90 per night), but this is an example of the kind of inn in which some rooms are definitely more desirable than others. For example, it's quite a hike from the least expensive room (the Solarium) to the shared bathroom. You might prefer spending the extra $20 to $25 for the space and bathroom facilities in the Aunt Rose, Aunt Anne, or Margaret rooms.

All in all, this is the kind of place where you can feel right at home as soon as you walk in. The house is not spectacular and there aren't the showy flourishes of some of the more lavish Victorians, but there is a comfortable quality and the feeling that people actually live and have a good time here. This is another case in which the friendliness of the innkeeper was a major attraction.

Breakfast is hearty, featuring an egg dish and those prize-winning baked goods, and is served downstairs in the dining room. There's a hot tub in the patio out back.

AUNT ABIGAIL'S, *21120 G Street, Sacramento, CA 95816; (916) 441-5007. Five-bedroom bed-and-breakfast inn. Three rooms with private baths. Full breakfast. Phone and TV upon request. No pets. Children "negotiable." No smoking inside. Rate range: $65 to $90 midweek, $65 to $105 weekends, plus 10% tax. MC, Visa, Am Ex, Diners, Carte Blanche. Two-night minimum stay on holidays and holiday weekends.*

✔ Driver Mansion Inn.

This is the bed-and-breakfast inn that could change the minds of those who have never dreamed of going to Sacramento for a romantic getaway. This three-story Colonial Revival mansion was built in 1899 for a prominent attorney, Philip S. Driver, whose father had been lured to California by gold rush fever. The mansion remained in the family until 1977; it was converted into a bed and breakfast in 1985.

Even from the street, you know you have arrived at a truly grand mansion, especially at night when the gleaming white building, with a columned porch and a turreted roof, is bathed in light. After you walk up the steps and through the entrance, you'll be ushered into a tastefully furnished sitting room complete with piano.

The bedrooms are on the second and third floors and in the Carriage House, behind the main house. Each of the rooms is decorated differently, and all have special touches; a fireplace here, a four-poster bed there. The climb up the stairs to the third-floor suite is worth the effort, if you are looking for a roomy, very private getaway. The bathroom alone is the size of some New York apartments; the sitting area is as large as some San Francisco apartments, and the bedroom is as cozy as can be.

Out behind the mansion in the Carriage House are three additional, spacious, romantic, and very quiet rooms, often happily occupied by honeymooners. These rooms have fireplaces and whirlpool tubs-for-two. The main house and the Carriage House are divided by a lovely Victorian garden, complete with gazebo. A full breakfast is served in the formal dining room; if you prefer a tray served in the privacy of your room, there is a $15 charge.

DRIVER MANSION INN, *2019 Twenty-first Street, Sacramento, CA 95818; (916) 455-5243. Eight-bedroom bed-and-breakfast inn. All rooms with private baths. Full breakfast. Phone and TV in all rooms; down pillow optional. No pets. Children over ten welcome. No smoking in rooms. Rate range: $85 to $155 midweek, $95 to $225 weekends, plus 10% tax. MC, Visa, Am Ex, Diners. No minimum stay.*

CHAPTER 26 Gold Country

The Gold Country is a huge region of California, spanning nine counties. With all that territory, and with the economy geared toward the tourist industry, it's a place you can visit over and over again and always go to an area you haven't seen. There are other bonuses to a visit to the Gold Country. It's very informal and friendly, with no pretensions of chic, and its location in the foothills of the Sierra makes for spectacular scenery. History buffs encounter major finds at every turn. And, it's much less expensive than most of the other destinations.

To add to all that good news, there are several places to stay in the Gold Country that are as comfortable and professionally run as places you would expect to find in, say, Napa or Sonoma.

✔ **City Hotel/Fallon Hotel.** There are two hotels within Columbia State Historic Park, both run by the state, but each with a different atmosphere.

The City Hotel is the more formal of the two and is famous for its street-level restaurant, considered to be one of the best places to eat in the entire Gold Country. Built in 1856, the City Hotel's bedrooms are on the upper floors of the building. The rooms are furnished with museum-quality antiques that are so lovely that they are a tourist attraction; unoccupied rooms are on display to visitors. A parlor on the second floor offers comfortable seating for reading and conversation; here a continental breakfast is laid out each morning; hotel guests may eat it there or take a tray back to their room.

The Fallon Hotel is on the other side of town—in other words, about a block away. The Fallon is a bigger hotel than the City (fifteen rooms compared to nine), and is more modern (vintage 1890s). It also has a more casual atmosphere, probably because it was originally built as a family hotel. The advantage of this hotel to the other is its proximity to the town ice cream parlor; in the morning, this is where a continental breakfast is served to Fallon Hotel guests.

The two hotels have several things in common. Both hotels (and the City Hotel's restaurant) are staffed by students in the "Hospitality Management Program" at nearby Columbia College. It's refreshing to encounter so many enthusiastic young people doing their best to get an A by checking in guests at the front desk, cleaning the rooms, and waiting tables.

Also, both hotels were renovated at the same time, with historical accuracy in mind. Original wallpaper prints were reproduced, and the furnishings are true to the era in which the hotels were built. To totally preserve historical accuracy, all bathroom facilities are shared and located down the hall. But since modern American travelers prefer private bathrooms, a happy medium was struck: rooms at both the City and the Fallon have private sinks and toilets; shower facilities are shared. In addition, the Fallon Hotel has one room with a private bath reserved for disabled persons.

You may want to note that the Fallon and City hotels offer special getaway packages at various times of the year. These special deals usually include lodging accommodations, dinner at the City Hotel, tickets for the current production at the Fallon Theatre, dessert in the town's ice cream parlor, and a night cap at the saloon. Contact the hotels for current offerings.

CITY HOTEL, *Main Street (mailing address: P.O. Box 1870, Columbia, CA 95310); (209) 532-1479. Nine-bedroom hotel. All rooms with private half baths and shared showers. Continental breakfast. No phone or TV in rooms. No pets.*

Children welcome. Rate range: $54.80 to $81.00, tax included. MC, Visa, Am Ex. No minimum stay.

FALLON HOTEL (mailing address: P.O. Box 1870, Columbia, CA 95310); (209) 532-1470. Fifteen-bedroom hotel. All rooms but one with private half baths; shared showers. Private bath for disabled persons. Continental breakfast. No phone or TV in rooms. No pets. Children welcome. No smoking inside. Rate range: $43.20 to $81.00, tax included. MC, Visa, Am Ex. No minimum stay.

GEORGETOWN ✔ **American River Inn.** Georgetown is about fifteen minutes up the hill from the state historic park at Coloma, where California gold was first discovered. The state park is worth a visit, and the nearby American River Inn is a good place to spend the night.

This is a beautifully renovated hotel and former stagecoach stop that has such civilized amenities as a swimming pool, hot tub, gardens with an aviary, and a vegetable garden. When the weather is right, breakfast can be served on the very pleasant redwood deck. Inside, the common rooms are particularly inviting, what with a player piano and loads of magazines in the parlor and a large Victorian-style dining room.

The sleeping accommodations range from small rooms with shared baths to a huge modern downstairs room with its own bathroom and private entrance to the pool and garden. Be sure to request this room; it's located behind the kitchen and is definitely worth the extra money.

A fully cooked breakfast is offered, and the staff goes all out to prepare a different feast each day. Our hostess was very knowledgeable about different ways to spend time in the area. She even knows about some secret lakes that sounded adventurous, but we didn't have time to explore them; maybe you will. The inn also provides bicycles for pedaling around town, and, if you would prefer to do your own cooking in the evening, barbecue grills are available.

AMERICAN RIVER INN, 6600 Main Street, at Orleans (mailing address: Box 43, Georgetown, CA 95634); (916) 333-4499. Twenty-seven bedroom bed-and-breakfast inn. Nine rooms with private bath. Full breakfast. One room with TV; no phone in rooms. Down pillow optional. Pool, Jacuzzi, croquet, Ping-Pong, and horseshoes on premises. No pets. Children over nine welcome. Rate range: $65 to $140, plus 8% tax. MC, Visa, Am Ex. No minimum stay.

JAMESTOWN ✔ **Palm Hotel.** Ahhh—a touch of class and comfort in a town that subsists largely on hokum. The Palm Hotel was originally built in the 1890s as the modest home of Jamestown's newspaper editor. Later it was turned into a boarding house for men working on the railroad and in the mines. The current owner, Jacob Barendregt, added on to the original house, giving it the appearance of a grand old

Victorian. He's got pictures of the original structure he bought, and it barely resembles the lovely inn it is today. In fact, the only recognizable landmark is the namesake palm tree out front.

The best rooms are the two suites on the top floor. These have vaulted ceilings and skylights. And though the various accommodations are decorated with period antiques, there's a modern, airy feeling about the place. Some of the rooms do not have private baths, but the Palm Hotel has one of the nicest shared baths we've ever seen, complete with a large, marble-lined shower-built-for-two.

The breakfast fare depends on how filled the place is. On slow days, Jacob will fix you pretty much anything you'd like; however, if it's filled to capacity, breakfast becomes a buffet, served from the ornate carved bar in the parlor lobby.

We should note there are no manicured gardens to stroll about; you will probably want to spend your days out sightseeing instead of lounging around the inn. The Palm Hotel is located a block from Jamestown's main drag of shops, restaurants, and gold-panning concessions, and just five blocks from Railtown Historic Park.

PALM HOTEL, *10382 Willow Street, Jamestown, CA 95327; (209) 984-3429. Nine-bedroom bed-and-breakfast inn. Five rooms with private bath. Full breakfast. No phone in rooms; TV and down pillows optional. No pets. Children "negotiable." No smoking in rooms. Rate range: $55 to $100, plus 8% tax. MC, Visa, Am Ex. No minimum stay. One room is handicapped accessible.*

✔ **Railtown Motel.** Sometimes it's nice to stay in a motel, where you can have privacy, a pool, air-conditioning, a phone, and TV. The Railtown Motel is one of the nicest in the Gold Country and is located far enough off Main Street to escape the noise but near enough to walk to the shops, restaurants, and to see the dummy hanging from a hangman's noose above the Gold Prospector's shop.

Inside, the rooms are your typical, modern motel rooms, though eight of them do have spa tubs-for-two in the room. One room is equipped for handicap access.

RAILTOWN MOTEL, *10301 Willow Street (mailing address: Box 1129, Jamestown, CA 95327); (209) 984-3332. Twenty-bedroom motel; eight have private Jacuzzi tubs. Phone, TV, and radio in rooms. Pool on premises. No pets. Children welcome. Rate range: $50 to $65, plus 8% tax. MC, Visa, Am Ex, Diners. No minimum stay.*

✔ **Downey House.** A number of bed-and-breakfast establishments have opened in Nevada City. Though others are grander, others are cuter (with lots of stuffed animals and dolls on the bed, that sort of thing), Downey House is the one we like best. For one thing, the location is ideal, within walking distance of downtown shopping and historical sites but far enough from the same to be reasonably

NEVADA CITY

immune from traffic noise and congestion. For another, the innkeepers have done a wonderful job of combining the old (an Eastlake-style Victorian home, vintage 1869) with the new (simple and elegant contemporary furnishings). An artist was commissioned to create a painting for each room; the hallways are decorated with attractive stenciling. Another nice touch: Each room comes equipped with a small tank of live goldfish; we're not sure why this is so appealing (instant pets?), but it is. Last but not least, the rates are modest: $60, $70, and $80 for two, including a full breakfast.

The only possible drawback is that the rooms are small. However, the inn does have a comfortable parlor, a cozy upstairs sun porch, and a landscaped garden out back where guests can relax and stretch their legs. The inn does allow children, but due to room size the parents must pay for a separate room for them.

DOWNEY HOUSE, 517 West Broad Street, Nevada City, CA 95959; (916) 265-2815. Six-bedroom bed-and-breakfast inn. All rooms with private baths. Full breakfast. No phone or TV in room. No pets. Children welcome. No smoking inside. Rate range: $54 to $72 Monday through Thursday, $60 to $80 weekends, plus 8% tax. MC, Visa. No minimum stay.

✓ **National Hotel.**   There seems to be a National Hotel in every major town in the Gold Country, but probably none is more historic than the one in Nevada City. This is said to be the oldest continuously operating hotel in California, and it's now a state historic landmark.

Rooms are comfortable and nicely furnished, if not lavish. There's an antique quality to the decor with brass beds, old-style lamps, and everything looking as it might have 100 years ago. When it comes to comforts, however, like a good mattress and functional plumbing, everything is up-to-date.

We stayed in the room where the papers that created the Pacific Gas and Electric Company were signed; another in our party had the room young Herbert Hoover used to stay in when he was a mining engineer. And sure enough, our lights worked, and our friend spent the evening in a depression.

NATIONAL HOTEL, 211 Broad Street, Nevada City, CA 95959; (916) 265-4551. Forty-three-bedroom hotel. Thirty rooms with private baths. Phone and TV in rooms. Pool on premises. Pets "negotiable." Children welcome. Nonsmoking rooms available. Rate range: $39 to $95, plus 8% tax. MC, Visa, Am Ex. No minimum stay.

SONORA   ✓ **La Casa Inglesa.**   On the outskirts of town, in a pleasant, rural neighborhood, is a good place to stay after exploring the southern region of the Gold Country. La Casa Inglesa is a modern, private home that looks like a place one might find in the English countryside. The four upstairs bedrooms and a large suite are the

guestrooms, and each has a private bath. The suite has a private whirlpool tub, and all guests have access to the hot tub in the backyard. The bedrooms are quite comfortable and cheerful, decorated with antiques and colorful fabrics. A full breakfast is served on china in the oak-paneled dining room, and the menu changes each day.

The hard-working couple that lives in La Casa Inglesa, Mary and John Monser, always seem to be on hand to do something for you, whether it's make a dinner reservation or offer a cup of coffee. We even got the feeling they were waiting up for us to come home in the evening, not quite ready to retire until they were sure we made it home safe and sound. Staying here is not an impersonal matter; it's being a guest in someone's home.

LA CASA INGLESA, *18047 Lime Kiln Road, Sonora, CA 95370; (209) 532-5822. Five-bedroom bed-and-breakfast inn. All rooms with private bath. Full breakfast. Phone and TV in suite accommodations only. Hot tub on premises. No pets. Children "not encouraged." No smoking in rooms. Rate range: $70 to $95, tax included. MC, Visa accepted, but cash or checks preferred. Two-night minimum stay on holiday weekends.*

✔ Llamahall Guest Ranch. This is a very special place, one of the more unusual bed-and-breakfast establishments we've seen anywhere on the Backroads. The Llamahall Guest Ranch is a working ranch; the main order of the day is llama breeding and sales. You'll see the wooly, long-necked animals as you drive down the long driveway entrance to the ranch house. The owner, Cindy Hall, has achieved a remarkable combination of ranch practicality and elegance; you could happily spend a few days on the property and forget you may have come to explore the surrounding Gold Country.

The guest accommodations are two elegant bedrooms downstairs in the ranch house building, each with a private entrance. Both rooms are graced with exquisite antiques and ornate wallpaper. The larger of the two bedrooms has one of the world's great bathtubs; it was handmade and tiled and is beautiful to look at. Even better, it is deep and egg-shaped, meaning it's deeper and wider in the middle than on the ends—big enough to accommodate two regular-size folks, and deep and long enough to give a football-player-size person a good soak.

Though the ranch is a good place for a romantic getaway, children can be easily accommodated. One of the rooms has a day bed that can turn into two single beds for the kids ($10 extra per person). Upstairs is a parlor and library with a fireplace, comfortable places to sit, and lots of books and box games.

The ranch includes several acres of wooded land, just right for a romantic stroll or for letting the little ones burn off some steam. A creek runs right by the house, and a well-worn trail leads out to an area of Indian grinding rocks, where the original inhabitants of the property made their acorn flour. Ranch guests can take a picnic lunch down there, or, by prior arrangement, lead the llamas on a short hike through the oak trees. Inn guests are also invited to visit the llamas in their pens and feed them an oatmeal snack.

A full breakfast is served, upstairs in the big country kitchen.

LLAMAHALL GUEST RANCH, *18170 Wards Ferry Road, Sonora, CA 95370; (209) 532-7264. Two-bedroom bed-and-breakfast ranch. Both rooms with private bath; share a phone and minirefrigerator in hallway. No TV in rooms. Full breakfast. Sauna and hot tub on premises. No pets. Children welcome; $10 extra per child. Rate: $85, plus 8% tax. No credit cards. Two-night minimum stay on holiday weekends.*

✔ **Serenity.** The innkeepers must have been tempted to name this place The Phoenix. Several years ago, Fred and Charlotte Hoover retired from their respective jobs in San Diego (he was a navy man, she a schoolteacher) and moved up to the Gold Country to do what lots of people dream of doing: run a little bed-and-breakfast inn. The Hoovers designed and built their own place. He did the carpentry, milling ornate door frames and kitchen cabinetry; she sewed comforters and crocheted edging for the bed linen and curtains. The inn opened in May 1986. One day they left to do some shopping; when they returned the place had been burnt to the ground. So they started all over again and built a second bed-and-breakfast inn from the blueprints of the first, remilled the door frames and sewed new curtains.

From the outside, Serenity resembles a nineteenth-century Colonial farmhouse. Like La Casa Inglesa (see page 220), the accommodations are more like staying in someone's home than in an inn. Each of the four bedrooms is named after a flower and decorated accordingly (so beware of the Lilac Room if you hate purple). The furnishings are white wicker. Though the bathrooms are spare, they are brand-new and each room has its own. Two of the bedrooms are on the first floor, which is handy for those who don't like climbing stairs.

The inn is situated on six acres, very nice for an early-morning or late-afternoon stroll, and is near Phoenix Lake, which offers swimming and other recreational activities. Also, this is one of the few inns in the county that has a liquor license, so wine and cheese will be served in the afternoon if you so desire.

SERENITY, *15305 Bear Cub Drive, Sonora, CA 95370; (209) 533-1441. Four-bedroom bed-and-breakfast inn. All rooms with private baths. No phone or TV in rooms. Full breakfast. No pets. Children "not encouraged." No smoking in rooms. Rate: $70, including tax. MC, Visa, Am Ex. No minimum stay.*

SUTTER CREEK

✔ **Hanford House.** The Hanford House is a modern bed-and-breakfast inn, but one with a definite charm. Part of that comes from the fact that the nine spacious rooms are decorated with antiques, which makes a nice contrast to the contemporary bathrooms. After all, the quaintness of an old building goes only so far. When it's time to shower or shave or put on your makeup, there is something to be said for new-fangled lighting and modern plumbing. The rest of the charm comes from the friendly proprietors, Lucille and Jim, who moved out from Oakland about five years ago and fulfilled their country dreams. They did their research well, picking a town that is one of the most appealing in the Gold Country. Their inn is located within walking distance of the main shopping area, which is filled with antique stores.

A decanter of wine and some cheese await guests on their arrival, to be enjoyed in the large living room that is for all guests at the inn. The guestrooms offer privacy for those who prefer to "get lost," and they are spacious enough to make you feel like camping out there. They are also well-lighted for those who love to crawl into bed and read.

Breakfast is described as expanded continental, meaning lots of fresh fruit, juice, coffee, and more pastries than you could possibly eat.

HANFORD HOUSE, *61 Hanford Street (Highway 49), Sutter Creek, CA 95685; (209) 267-0747. Nine-bedroom bed-and-breakfast inn. All rooms with private baths. Continental breakfast. No phone or TV in rooms. No pets. Children welcome. No smoking inside. Rate range: $55 to $75 in winter, $65 to $100 in summer, plus 6% tax. MC, Visa. Two-night minimum stay on weekends.*

✔ **Sutter Creek Inn.** Hostess Jane Way was one of the West Coast bed-and-breakfast pioneers, and she has done everything right. Her New England–style Sutter Creek Inn is a surprisingly large compound, with rooms surrounding a shaded garden. There are several varieties of unusual accommodations, featuring such items as beds that swing (suspended by chains in the ceiling) and at least one enormous suite that is like a country cottage, complete with a large front porch overlooking the garden.

Here you are insulated from such modern appliances as the telephone and the television set. True to the genre, two features make this place stand out. Breakfast is a full-blown meal with eggs, freshly baked pastries, juice, and good coffee. As for the bed, Jane sends away to France for some of the most comfortable feather pillows around. This is a nice place for a romantic getaway; no children under fifteen or pets allowed.

SUTTER CREEK INN, *75 Main Street, Sutter Creek, CA 95685; (209) 267-5606. Nineteen-bedroom bed-and-breakfast inn. All rooms with private baths. Full breakfast. No phone or TV in rooms; down pillows optional. No pets. No children under fifteen. Nonsmoking rooms available. Rate range: $50 to $95 midweek, $70 to $125 weekends, plus 6% tax. No credit cards. Two-night minimum stay on weekends.*

CHAPTER **27** Yosemite

Outside of pitching a tent or unrolling a sleeping bag in the woods, if you want to spend the night in the Yosemite National Park, you are going to have to work through the company that has the concessions for most of the services in the park, the Yosemite Park and Curry Company, which is a division of the show business firm MCA. They offer several different types of accommodations, and information and reservations can be handled through one central address: Yosemite Park & Curry Company, Yosemite National Park, CA 95389. In this section, we'll cover the three most accessible places.

YOSEMITE VALLEY

✔ **Ahwahnee Hotel.** This is a luxury lodge, the kind that just isn't being built anymore. Walk-in fireplaces warm enormous common rooms with high ceilings and gigantic timbers. Everybody who is anybody has stayed here, including Queen Elizabeth. Her room was quite large, with a great view of the valley. Some of the other rooms are on the small side, but it doesn't matter since the public rooms of the hotel offer so much space and such an inviting setting for lounging, reading, or having conversations.

The hotel has all the trappings of a fine resort, with pool, tennis courts, shops, and even phones and TV in the rooms. Guests may choose a variety of options: European Plan (no meals), American (breakfast, lunch, dinner), or Modified American (lunch and dinner).

This is an extremely popular hotel, likely to be well booked in the summer and at Christmastime. The management recommends reservations nine months in advance.

AHWAHNEE HOTEL, *(209) 372-1407. Mailing address: Yosemite Park & Curry Company, Yosemite National Park, CA 95389. 124-bedroom hotel. All but five have private baths. Full or continental breakfast. All rooms with phone, TV (some with VCR); down pillow optional. Pool and tennis courts. No pets at the hotel, but kennel facilities are available. Children welcome. Nonsmoking rooms available. Rate range: $187.50 to $238.50, plus 7% tax; slightly lower rates in winter. MC, Visa, Am Ex, Diners. No minimum stay.*

✔ **Wawona Hotel.** This lovely inn is in another section of the park, higher up in elevation and closer to Fresno than the Bay Area. It is near the Mariposa Grove of sequoia trees and is adjacent to the Pioneer History Center. The stately white hotel looks more like a Southern antebellum mansion than a lodge in Yosemite, and, in fact, it offers a much different experience than a visit to the valley, as the area tends to be less crowded.

This is a good stop for families because of the living history exhibits at the pioneer center and because there are many activities available, including golf, tennis, and horseback riding. In terms of elegance and formalities, the Wawona is a good middle ground between the Ahwahnee and the Yosemite Lodge (see below).

Lodging here is all on the European plan, so you pay extra for your meals, which are all served in the hotel dining room.

The Wawona Hotel is closed from January through the week before Easter. Open all week until Halloween; in November and December, open only on weekends and holidays.

WAWONA HOTEL, *(209) 375-6556. Mailing address: Yosemite Park & Curry Company, Yosemite National Park, CA 95389. 105 rooms. Fifty rooms with private baths. Breakfast not included in price. No phone or TV in rooms. No pets. Children welcome. Nonsmoking rooms available. Rate range: $54.25 to $73, plus 7% tax. MC, Visa, Am Ex, Diners. No minimum stay.*

✔ Yosemite Lodge.   This is where you stay when you can't get into the Ahwahnee, or don't want to pay that much for a room. After all, most of your time should be spent in the great outdoors. Otherwise, why come to Yosemite?

The lodge offers no-nonsense motel-type accommodations, plus such features as an Olympic-size pool and an inexpensive cafeteria for breakfast. Since the price is low, it is ideal for families, so expect the pool to be crowded in the summer and expect to wait in line for breakfast in the cafeteria.

There are actually several lodge buildings, plus some cabins scattered around the grounds. The rooms have good comfortable beds and nondescript furniture, and are well maintained. Most of them have private bathrooms. Let's face it, it's hardly roughing it.

YOSEMITE LODGE, *(209) 372-1274. Mailing address: Yosemite Park & Curry Company, Yosemite National Park, CA 95389. 495-room lodge with cabins. 390 rooms with private bathrooms. Breakfast not included in price. All rooms with phone; no TV. No pets. Children welcome. Nonsmoking rooms available. Rate range: $37.50 to $89 in summer, $27 to $60 in winter, midweek plus 7% tax. MC, Visa, Am Ex, Diners. No minimum stay.*

CHAPTER **28** Lake Tahoe

Because of the lure of the casinos on the Nevada side of the lake, this is big hotel country. Even though some of them have very attractive and well-equipped rooms, these hotels are designed so you must pass through the casinos to get to your room. Few guests make it without at least one stop at a slot machine. That leaves two options: find a place out in the country or off the beaten path, or rent a condo out in the woods. For information on the latter, call the following numbers: Tahoe North Visitors and Convention Bureau: 1-800-822-5959 from California, 1-800-824-8557 from out of state; Tahoe South Visitors Bureau: 1-800-822-5922 from California, 1-800-824-5150 from out of state.

HOPE VALLEY ✔ **Sorenson's Resort.**   There's not much out in the Hope Valley except beautiful vistas, snow-covered purple mountain majesties, wildflowers in the spring and summer, clear starry nights, clean air, and a comfy, rustic resort and conference center called Sorenson's. The valley is about a half hour away from South Tahoe, out Route 88.

In 1902, the Sorenson family built a small cluster of cabins for use during the fishing and hunting seasons. The family kept building more cabins into the forties. Then in 1981 Patty and John Brissenden, with the help of friends and relations, bought the old-fashioned resort.

Now Sorenson's is open all year, offering twenty-five different activities, some on the property, others organized as group outings. These include cross-country skiing, fly fishing, hiking, river rafting, llama treks, bicycling, hot springs soaks, and star gazing. If you prefer, you can sequester yourself in your cabin with a book or head out on your own to Kirkwood ski area and casinos in South Lake Tahoe.

The accommodations are far from luxurious. The Sorensons built practical cabins; the Brissendens maintain them as quaint, rustic, and warm accommodations.

The three top-of-the-line cabins (called Rockcreek, Tanglewood, and Wa-She-Shu) are recently constructed log cabins. Each has a living room, separate bedroom, bathroom with shower, and a sleeping loft.

For those interested in no-frills bed-and-breakfast accommodations, the Lupine and Larkspur rooms are real bargains: $45 to $50, though they share a bathroom and a small sitting area. These rooms can be reserved together or for separate parties.

All cabins but one have cooking gear. In the upper-end cabins, the kitchen consists of stovetop cooking and microwave ovens. Smaller cabins feature stoves with regular ovens; so, if you're planning to bake, be sure to inquire about the cooking facilities of the place you reserve. The Lupine and Larkspur rooms have no cooking facilities.

If you don't feel like cooking, Sorenson's has a wonderful country cafe (see Dining section, page 131), with lots of housemade breads, stews, and desserts made fresh daily. A full breakfast is included in the price of bed-and-breakfast rooms.

The resort is also set up to accommodate large groups like company retreats and family reunions.

All accommodations have six different prices, including mid-week/nonholiday rates, weekend rates, holiday rates in winter and summer (less expensive in summer), plus an additional scale for large groups. But for the most part, this place is a real bargain.

By the way, this is a totally nonsmoking resort; cigarettes must be smoked outdoors. Those with pets take note: pets are allowed in two of the cabins at no extra charge; in other accommodations an additional $25 cleaning fee will be charged.

SORENSON'S RESORT, *Highway 88, Hope Valley, CA 96120; (916) 694-2203. Twenty-two cabins, plus two bedrooms in main house. All cabins with private baths; rooms share one bath. Full breakfast included with some accommodations. No phone or TV in cabins or rooms. Sauna and volleyball on premises. Pets OK. Children welcome. No smoking inside. Rate range: $45 to $105 midweek in summer, $50 to $115 weekends in summer, $60 to $115 midweek in winter, $60 to $140 weekends in winter, plus 8% tax. MC, Visa accepted; additional 5% charged for using cards instead of cash or check. Minimum stay: three nights on weekends, three or four nights on holidays.*

✔ **Clair Tappan Lodge.** For hostellike accommodations for the whole family, this lodge run by the Sierra Club is a popular spot. The facility offers some large common rooms for conversation and reading by the fire, plus a library, hot tub, and Ping-Pong table. Sleeping accommodations are either same-sex dorm-style or in small family rooms. They provide cots and bunk beds plus three good meals a day; you provide the bedding and soap and towels, and you pitch in on chores, such as clearing the table in the communal dining hall.

NORDEN

Even though this lodge is huge and can accommodate 140 people, it is usually booked well in advance, especially during ski season. The rate is very inexpensive. Rates below are for individual persons.

CLAIR TAPPAN LODGE, *on Old Highway 40 (mailing address: P.O. Box 36, Norden, CA 95724); (916) 426-3632. 140 beds in hostellike accommodations. No private bathrooms. Full breakfast. Hot tub on premises. No pets. No children under four on winter weekends. No smoking inside. Rate range: in winter, $53* *for Sierra Club members, $59 for nonmembers; in summer $22.50 for members, $25.50 for nonmembers. Tax included. No credit cards. Two-night minimum stay on winter weekends.*

SUNNYSIDE   ✓ **The Cottage Inn.**   Maybe we've seen too many old movies on the late show, but there's something very romantic about staying in little roadside cabins. In black-and-white movies, aren't these the kind of places lovers-on-the-run would end up at night? Anyway, in the little north shore town of Sunnyside, near Tahoe City, is a collection of little tourist cottages clustered around a cozy-looking main house. Though there are similar roadside cabins in the area, The Cottage Inn is a particularly well-run place. The cabins were originally built in 1938, but the furnishings and decor give the place a modern feeling. There's a sauna on the premises; if you make arrangements in advance you can have it all to yourself.

Each cabin has its own bathroom, and the larger accommodations have additional futons and daybeds for the kids.

A hearty breakfast is served each morning in the main house, where a fire will be roaring on cold mornings, and there is even an espresso maker. You have the option of joining other guests in the dining room or having a tray delivered to your private quarters.

The Cottage Inn also has access to a private beach that has picnic tables and volleyball; swimming is permitted, but because boats are launched off the dock the swimming might not be that great. Guests who arrive by or with a boat can "park" it off this dock.

THE COTTAGE INN, *1690 W. Lake Boulevard (mailing address: P.O. Box 66, Tahoe City, CA 95730); (916) 581-4073. Reservations can also be made toll-free by calling the North Tahoe Visitors Bureau, 1-800-824-6348. Fifteen cabinlike rooms. All rooms with private bath. Full breakfast. Black-and-white TV available upon request. Sauna and private beach on premises. No pets. Children welcome. No smoking inside. Rate range: $70 to $100 in spring and fall, $100 to $110 winter and summer, plus 8% tax. MC, Visa. Minimum stay: two nights on weekends, two to four nights on holidays.*

TRUCKEE   ✓ **Best Western.**   Normally we don't spend much time in chain-type motels or recommend them. But special mention is due to the Truckee Best Western. Though the bed-and-breakfast boom has not yet swept the Tahoe area, someone involved with this place has been incorporating the special touches one expects at a bed and breakfast.

For starters, when you check in you are invited into a reception room behind the lobby for cherry cobbler, coffee, tea, hot chocolate, soft drinks, and video movies. Okay, the coffee is not freshly ground French roast and the cobbler was not made by your grandmother. But it's the thought that counts. And if you have kids they'll probably love it.

Then there's the complimentary breakfast served upstairs. You'll have sweet rolls, muffins, hot and cold cereals, and hot beverages.

The rooms are about what you'd expect: basic beds and bathrooms and motel decor, but guests do have access to a hot tub and sauna. Nonsmoking rooms are available.

BEST WESTERN, *11331 Highway 267, Truckee, CA 95734; (916) 587-4525, or call toll-free in California 1-800-824-6385. 100-bedroom motel. Continental breakfast. All rooms with private bath, phone, TV, radio; down pillows optional. Pool, Jacuzzi, and sauna on premises. No pets. Children welcome. Nonsmoking rooms available. Rate range: $56 to $77, plus 8% tax. MC, Visa, Am Ex, Discover, Diners. No minimum stay.*

✔ **Richardson House.** As just mentioned, the bed-and-breakfast boom has not yet hit the Tahoe area, but there is a good one in Truckee. The Richardson House is a Victorian mansion on a hillside above the town of Truckee. This was the home of lumber baron Warren Richardson, who built this place in the late 1800s.

There are not many Victorian mansions in this part of the world, so the restoration and conversion of this historic home into a bed and breakfast was practically a public service. Currently it is run by Mary Lou Huebner, who is continuing the restoration to bring the place back to its original splendor.

Already it's pretty ornate and snazzy. Unlike city Victorians, which tend to be dark and full of tiny rooms, country Victorians like this one have large, airy, welcoming rooms. Period antiques adorn the place.

With a panoramic view of the mountains, the large living room is a comfortable place where guests can chat, read, or simply gaze out the windows. The bedrooms are quite large if you prefer privacy. Wine and cheese are served in the evening, and a full breakfast comes with the price of the room.

There is one possible drawback to this inn, however. All seven guest rooms share bathrooms. This is less of a problem when the inn is not full, which usually means week nights. You can inquire about the chances of having a bath to yourself if that's important to you.

RICHARDSON HOUSE, *corner of Spring and High streets (mailing address: P.O. Box 2011, Truckee, CA 95734); (916) 587-5388; collect calls accepted for reservations. All rooms share baths. Full breakfast. No phone or TV in rooms. Jacuzzi on premises. No pets. Children over twelve "preferred." No smoking in rooms. Rate range: $55 to $70 in winter, $45 to $60 in summer, plus 8% tax. MC, Visa. Two-night minimum stay during ski season and on holiday weekends.*

CHAPTER **29** Mendocino County

Whenever we need a "can't miss" location for a TV segment, we head for Mendocino. This area is simply one of the most beautiful in California, with its rugged coastline, dense forests, and quaint towns. It's been the setting for countless films and television shows, often passing for New England.

The County of Mendocino includes such inland towns as Boonville and Ukiah; Ft. Bragg and the village of Mendocino are the main population centers on the Coast and draw the most visitors. Here, and in the coastal towns of Albion and Elk, you will find a wide selection of accommodations, ranging from historic old hotels to very cozy bed-and-breakfast inns. Be advised that most of the smaller places do not accept credit cards nor do they offer phones or TVs. Also, many operations are closed mid-December through February, so if you have your heart set on one place be sure to call ahead to make sure the innkeeper doesn't have plans to be in Tahiti. The good news is that winter time can be perfect for visiting the area. The summer coastal fog takes a vacation and you can get wonderfully clear, sunny days. What's more, there are few tourists in the winter.

Also included in this section are a few places on the way to Mendocino, in Philo, which is north of Boonville, and near Gualala, on the coastal route.

ALBION

✓ **Fensalden Inn.** To get to this former stagecoach stop, you turn off Highway 1 and head east for about a quarter of a mile on Navarro Ridge Road. Suddenly you find yourself in the rural countryside. If you stay at Fensalden Inn, what is sacrificed by not being right on the ocean is made up for the peace and quiet of the countryside. That is, of course, unless the cows across the street start making a racket; they moo very loudly in the morning before they've been fed, but for our money it's better than listening to trucks going by on Highway 1.

Fensalden Inn was built in the 1860s and has evolved into a very gracious homelike setting that looks brand-new. It is on twenty acres of land that include a barn and rolling hills. Within the main house is a large and comfortable common room with a baby grand piano and view of the fishing boats, and if your timing is right, of the migrating whales in the distance. Guests may have breakfast here, or be served in their room. Two bedrooms are downstairs, and three are upstairs. Particularly comfortable is the upstairs Pearl Suite, complete with a sitting room, fireplace, and ocean view.

Out back is the water tower, which has two bedrooms, including the Cypress, which has a fireplace, queen-size bed, and private entrance. The Captain's Walk Suite has an upstairs loft with queen-size bed and downstairs sitting room with fireplace and kitchen.

FENSALDEN INN, *33810 Navarro Ridge Road (mailing address: P.O. Box 99, Albion, CA 95410); (707) 937-4042. Eight-bedroom bed-and-breakfast inn. All rooms with private bath. Full breakfast. No phone or TV in rooms. No pets. Children twelve and over allowed. No smoking in rooms. Rate range: in winter, $60 to $115, summer $70 to $105 midweek, $80 to $125 weekends, plus 8% tax. MC, Visa. Two-night minimum stay on weekends.*

✓ **Toll House Inn.** When you pull into the gravel parking lot adjacent to the Toll House Inn, one of the first things you see is a satellite TV dish. Not to worry; there's only one television in the place, and it's in the innkeeper's quarters. For big media events like Academy Awards or Olympics, owner Beverly Nesbitt will invite her guests to watch, but most of the time you'll be cut off from the world. There's no phone in the room, just lots of old magazines lying around in baskets, mostly back issues of *National Geographic* and various food and wine publications.

BOONVILLE

In other words, this is a place to get away from it all, whatever "all" may be. There's nothing fancy about this homey country inn, but it has the appeal of a lovely garden, a porch swing, hammocks, lawn chairs, and a hot tub. Beverly is a very youthful grandmother and a former professional photographer from Laguna Beach who decided to get out of the Southern California rat race and into the quiet of the boonies. At breakfast you'll be awfully glad she did. She can cook wonderful omelets and bake perfect muffins accompanied by a variety of local products, including Thanksgiving coffee and Tinman apple juice. She seems to be having a ball.

Her house was originally built in 1912 for the Miller Family, who maintained the road out front and extracted a fee from passers-by. Thus the name Toll House. Today that road is State Highway 253, and it is the connecting route between Highway 128 and Boonville to U.S. Highway 101 and Ukiah. Trucks use the road, and you can hear them at night, so if you book one of the front rooms—the Library downstairs or the Blue Room upstairs—you might want a pair of earplugs with you. The advantage of those two rooms is that they both have fireplaces and private bathrooms.

The least expensive room is called The Bicycle Shed, so called because it seems to appeal to those cycling through the area, i.e., willing to rough it a bit. This bare-bones room has twin beds, and the occupants must traipse across the yard into the house to use bathroom facilities. But it is charming, and the room rate includes the full breakfast.

TOLL HOUSE INN, *15301 Highway 253, Boonville, CA 95415; (707) 895-3630. Five-bedroom bed-and-breakfast inn. Three rooms with private bath. All rooms have cassette tape player and radio; two rooms have the option of telephone, upon request. Full breakfast. Hot tub on premises. No pets. Children "negotia-*

ble." Rate range: $70 to $120, plus 8% tax. No credit cards. Two-night minimum stay on weekends, three nights on holidays.

ELK   ✔ **Harbor House.**   Around the turn of the century, the town of Elk was a busy seaport for the lumber industry. In 1916 the Goodyear Redwood Lumber Company built an executive residence for entertaining clients. The main house was built as a commercial showroom, featuring vaulted ceilings and elaborate fireplace mantels made of gorgeous virgin redwood.

Today the former executive guest home is a bed-and-breakfast and dinner inn called the Harbor House. It rests on the bluffs above the ocean, surrounded by landscaped gardens with a path leading down to a beach. In the main house are six bedrooms, each with a private bath and wood stove or fireplace. In the yard are four guest cabins, which offer a greater sense of privacy than the rooms in the main house; one cottage has a spectacular ocean view. All accommodations are decorated in period furnishings.

Staying here requires you to agree to have dinner at the inn, or at least to pay for it. Even though this may prevent you from sampling some of the other places in the area, you should know that the evening meal at Harbor House is good enough to attract customers from other towns. There's a full-time gardener on staff, and many of the vegetables come from the backyard.

HARBOR HOUSE, *5600 South Highway One (mailing address: P.O. Box 369, Elk, CA 95432); (707) 877-3203. Six bedrooms in main house, plus four cottages. All accommodations have private baths. Full breakfast. No phone or TV in room; down pillow optional. No pets. No children. Rate range: $135 to $200, plus 8% room tax and 6% food tax. Room rate includes breakfast and dinner for two; midweek in winter, rates drop $10 to $20. No credit cards. Two-night minimum stay on weekends.*

GUALALA   ✔ **Old Milano Hotel.**   The Old Milano Hotel is so unique and well positioned on the ocean side of Route 1 that it is worth the inconvenience and/or lack of privacy and/or whatever reasons people don't like sharing bathrooms.

The original hotel was built in 1905 by an Italian couple who named their restaurant, pub, and inn after their hometown. Their customers were the travelers on the old coastal route.

Not a lot has changed inside the old hotel. Today it is furnished in gracious Victorian style—a contrast of civilization and fine china against a backdrop of nature and rugged coastline. Upstairs, the hotel has six guestrooms that share two bathrooms. Downstairs, the original quarters of the Lucchinetti family is now a master suite, featuring a private sitting room with ocean view, separate bedroom, and a private bath. The only potential drawback to this suite is that it is located right off the wine parlor, where guests sometimes gather for breakfast.

For more privacy, two accommodations separate from the hotel building are available. One is called the Passion Vine cottage and is separated from the hotel by a lush garden. This has a kitchenette, wood stove, a loft for reading and other lounging activities, and bathroom with shower. It is very cute, but not recommended for tall people; the bathroom in particular is very tiny.

The other private accommodation is called The Caboose, and it really is a caboose, from the old Pacific North Coast Railroad. It has been remodeled to have a private bath, kitchenette, and cupola. It is tucked away in the woods and far enough from other guests that the hotel's usual "no children" policy can be waived for this room.

All in all, the setting is spectacular, on three acres of pine and cedar trees, flowers, and bluffs overlooking some of the most beautiful coastline in the world. In front of the hotel is a manicured lawn on which one may play croquet; out back is a hot tub, positioned to take advantage of the cliffside view.

The hotel operates a restaurant that is a very popular place for dinner. The kitchen also prepares a generous breakfast for hotel guests; this may be enjoyed in the bedroom, on the patio, or by the fireplace in the wine parlor.

OLD MILANO HOTEL, *38300 Route One, Gualala, CA 95445; (707) 884-3256. Nine-bedroom hotel. Three rooms with private baths. Full breakfast. No phone or TV in rooms. Hot tub on premises. No pets. No children, except in The Caboose. No smoking inside. Rate range: $75 to $160, plus 6½% tax; in winter, 25% discount Monday through Thursday. MC, Visa, Am Ex. Two-night minimum stay on weekends.*

✔ **Serenisea.** What if you're traveling with the kids and a dog? Or what if you want to stay put for many nights in a row? You can check out the rustic and comparatively cheap cottages in Serenisea. A group of four is set on the bluffs above the ocean in a semicircle, with a basketball hoop in the center.

One of the best deals on the Mendocino coast is Cottage Number 5: two bedrooms, sauna, cable TV, stereo, full kitchen, sundeck with grill and picnic table, all overlooking the ocean, and with views from every room—$95 a night for two persons in winter, $110 summer. Also on the property is a cabin with one bedroom, a tiny kitchenette and a bathroom, a bit beat-up and well worn but only $45 a night in winter, $50 in summer. So what if the tile in the kitchen is askew? All these cottages have fireplaces, kitchens, or kitchenettes and come equipped with linens, pots and pans, dishes and firewood; most have phones and TVs. The price drops 30 percent after a three-night stay.

The folks who run Serenisea also make arrangements for the rental of vacation homes in the area.

SERENISEA, 36100 Highway One South, Gualala, CA 95445; (707) 884-3836. Hot tub on premises. Pets OK. Children welcome. Four oceanfront cottages plus a variety of vacation homes in the area. Cottages range from $45 to $90 a night during winter, $50 to $120 in summer, plus 8% tax. No credit cards. Two-night minimum stay in vacation homes.

LITTLE RIVER

✔ **Glendeven.**   Glendeven is a large operation, a two-acre compound that includes gardens, bedrooms within a Victorian farmhouse, accommodations for families or groups in a converted barn, four suites in a recently constructed building, plus a crafts gallery featuring one-of-a-kind fine furniture.

A variety of rooms is offered within the old farmhouse, built in 1867. One of the most elaborate is the Eastlin Suite, with its own sitting room, fireplace, French doors looking across the brick terrace to the bay, and a secret doorway hidden behind a bookcase—just like in old British murder mysteries. Another special room is The Garret, which is, of course, in the attic and features dormer windows, an elaborate antique bed, and a private bath. The least expensive rooms in the house share a bath; these two bedrooms are offered at a reduced rate when rented together.

The top-of-the-line rooms are the four newly constructed suites in the Stevenscroft building, two on the ground level, two up a flight of stairs, each with a private entrance. These are the ultimate in tasteful interior design, combining period wallpaper prints and furniture with modern art. The Bayloft features a fireplace and bay view window, the Briar Rose has a private balcony overlooking Glendeven's gardens and the bay in the distance; the Pinewood has a fireplace and Swedish tub and shower, and the East Farmington has a private deck.

The Barn Suite is the farmhouse's original hay barn; the innkeepers remodeled it as their home. They have taken up residence elsewhere, but the barn is available to accommodate parties of two to five.

Breakfast is of the type that serves warm muffins and hard-boiled eggs. You have the choice of having it delivered to your door or of socializing with other guests in the dining room of the main house.

As with most places, you get what you pay for. The more expensive rooms are larger and more gracious than the less expensive rooms. Also, bear in mind that the main house is located near the road, while the suites building is set back, away from the possible intrusion of highway sounds.

GLENDEVEN, 821 N. Highway 1 (Shoreline Highway), Little River, CA 95456; (707) 937-0083. Eleven-bedroom bed-and-breakfast inn. Eight rooms with private baths. Continental breakfast. No phone or TV in rooms; down pillow optional. Hot tub on premises. No pets. Children welcome. No smoking in rooms. Rate range: $70 to $120 midweek, $80 to $140 weekends, plus 8% tax. Large *barn suite $185 to $220, plus 8% tax. MC, Visa. Two-night minimum stay on weekends.*

✔ **The Inn at Schoolhouse Creek.** When innkeepers Linda Wilson and Peter Fearey left their political jobs in Sacramento to open an inn in Mendocino, they set out to do what everyone said was impossible: to offer nice accommodations at a bargain price. They've managed to do it by cutting out the frills. What's left is the best lodging deal near Mendocino, especially for those traveling with children and pets. This is the only place we've found in the entire area that offers a $37 room with a private bath.

Linda and Peter took over The Lazy Eye Motor Court, an odd conglomeration of five cabins and seven motel rooms—some built in the 1800s, others in the 1930s, others in the 1960s—cleaned them up, painted them light blue, and named the place The Inn at Schoolhouse Creek (yes, Schoolhouse Creek does run through the property). One way they've cut corners is by not providing breakfast. Instead, there's a Coffee Room; in the morning guests can help themselves to a fresh brewed pot and a bowl of fruit. In the Coffee Room is a collection of box games, which guests can borrow, and a bulletin board posted with notices of local events.

The old miners' cabins have full kitchens, separate bedrooms, queen-size hide-a-beds in the living room, a dining area, fireplace, and deck with view. Other accommodations have kitchenettes, and some are simply rooms with a bath (the $37 room is a simple room-and-bath arrangement). All rooms come equipped with a pot for boiling water and the makings for instant coffee and tea.

Pets and children are welcome, and as a result the rooms show the wear and tear. The advantage of these modest accommodations is that it is possible to set up housekeeping for a week or more, cooking your own meals and whiling away the time on your own little terrace area with ocean view. Also, the inn is located on ten acres of land leading down to the creek, which makes for a very pleasant morning or afternoon walk without having to drive anywhere. Picnic tables are provided on the lawn area.

THE INN AT SCHOOLHOUSE CREEK, *7051 North Highway 1, Little River, CA 95456; (707) 937-5525. Twelve-bedroom inn, including five cabins. All rooms with private baths. No phone or TV in rooms. Pets OK. Children welcome. Rate range: $37 to $80, plus 8% tax. No credit cards. Two-night minimum stay on weekends, three nights on holidays.*

✔ **Rachel's Inn.** This is a small operation, run by Rachel Binah, one of the leading activists in the struggle to prevent off-shore drilling on the Mendocino Coast. In the area you'll see lots of businesses with a picture of a floating oil well with a red slash through it (it's a very popular cause in these parts). At the check-in desk at Rachel's is a large jar filled with the business cards of inn patrons who support the cause; Rachel has several of these jars filled to the brim; she hopes to drop them off in Washington, D.C., someday.

In addition to fighting the good cause, Rachel runs a first-class inn. She started out in 1984 by buying an 1860s vintage drugstore. It was a wreck, and Rachel will happily show you her photo album documenting the inn's transformation to its present condition. Today it's hard to imagine that this wasn't always a lovely country inn, decorated in soothing colors, antique furniture, and modern art.

The rooms are all different and have special touches. Downstairs, the Garden Room has its own fireplace, and the Parlor Suite has its own piano. Upstairs is a sitting room for inn guests and some bedrooms with an ocean view.

Rachel's breakfast is substantial and may include omelets, creamy polenta, and ratatouille; with advance notice she can prepare dinner for her guests.

The inn itself is adjacent to eighty-two acres of state park land; paths meander from the inn through woods and down to the ocean.

RACHEL'S INN, *on North Highway 1, two miles south of Mendocino (mailing address: P.O. Box 134, Mendocino, CA 95460); (707) 937-0088. Five-bedroom bed-and-breakfast inn. All rooms with private bath. Full breakfast. No phone or TV in rooms. No pets. Children welcome. Rate range: $89 to $100, plus 8% tax. No credit cards. Two-night minimum stay on weekends, three to four nights on holidays.*

MENDOCINO ✔ **Big River Lodge/The Stanford Inn by the Sea.** Not only is this the longest name for a bed-and-breakfast inn in the area, it is also the best place to stay when you want the convenience of a telephone and TV in your room. This former motel has been converted into an attractive antique-and-modern-art-filled inn. Each room has its own deck, a minirefrigerator and an automatic drip coffee maker for brewing a fresh pot of Thanksgiving coffee each morning. Some rooms have a view of the ocean, others a view of Mendocino, some have a wood-burning fireplace, others a wood-burning stove.

Also available is a two-bedroom cottage with all the comforts of home, including a kitchen and maid service.

The inn is located a bit south of town, so you are away from the hubbub of the village yet nearby. Breakfast usually consists of warm coffee cake, fresh fruit, and granola, which you can eat with fellow guests in the parlor off the lobby or you can take a tray to your room. The staff is quite knowledgable about the best places for dinner and sightseeing, and bicycles are available to guests free of charge.

On the property is a pond with black swans, a family of llamas, and a fruit and vegetable garden; the organically grown lettuces, spinach, and so on are sold to local restaurants and donated to a local food bank and senior center.

BIG RIVER LODGE/THE STANFORD INN BY THE SEA, *Highway 1 and Comptche-Ukiah Road, ¼ mile south of Mendocino (mailing address: P.O. Box 487, Mendocino, CA 95460); (707) 937-5615. Twenty-four-bedroom lodge, plus a two-bedroom cottage. All rooms with private bath. Continental breakfast. All rooms with phone, TV, VCR, cassette player, radio, down pillows, and minirefrigerator. Pets OK. Children welcome. Rate range: $135 to $205, plus 8% tax; reduced rates midweek in winter. MC, Visa, Am Ex, Diners, Discover. Two-night minimum stay on weekends; three to four nights on holidays.*

✔ **Blue Heron Inn.** Here's a hidden little three-room inn that's a big bargain. Right in the heart of Mendocino village, the Blue Heron offers two rooms above a cafe called The Chocolate Moose and a private bungalow in the courtyard behind. The rooms are small but tastefully decorated in pastels and with contemporary furnishings, lending an airy feeling to the rooms.

The two rooms above the cafe share a bath; the Bay Room has a view of the ocean from one window and of the village rooftops from the other; the Sunset Room is a perfect writer's garret, built into the slope of the roof with a window desk facing the garden below and the ocean at a distance. The two rooms can be rented together at a reduced rate, and children are welcome at the inn if parents rent both rooms.

The Garden Room, which is the bungalow located behind the cafe, has a private entrance on Albion Street, private bath, a fireplace, deck, and garden. All accommodations are graced by down comforters, feather pillows, and fresh flowers. Room rate includes a continental breakfast in the cafe, consisting of freshly squeezed orange juice, hot homemade coffeecake or croissant, and a good cup of coffee.

BLUE HERON INN, *390 Kasten Street, Mendocino, CA 95460; (707) 937-4323. Three-room bed-and-breakfast inn. One room with private bath. Continental breakfast. No phone or TV in rooms; down pillow optional. No pets. Children welcome. Rate range: $58 to $90, plus 8% tax. No credit cards. Two-night minimum stay on weekends, three nights on holiday weekends.*

✔ **Brewery Gulch Inn.** Did you get to visit a kindly grandma and grandpa who lived in a big farmhouse out in the country? If you didn't, here's your chance. Marge and Dean Alexander have a storybook white farmhouse on ten acres down the road from Mendocino village. It's the oldest farm on the Mendocino coast, established in the 1860s as a brewery and dairy operation (talk about contented cows . . .). If you walk out into the orchard you'll find the old copper beer-brewing pots.

Once you check into the main house, you've got the run of the place. The Alexanders live in separate quarters on the property and come back in the morning to fix your breakfast. The wonderful farmhouse kitchen—featuring a huge, antique wood-burning oven and stove—is open to guests at all hours for making tea, coffee, and hot chocolate. Families or large parties traveling together can rent the entire house at a reduced rate.

This is the sort of inn that feels like you're staying in someone's home. There's nothing fancy about the place; no interior designer has made things just so. The decor is an informal collection of handmade quilts, some antiques, and furniture you can put your feet up on. Particularly pleasant are the downstairs Garden Room, with a fireplace and huge picture window, and the upstairs suite, which has a private sitting area.

Breakfasts are full and plentiful and can be served in your room or downstairs at the dining room table or outside in the garden, weather permitting.

BREWERY GULCH INN, *9350 Coast Highway 1, Mendocino, CA 95460; (707) 937-4752. Five-bedroom bed-and-breakfast inn. Three rooms with private bath. Full breakfast. No phone or TV in rooms. Croquet and horseshoes on premises. No pets. No children, unless entire house is rented. No smoking in rooms. Rate range: $70 to $110, plus 8% tax; entire house $400 plus tax; midweek in winter 25% discount on all accommodations. MC, Visa. Two-night minimum on weekends, three nights on holidays.*

✔ **Mendocino Village Inn.** For years, the Mendocino Village Inn was the wreck of an elaborate Queen Anne Victorian, a landmark as you'd approach the main drag of shops and restaurants. Now it is a cheerfully restored bed-and-breakfast inn, thanks to the efforts of Sue and Tom Allen. This sprawling home, built in 1882, offers a range of accommodations. At the modest end is one of the better deals in town: two attic rooms that share a bath—$55 each. At the top of the line is the Diamond Lil Room, which was once a parlor; guests who stay here have a private fireplace, a crystal chandelier, a claw-foot bathtub, and various frilly excesses a Victorian lady would enjoy. Another room of note is the Teddy Roosevelt on the second floor; it comes complete with a fireplace, private bath, ocean view, and rough rider–style hat.

Breakfasts are elaborate, with housemade breads, fresh fruit and juice, plus a breakfast entree along the lines of savory cheesecake and blue cornmeal pancakes.

MENDOCINO VILLAGE INN, *44860 Main Street, between Evergreen and Howard (mailing address: P.O. Box 626, Mendocino, CA 95460); (707) 937-0246, or toll-free in California 1-800-882-7029. Twelve-bedroom bed-and-breakfast inn. Ten rooms with private bathrooms. Full breakfast. No phone or TV in rooms; some rooms with down pillows. No pets. Children over ten OK. No smoking in rooms.*

Rate range: $55 to $120, plus 8% tax. MC, Visa. Two-night minimum on weekends.

✔ **Philo Pottery Inn.** This former stagecoach stop has been a bed-and-breakfast inn and pottery gallery since 1986, founded by a potter who has since decided to devote full time to her art. The operation was sold to Bill Hardart, a former insurance salesman from New Jersey who decided to live yet another version of the American Dream. He and his wife, Judy, offer very nice accommodations with creature comforts like antiques, down comforters, and a hearty breakfast.

Most of the guestrooms are in the main house. The rooms upstairs have private bathrooms; one has a claw-foot tub. The least expensive room is a garden cottage out back near the pottery gallery. The good news is it has a cozy wood-burning stove; the bad news is you have to go outside to the main house to use bathroom facilities.

The inn is situated on an acre of land shaded by a grove of trees, including a remarkable pair of cedars probably planted by some pioneering resident of long ago. Bill also tends two small gardens on the property, one with herbs and other edible things that make their way into the morning meal.

Rooms are small, so you'd probably want to spend reading and relaxing time in the library–living room. The pottery gallery is in a log cabin behind the main house; if you don't have the time to spend the night, you might enjoy checking out the craftwork of the locals.

PHILO POTTERY INN, *8550 Highway 128 (mailing address: P.O. Box 166, Philo, CA 95466); (707) 895-3069. Five-bedroom bed-and-breakfast inn. Three rooms with private bath. Full breakfast. No phone or TV in rooms. No pets. Children over six OK. Rate range: $65 to $82, plus 8% tax. No credit cards. No minimum stay.*

CHAPTER **30** Redwood Empire

The area that features some of the oldest living creatures in the world, the great coastal redwoods, also offers some very nice places to stay. The natural surroundings of this part of the country are all on a grand scale, and possibly taking inspiration from the great trees, the hotels and inns seem to follow suit. There are some very ornate and impressive hostelries in this neck of the woods, and since Eureka and Ferndale are not the tourist draws of Carmel or Mendocino, the innkeepers are more than hospitable.

EUREKA ✓ **Carter House Inn and Hotel Carter.** Just down the street from the fabulous Carson Mansion—the most elaborate Victorian building you can imagine, now used as a private men's club—is a dual set of accommodations run by the Carter family. (No, not the country-and-western singers.) Both offer the ultimate in comfort and style, though in concept they are as different as night and day.

The Carter House Inn, a bed-and-breakfast establishment, came first. By appearances you'd bet money that the place was built at the turn of the century. However, the original Victorian that stood on this site was destroyed in the 1906 earthquake, the same jolt that wrecked much of San Francisco. Several years ago, Mark and Christi Carter built this current structure from the plans of an 1884 San Francisco house designed by the same architects that created the Carson Mansion.

The result is a lovely combination of Old World charm, the design of the Victorian era, and the niceties of a modern inn. This is a place to stay when you're trying to get away from it all. The elegant atmosphere includes a leisurely full breakfast and no phones or television. Art by local painters is displayed in the hallways, and there are lots of books lying around for your reading pleasure.

For those traveling on business, or who simply prefer more action, the Carters also have a modern hotel right across the street. This is the kind of place that would be right at home in downtown San Francisco, its lively yellow exterior contrasting with the staid, grand Victorian accommodations of the Carter bed and breakfast. The rooms are spacious, the interior furnishings very jazzy and elegant in a modern way. Yes, there are phones and television, and continental breakfast is meant for people on the move.

Yet the hotel is small enough to be a warm and intimate place. The hosts are very congenial, and wine is served in the lobby in the afternoon. A huge bowl of fruit is available to guests at all times, which comes in handy when you're on the road and need a quick snack.

CARTER HOUSE INN, *1033 Third Street, at L Street (mailing address: 301 L Street, Eureka, CA 95501); (707) 445-1390. Seven-guestroom bed-and-breakfast inn. Four rooms with private bath. Full breakfast. No phone or TV in rooms; down pillow optional. No pets. No children under twelve. No smoking in rooms. Rate range: $75 to $165, plus 8% tax. MC, Visa, Am Ex. No minimum stay.*

HOTEL CARTER, *301 L Street, Eureka, CA 95501; (707) 445-1390. Twenty-bedroom hotel. All rooms with private baths, phone, TV. Continental breakfast. Pets "not encouraged." Children welcome. No smoking in rooms. Rate range: $89 to $169, winter rates $10 less plus 8% tax. MC, Visa, Am Ex. No minimum stay.*

✓ **Eureka Inn.** This is a fine place to stay if you want to be in the center of town.

The inn is a block-long 1920s English Tudor building, now a historic landmark. Though the bedrooms are nothing special, the rest of the hotel is a throwback to an era of stately elegance that is hard to find these days. The lobby, with its huge roaring fireplace, is particularly inviting. It was built in the era when redwood was as plentiful as toothpicks, so you'll find beautiful paneling everywhere, even in the lobby level men's room.

The inn offers many hotel-type services, including a pool, Jacuzzi, sauna, and a very large dining room. If you like to dance, there's usually a party of some sort in the ballroom, complete with a good swing band.

EUREKA INN, *Seventh and F Streets; (707) 442-6441, or toll-free in California 1-800-862-4906. 105-bedroom hotel. All rooms with private bath, phone, TV. Pool, sauna, Jacuzzi. Small pets OK. Children welcome. Nonsmoking rooms available. Rate range: $96 to $250, plus 8% tax. MC, Visa, Am Ex, Diners. No minimum stay.*

√ Gingerbread Mansion.   Usually a cute name like this would be a turnoff to us, but after a visit to the place we realized there is no more appropriate name for this splendid Victorian inn. It is truly an incredible building, and the innkeepers who run it make sure every touch is just right. Wendy and Ken never seem to rest, dividing their time between making sure their guests are enjoying themselves and figuring out how and where to add more rooms and bathrooms.

The latest additions to their huge home are two new suites, plus a new garden room. Each room is filled with Victoriana, and special attention is given to bathrooms. If you like to soak and then fall into bed, ask about the downstairs room with two claw-foot bathtubs facing each other. Very romantic. Afternoon tea is served in the four large parlors, and in the morning a tray of coffee, tea, or juice is placed in the hallway and you can take your wake-up beverage into your room. Then a breakfast of juice, fresh fruit, home-baked coffee cake, and hard-cooked eggs is served in the formal dining room, overlooking one of the gardens.

GINGERBREAD MANSION, *400 Berding Street (mailing address: P.O. Box 40, Ferndale, CA 95536); (707) 786-4000, national toll-free 1-800-441-0407. Nine-bedroom bed-and-breakfast inn. All rooms with private bath. Expanded continental breakfast. No phone or TV in rooms. No pets. Children over ten OK. No smoking in rooms. Rate range: $75 to $135 midweek, $90 to $150 weekends, with slightly lower rates in winter, plus 8% tax. MC, Visa. Two-night minimum stay holidays and some summer weekends.*

√ Scotia Inn.   The grandest building in the company town of Scotia was built as a tourist attraction for the wealthy. In recent years the class distinction has eroded somewhat, as has the company town, but the elegant old hotel stands and offers overnight accommodations for all. Rooms are attractive, and the din-

FERNDALE

SCOTIA

ing room is a classic from a bygone era. But be advised that the company whistle goes off to wake the entire town—including hotel guests—at 6:30 A.M. each workday.

SCOTIA INN, *corner of Main and Mill streets (mailing address: P.O. Box 248, Scotia, CA 95565); (707) 764-5683. Eleven-bedroom hotel. All rooms with private bathrooms. Continental breakfast. No phones in rooms; some have TV. Jacuzzi on premises. No pets. Children welcome. Rate range: $50 to $125, plus 8% tax. MC, Visa. No minimum stay.*

TRINIDAD ✓ **Trinidad Bed and Breakfast Inn.** Trinidad, about thirty miles north of Eureka, is one of the surprise beauty spots on the coast. It's definitely worth a trip and offers lots of motel accommodations and camping facilities. We recommend the Trinidad Bed and Breakfast with some trepidation: When you call for a reservation, it will probably be full. That's because there are just four pleasant rooms in this Cape Cod–style house overlooking the ocean. The original owner of the house hailed from the East Coast, thus the unusual architecture.

The current owners, Carol and Paul Kirk, moved up from Southern California several years ago and have become the town's biggest boosters. Their inn is across from the prettiest spot on the harbor, where most visitors park and look out at the views. They carry brochures on all the attractions in the area and act as the unofficial chamber of commerce.

TRINIDAD BED AND BREAKFAST INN, *560 Edwards Street (mailing address: P.O. Box 849, Trinidad, CA 95570); (707) 677-0840. Four-bedroom bed-and-breakfast inn. All rooms with private bath. Full breakfast. No pets. Children over ten OK. No smoking in rooms. Rate range: $75 to $110, less $15 midweek in winter, tax included. No credit cards. Two-night minimum on weekends in Bay View Suite.*

CHAPTER **31** Monterey Peninsula

If you've ever been caught in a traffic jam in the besieged town that calls itself Carmel-by-the-Sea, you know that this is as far from a Backroad as you can get. Even though it is still a village of amazing beauty, the central area can be a bit frazzling. In this section, we suggest some out-of-the-way places to stay that allow you to enjoy the splendor of the Monterey Coast and still have some peace and quiet. Most of these places are in the town of Pacific Grove, which provides its own special ocean drive and is a short hop from the Monterey Bay Aquarium.

✔ **Mission Ranch.** Although Clint Eastwood is no longer mayor, he has taken a personal step to preserve one of Carmel's landmarks. Located directly behind the Carmel Mission, about ten minutes away from the commercial (and busy) part of town, is the Mission Ranch, which operates as a large yet modest inn. When there were plans to sell the place and develop the land, Eastwood stepped in to help preserve it as it is, though he is not involved with the day-to-day operation.

Originally this was a dairy farm settled by a family of Scottish immigrants lured to California by the Gold Rush. Most of the original buildings have been saved and given new uses. The original Victorian farmhouse, built in the 1850s, has been divided into six guestrooms. The restaurant is the site of the original creamery, the old cow barn has been turned into a party-and-dance hall, the old bunkhouse for farmhands now can sleep three couples or a family. It has its own kitchen.

There are many random buildings on the property and various accommodations. This is a twenty-acre ranch, complete with nature trails, tennis courts, a lagoon for swimming, plus a collection of cottages and motel rooms, some with ocean views, others with fireplaces. It's far from luxurious, but the ranch does offer a lot of options for sleeping space, and the grounds are a pleasant respite from the tourist crush.

MISSION RANCH, *26270 Dolores, Carmel-by-the-Sea, CA 93923; (408) 624-6436. Twenty-six-bedroom ranch operation, with accommodations in a farmhouse, cottage, and motel units. All rooms with private baths. Continental breakfast. Most rooms with phone and TV. Tennis courts on premises. Pets OK. Children welcome. Rate range: $49 to $115, tax included. MC, Visa, Am Ex, Diners. Two-night minimum stay on weekends; three nights on national holidays.*

✔ **Stonepine.** If it's luxury you're after, go east, away from the water. About thirteen miles inland, in the hot and dry Carmel Valley, is a luxury equestrian center, though you don't have to ride horses to enjoy a stay at Stonepine. This exclusive estate was built in the thirties for the Crocker banking family; in its heyday the ranch was one of the country's top breeding farms of thoroughbreds and the site of many a Gatsby-like party for the polo set.

The main house is called Château Noel, the kind of Mediterranean-style mansion that simply isn't built anymore, with stone arches supported by centuries-old columns imported from Rome and interior oak paneling from early nineteenty-century France. You can imagine the Crockers habitating these rooms, adorned by tapestries, marble fireplaces, and Lalique *objets*. Upstairs are eight elegant suites, each individually appointed with antique furniture, down comforters, and fresh bouquets, and featuring such modern conveniences as phones, TV with VCR, and Jacuzzi tubs. The Château is surrounded by spectacular gardens and the namesake Stone Pines, planted as eighteen-inch saplings, now sixty feet tall.

Down the road, next to the equestrian facilities, is the less formal Paddock House. Here you'll find four deluxe suites, decorated in a style reminiscent of Ralph Lauren ads and suitable for accommodating families.

Guests of Stonepine may, for an additional fee, take instruction in English and Western horseback riding. Those not interested in horsey activities can amuse themselves with tennis, archery, swimming (in a pool or in a swimming hole), croquet, and health club facilities like weight-training machines and a steam bath. All guests are invited to see the owner's collection of antique carriages, including an 1860-vintage farmer's buggy, 1875 stagecoach, and horse-drawn chariots available for children to take a romp around the property.

STONEPINE, *150 East Carmel Valley Road, Carmel Valley, CA 93924; (408) 659-2245. Twelve-bedroom resort. Continental breakfast. All accommodations with private baths, phone, TV, VCR, whirlpool tubs; down pillow optional. Pool, tennis courts, gym, and equestrian activities on the premises. No pets. Children welcome. Rate range: $160 to $550, plus 10% tax. MC, Visa, Am Ex, Diners. Two-night minimum stay on weekends, three to four on various holidays.*

PACIFIC GROVE   ✓ **Asilomar Conference Center.**   In 1913, Phoebe Apperson Hearst, a champion of women's rights and mother of newspaper magnate William Randolph Hearst, donated this wooded oceanfront property to the YWCA to be used as a conference center. Phoebe hired her favorite architect, Julia Morgan (who would later design Hearst Castle), to design and build a social hall, dining hall, chapel, lodges, and cottages. Asilomar was used by the YWCA for retreats and conferences until the 1950s.

Today Asilomar Conference Center is owned by the California State Park System, which preserved the historic buildings and built additional modern accommodations. Located on 105 acres of sand dunes, pines, oaks, and Monterey cypress, Asilomar is a spectacular place, a destination unto itself. Although most of the large facility is booked by groups for meetings, some rooms are usually available for individuals or families. Be sure to call ahead. The rooms are adequate, if not elaborate, but the grounds and the neighboring beach are spectacular, and you can't beat the price.

You check in inside the Morgan-designed Administration Building, a long, rectangular lodge where you will also find Ping-Pong tables, a huge fieldstone fireplace, comfy chairs, and a series of historic photographs telling the saga of the building of Asilomar (the name comes from Indian words meaning "refuge by the sea").

You'll find pleasant walks on the property, a swimming pool, and beach access. If you want to save money but stay in beautiful surroundings near Carmel, try to get a room at Asilomar.

ASILOMAR CONFERENCE CENTER, *800 Asilomar Boulevard (mailing address: P.O. Box 537, Pacific Grove, CA 93950); (408) 372-8016. 313 bedrooms in 28 lodges. All rooms with private baths. Full breakfast. No phone or TV in rooms. Pool and volleyball on premises; beach access. No pets. Children welcome. Rate range: $46.98 to $75.28 for rooms, $101.98 to $179.90 for cottages, tax included. No credit cards. No minimum stay.*

✔ **Martine Inn.**   Along Oceanview Drive in Pacific Grove are a number of spectacular homes, several of which have been converted into bed-and-breakfast inns. The Martine Inn is one of the most elegant. This rambling pink mansion, built in 1899, is perched on a hillside; you must climb a number of steps to get to the front door. Once inside you are confronted with a variety of options: to head upstairs, into a parlor, into a dining area, or down a hallway. In other words, this place is huge, with thirteen bedrooms (all with private baths) in the main house alone; additional rooms are out back in the Carriage House.

Each guestroom has an individual character. Some are very elegant, decorated with such furnishings as an 1860s Chippendale Revival canopy bed and a mahogany bedroom suite exhibited at the 1863 World's Fair. Other rooms are more fanciful. A personal favorite is the art deco room, featuring a Coca-Cola sign from an old movie theater candy counter. The innkeepers are proud of their silver collection, which is used each morning at breakfast and includes a large Sheffield serving dish dated 1765.

MARTINE INN, *255 Oceanview Boulevard, Pacific Grove, CA 93950; (408) 373-3388. Nineteen-bedroom bed-and-breakfast inn. All rooms with private baths and phones. Full breakfast. Jacuzzi on premises. No pets. Children "not encouraged." Nonsmoking rooms available. Rate range: $99 to $205, plus 10% tax. MC, Visa, Am Ex. Two-night minimum stay on weekends, three nights on holidays.*

✔ **Pacific Gardens Inn.**   We found this place by accident on New Year's weekend. Every inn, motel, and bed and breakfast in the area was booked solid, but the Pacific Gardens Inn had one room left and we took it. While we were checking in, the lady at the reception desk apologized profusely; since this was the last room, she said this was the least desirable one in the inn.

Expecting the worst, we were delighted to discover very pleasant accommodations. Not only was the room perfectly adequate and comfortable, it came equipped with a popcorn popper (and yes, they supplied the popcorn).

The Pacific Gardens Inn is really a nice, well-run motel. In addition to the popcorn poppers, all rooms have coffeemakers and minirefrigerators; every room with the exception of one (guess whose) has a wood-burning fireplace. The inn also has suites with one and two bedrooms; these have kitchens and a large living room.

A contintental breakfast is served in the lobby, and it includes fresh fruit, hard-boiled eggs, and pastries; you can sit by the fireplace there or take a tray back to your room.

The inn is located within hiking distance of Asilomar Beach.

PACIFIC GARDENS INN, *701 Asilomar Boulevard, Pacific Grove, CA 93950; (408) 646-9414, or toll-free in California 1-800-262-1566. Twenty-eight-bedroom motel. All accommodations with private baths, phone, TV. Continental breakfast. Two outdoor Jacuzzis. No pets. Children welcome. Rate range: $88 to $145 March through October, $70 to $125 November through February, plus 10% tax. MC, Visa, Am Ex. Minimum stay some holiday weekends.*

✔ **Pacific Grove Inn.**   If you don't mind being away from the beach you will have the opportunity to stay in a nicely appointed and inexpensive inn located near downtown Pacific Grove. The house was built in 1904 by the town's hardware store owner, a very successful businessman whose lavish home was the site of society gatherings. In 1985 the house was restored to open as an inn and was placed on the National Register of Historic Places.

Today the inn combines the niceties of a bed-and-breakfast inn (antique cherry furniture, brass beds, period wallpaper) with modern conveniences (phone, TV, minirefrigerators, heated towel racks). All accommodations have gas fireplaces, which also serve to heat the room. Somebody around here must like movies: The inn features an in-house closed-circuit channel for old films, and the current movie listings from the newspaper are posted in a downstairs hallway.

Breakfast is optional. For $5 you can be served the typical bed-and-breakfast fare: eggs, freshly baked goods, and so on. But if you're one of those people who simply can't face a plate of eggs in the morning, you can skip it and pocket the five bucks.

PACIFIC GROVE INN, *581 Pine Avenue, Pacific Grove, CA 93950; (408) 375-2825. Ten-bedroom bed-and-breakfast inn. All rooms with private baths, phone, TV, and radio. Breakfast optional. No pets. Children "not encouraged." No smoking in rooms. Rate range: $62.50 to $132.50, plus 10% tax. MC, Visa, Am Ex. No minimum stay.*

✔ **Seven Gables Inn.**   Even if you have no intention of staying here, it's worth driving by the Seven Gables Inn, a storybook Victorian located on the boulevard that runs along the ocean in Pacific Grove. The original house was built in 1886 as a rather conventional home. Then Lucie Chase, a well-to-do widow with a sense of humor and style, moved in. She added the gables, sun porch, and the plethora of windows that makes this house a one-of-a-kind architectural wonder. Today it's painted yellow with white trim, furnished lavishly with European antiques, Oriental rugs, and crystal chandeliers, and is surrounded by a lovely English-style garden.

Up in the third-floor attic of the main house is a special room worth noting, especially for those looking for a romantic getaway. This room, set off by itself, has a dormer ceiling and a cozy nook with pillows on the floor and windows looking out over the ocean. The innkeeper told us of a honeymoon couple who set up a chessboard and spent their afternoons in this unique and spectacular setting.

Breakfast is a sit-down affair, served between eight and ten in the morning, and High Tea is presented each afternoon from four to five. Home-baked goodies are featured.

SEVEN GABLES INN, *555 Oceanview Boulevard, Pacific Grove, CA 93950; (408) 372-4341. Fourteen-bedroom bed-and-breakfast inn. All rooms with private baths. Continental breakfast. No phone or TV in rooms. No pets. Children under twelve "discouraged." No smoking in rooms. Rate range: $95 to $165, plus 10% tax. MC, Visa. Two-night minimum stay on weekends.*

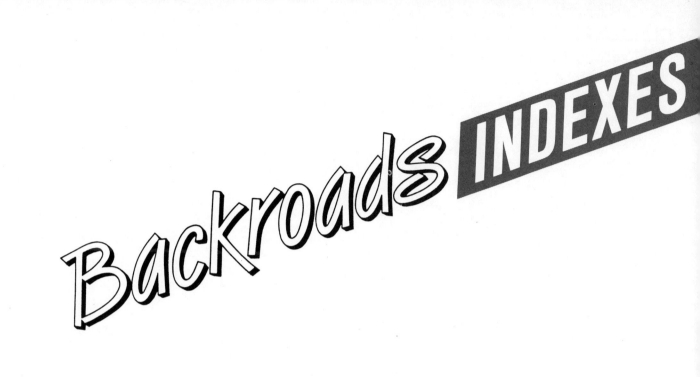

Backroads **INDEXES**

Restaurants

251

Inexpensive Restaurants

255

Moderate Restaurants

257

Expensive Restaurants

Lodging